99 HISTORIC HOMES OF *Indiana*

Bill Shaw

[signature]

HISTORIC
LANDMARKS
FOUNDATION OF
INDIANA

INDIANA
University Press
Bloomington & Indianapolis

99
HISTORIC
HOMES
OF *Indiana*

A LOOK INSIDE

Photographs by Marsh Davis

Text by Bill Shaw

With a foreword by J. Reid Williamson, Jr.

This book is a publication of

Indiana University Press
601 North Morton Street
Bloomington, IN 47404-3797 USA

http://iupress.indiana.edu

Telephone orders 800-842-6796
Fax orders 812-855-7931
Orders by e-mail iuporder@indiana.edu

The paper used in this publication meets the minimum requirements of American National Standard for Information Sciences—Permanence of Paper for Printed Library Materials, ANSI Z39.48-1984.

Manufactured in Canada

Library of Congress Cataloging-in-Publication Data

Davis, Marsh.
99 historic homes of Indiana : a look inside / photographs by Marsh Davis ; text by Bill Shaw with a foreword by J. Reid Williamson, Jr.
p. cm.
Includes index.
ISBN 0-253-34145-0
1. Architecture, Domestic—Indiana. I. Title: Ninety-nine historic homes of Indiana. II. Shaw, Bill. III. Title.
NA7235.I5 D38 2002
728'.37'09772—dc21

2002001481

1 2 3 4 5 07 06 05 04 03 02

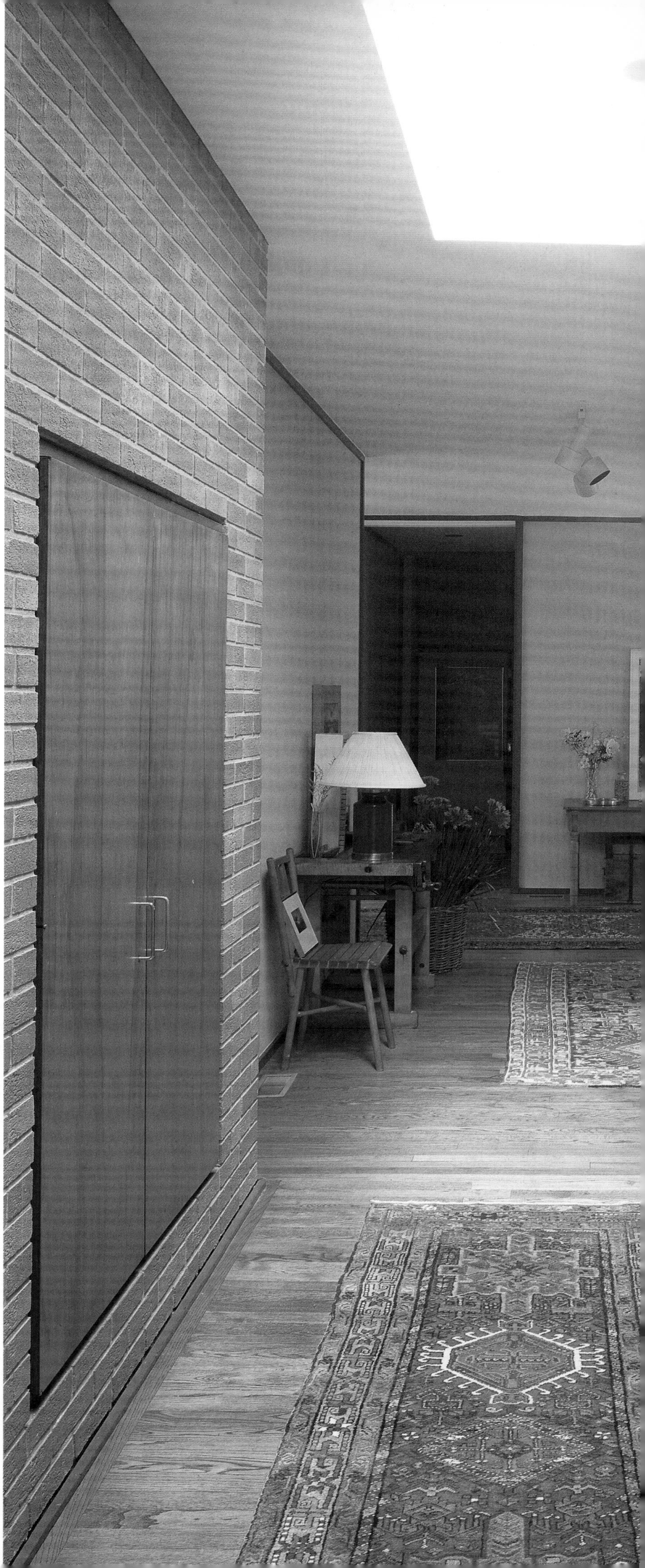

*Dedicated to the memory of
James E. Hughes, Chairman
of the Board of Directors of
Historic Landmarks
Foundation of Indiana
1999–2001*

CONTENTS

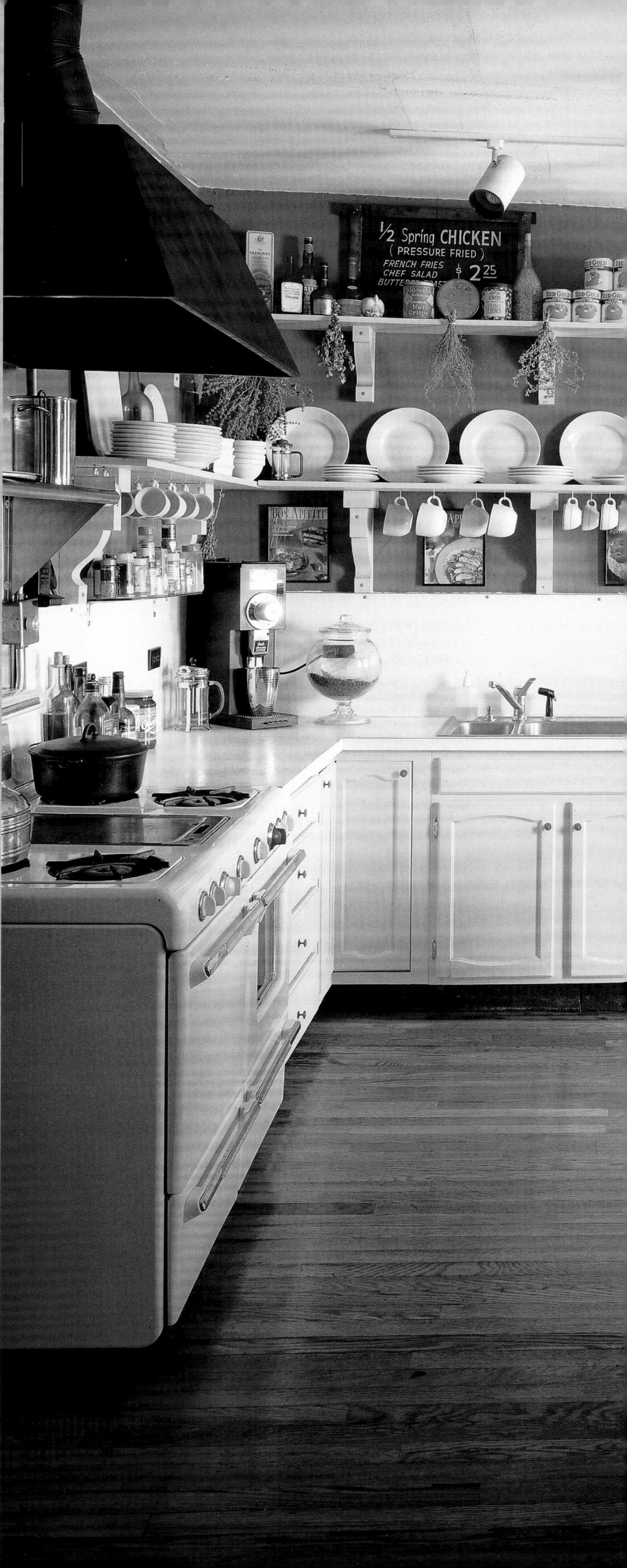
½ Spring CHICKEN
(PRESSURE FRIED)
FRENCH FRIES
CHEF SALAD
$ 2.25
BON APPETIT

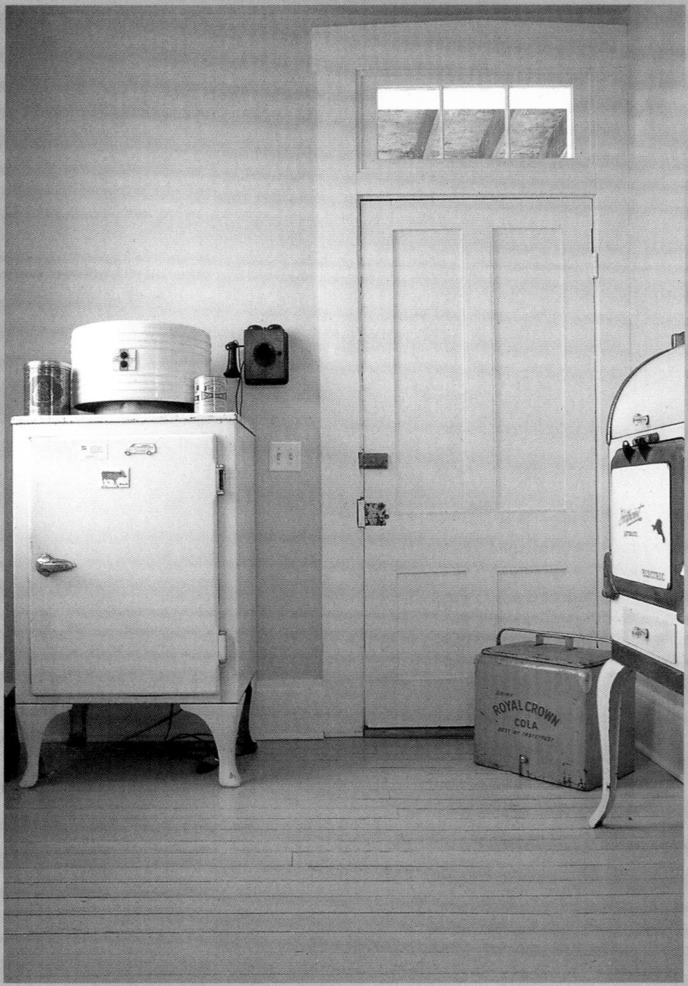
ROYAL CROWN
COLA

FOREWORD

There are about 180,000 historic buildings in Indiana. Unfortunately, Historic Landmarks Foundation of Indiana can't save them all. No organization can. Old buildings are saved one at a time by individual people, ninety-nine of whom are featured in these pages, along with pictures of their unique homes.

Putting a building in a book gives it a status and credibility that aids historic preservation efforts. For that reason, we were the first preservation organization in the country to publish historic-sites surveys on a statewide, county-by-county basis. This is only our second major book. The first was published ten years ago and focused on the architecture of the historic homes of Indiana's "main street," North Meridian Street in Indianapolis. It is entitled *The Main Stem.*

Prior to *99 Historic Homes of Indiana: A Look Inside,* the only other book devoted to historic homes throughout the state was Wilbur D. Peat's excellent work *Indiana Houses of the Nineteenth Century,* which was published forty years ago. Its primary purpose was architectural style and design.

This book differs dramatically from the Peat book in its theme. *99 Historic Homes of Indiana* is a book about people who, one by one, are responsible for preserving some of Indiana's finest historic houses and maintaining them as homes.

We have selected Marsh Davis as our photographer. We consider Marsh to be one of Indiana's premier architectural photographers. His work within these pages speaks to his rare talent and captures the striking visual essence of each home.

Bill Shaw was selected to write the narrative because of his longstanding body of work as a former feature writer for *The Indianapolis Star* and numerous national magazines. Bill has a well-known reputation for his human-interest approach to topics.

And human interest is important because this is not a book of houses and buildings, but of homes and people. *Home* is the essence of this book. The people are of varied backgrounds and status in life and are from all geographic parts of the state, but they are bound by a common passion and dedication to their homes. They also share a profound respect and reverence for those who preceded them as occupants over the decades.

These are people who understand the importance of preservation and history. For those who build anew, there is no past within the home. And yet we are defined by our past. We are who we have been. We are our legacies. It is important to have a balance of the old and the new. We can't just be a people who push for so-called progress. There must be those who push back and say, "Leave it alone."

The ninety-nine homeowners in this book reflect a growing number of people with an affection and deep appreciation for history, the importance of preservation and leaving buildings alone. Their contributions to saving, restoring, and living in old homes are at the heart of the preservation movement.

It all comes down to individuals saving one old house at a time.

When I return to my seaside home of Fairfield, Connecticut, I drive by the house where I grew up and the elementary school I attended. It's no longer a school, but the building is still there and provides me with a reassuring feeling, an important connection in my life. You don't know yourself until you know your past.

This book is dedicated to our former chairman of the board of directors, attorney Jim Hughes, who died in the summer of 2001. Jim and Sheila's home is featured in these pages. Bill Shaw's narrative perfectly captures their dedication to preservation, both intellectually and architecturally. Jim had a true sense of history and people's place in the world, and was intrigued by all things interesting and old.

I'd especially like to thank all those people who have been so considerate and generous with their financial contributions, which made this important book possible. They are acknowledged by name on page xiv.

We remain grateful to the homeowners who graciously opened their doors and their lives to Marsh Davis and Bill Shaw. They represent the heart and soul of the preservation movement in Indiana for one simple reason: They live it.

J. Reid Williamson, Jr.
President
Historic Landmarks Foundation of Indiana

PREFACE

by Bill Shaw

This book is about old houses and the people who live in them and why. It is a tribute to homeowners around Indiana who have chosen the path less traveled, seeking something substantial and enduring, something that is unfortunately disappearing at an alarming rate: old homes. They understand, as William Faulkner wrote, "The past is not dead. It's not even past." The houses featured in this book were built at a time when people cherished their individuality and independence. They didn't want a house that looked like the one next door. They built houses that were distinctive, unique, and imbued with a lasting belief in permanence.

Many of the people featured in this book restored or rehabilitated old, and in many cases crumbling, unwanted houses, and remade them into homes. And that's an important point. A house is a building, a structure, an object. A home has a life and personality unto itself and represents the human history that unfolded within its walls over the long years: births, deaths, and everything good and bad in between. The cycles of life. As Willie Morris, the great Southern writer, observed, history is not merely a series of events: "It is people acting and living their past in the present; the uniqueness of man, the pride in his gifts, his genius for flexibility and improvisation."

The homes are loosely defined as historic. Some are listed in the National Register of Historic Places. Some are not. Most date to the nineteenth century. Exceptions include John Christian's sleek Lafayette home near the Purdue University campus, which was designed by architect Frank Lloyd Wright and completed in 1956. Mark and Becca Ewing's home in the deep woods outside Vincennes was built by Mark's great-great-great-great-great-grandfather Nathaniel, around 1809, ten years before Indiana became a state. The house has been continuously occupied by Nathaniel Ewing's descendants for nearly two hundred years.

The past is certainly not dead, nor even past, in the Ewing house. Like dozens of other families, the Ewings display portraits or photographs of the previous occupants of the house, in addition to other memorabilia. Many people continue to use furnishings and other belongings left by former occupants, thus embracing history every day. The people I interviewed consider themselves "caretakers" of their homes, protectors not just of a structure, but of the legacies of those who preceded them.

The people, the stories of their lives, and the histories of their houses are intriguing. Take Robert Beardsley in Elkhart County, for example. His grandfather invented Alka-Seltzer. I didn't know a Hoosier invented Alka-Seltzer. Meg Shelly's father invented Pringles potato chips. It never occurred to me that someone actually invented Pringles. John Simmermaker of Winemac has the largest collection of coverlets in Indiana. I'd never heard of coverlets before meeting John.

I met farmers and factory workers, teachers, architects, lawyers and doctors, nurses, photographers, a world-renowned folklorist, professors, judges, a beautician, and a construction foreman, among others. Some of the people are wealthy, most are not. Some houses are big, some are small.

Brenda and Terry Blackburn live in an 1849, eighteen by thirty-seven–foot oak log cabin they rescued in Kentucky and reassembled and restored in rural Grant County. Six Rhode Island Red roosters peck around in the front yard.

Ted and Kim Reese live in a four-story, eight-thousand-square-foot mansion overlooking Lake Michigan with the Chicago skyline shimmering in the distance and four thousand bottles of vintage wine stored in the climate-controlled wine cellar. The house is in the unincorporated town of Long Beach in LaPorte County. It was built by William Scholl, son of a LaPorte County mint farmer. William later became Dr. Scholl and created a worldwide empire based on foot-care products. Ted and Kim live in his house. I didn't know Dr. Scholl was a Hoosier. I didn't even know there was a place called Long Beach.

Minimalist Sam Crane lives alone in an 1843 Shelby County farmhouse with no electricity or running water. He likes it that way. He happily exists on $200 a month, smokes twenty pounds of tobacco a year, speaks Japanese, bakes pies on a wood stove, sews his own clothes, and bathes in a galvanized tub in his kitchen. He has little and wants nothing. He is one of the most contented people I met on this long journey.

Robert Beardsley owns a ninety-acre estate on the Kennebunk River in Maine and a chateau in Normandy, France, but home base is an 1835 farmhouse in the Bristol Fruit Hills of Elkhart County, where he tends his beloved apple orchards.

I was astounded at the enormous effort some people make to live in their Hoosier homes. Jim King lives in Cambridge City on Old National Road with his wife Jill and their two children. He works in New York City where he is a vice president of

McGraw-Hill Company. On Monday morning he flies to work and returns on Friday afternoon. (In his previous job, he commuted to Seattle, flying thirty-five hundred miles a week.) U.S. Court of Appeals judge Jim Kanne lives in Rensselaer with his wife, Judy, and commutes to his federal courthouse offices in Chicago and Lafayette. Jim King, Judge Kanne, and others simply saw no reason to move, no matter how inconvenient the commute. They love their homes. It's just that simple. They are caretakers.

I was amazed at the number of people who bought homes they had admired decades before, as children. Huntington attorney Lee Bowers remembered walking past the big house on a hill as a kid. It scared and fascinated him. After law school, he returned home and bought it. When Mike Klink was a senior in high school, he drove his girlfriend, Deb, to the Eckhart mansion in Auburn and slipped an engagement ring on her finger. He promised her she would one day live in the Eckhart mansion. Now they do. I heard similar stories time and time again. A childhood dream come true.

I visited every home in this book, looked in bedrooms, bathrooms, and basements. I asked to see everything. Some are magnificently furnished with rare artwork, exceptional antiques, and family heirlooms. Bob and Ellie Haan's Lafayette home contains the second-largest privately held collection of T. C. Steele paintings in the world; Sam Crane has stick drawings of birds tacked to his walls; Kevin Cox in Farmland hung egg cartons from his ceiling; and Ted Toler's house in Richmond is decorated for Christmas 365 days a year.

I drove nearly fourteen thousand miles in ten months, crisscrossing Indiana, interviewing over 130 people in ninety-nine homes from Evansville on the Ohio River to Long Beach and Beverly Shores on the great white sand dunes of Lake Michigan. I don't wear a watch and tried never to be in a hurry. I avoided interstates whenever possible and mostly drove on state highways and county roads and arrived everywhere early with time to spare. I looked at farms and barns and big trees and Red-winged Blackbirds perched on fence posts. I skipped stones across rivers and lakes, climbed hills and poked through antique shops all over Indiana. I walked through courthouses, read local histories in Carnegie libraries, and ate too many good cheeseburgers.

That was the good part.

The bad part was seeing the speed with which suburbs and commercial development are overtaking vast chunks of Indiana. Ron and Sonja Halbauer must call the police to stop traffic to get in and out of their Lawrenceburg home along hopelessly congested U.S. 50, which runs through Dearborn County. It is possibly the most commercially overdeveloped stretch of road

in Indiana, except for U.S. 31 through Kokomo, U.S. 24 into Fort Wayne, U.S. 41 into Evansville, U.S. 52 through Lafayette, U.S. 30 through Merrillville, all of Indianapolis and Marion County, everything in and out of Bloomington, New Albany, Jeffersonville, Valparaiso, Richmond, Elkhart, South Bend, Gary, Hammond, Michigan City, . . . Harold Mailand spent years restoring a Shelby County farmhouse that once overlooked some of the prettiest green hills in central Indiana. The hills are now covered with "exclusive homesites" and Harold is sickened by it. Who can blame him?

Prior to this book project I wrote for *The Indianapolis Star.* I traveled throughout Indiana writing about people and situations I found interesting. On my long drives through the state, I'd pass old homes along country roads or around courthouse squares and wonder who lived in them, and why?

Who hasn't wondered that?

The caretakers featured in this book are from all points in the state and I liked them all, without exception. They were warm and gracious, patiently answered all my nosy questions, and showed me their stuff. Eleanor and Jake Arnold made me a fine lunch of chicken, mashed potatoes, gravy, salad, bread and butter, iced tea, and pie. I don't remember all the other food people fed me, but it was all good. (I well remember Helen Disler's oatmeal raisin cookies in LaPorte.)

This book opens the doors to ninety-nine of the most historically and architecturally interesting homes in Indiana. But more importantly, it introduces you to the good people who have chosen to live along the roads less traveled, caring for our irreplaceable historic homes and preserving a bit of our threatened Hoosier heritage.

PREFACE

by Marsh Davis

One might expect a book on historic homes to present a discourse on domestic architecture or to celebrate historical personalities of the past. But this book, as Reid Williamson clearly points out, is about old homes and the way present-day people inhabit them.

Indiana contains a wealth of historic homes—and that's good, but it made the process of selecting subjects for this book a difficult one. The selection process was aided immeasurably, thanks to the terrific staff of Historic Landmarks Foundation of Indiana and to numerous associates throughout the state who understand good preservation practice. With an eye toward geographic distribution, stylistic variety, and chronological breadth, ninety-nine entries were selected out of a vastly larger number.

"Historic" and "old" are, of course, relative terms. We chose a broad interpretation, including homes dating from the first decade of the nineteenth century through the late 1950s—even though counting late '50s architecture as "historic" hits a bit close to home for some of us.

The issue of age aside, the idea of inhabiting an old house forms the premise of this book. All of the houses featured are *homes*. None are museums or buildings maintained but not lived in. To be sure, a few are seasonal dwellings or second homes, but all are regularly occupied by people.

A variety of approaches to living in old houses are depicted. Some reveal an owner's tendency toward "purism" in the extraordinary care given to the selection of period-appropriate furnishings and surface treatments. Others mix contemporary design with historic architecture and furnishings. And some demonstrate completely unselfconscious, graceful ways of inhabiting a place.

The goal of the photographic component of this book was to depict the homes as naturally and accurately as possible. Only existing lighting was used, no props were employed, no furniture rearranged—even when doing otherwise would have made for an easier picture. Working primarily with an old Deardorf view camera, I wished for the camera work to become largely self-effacing, allowing the homes to speak for themselves.

Profound thanks are due to many who supported the production and publication of this book in a variety of ways. First, thanks must go to the leadership of Historic Landmarks Foundation of Indiana and its board of directors, and especially to the late Jim Hughes, chairman of the board, as work on this book unfolded, and to his successor, David Ross. Both saw the value of the project and never failed to support it. And to Reid Williamson, president, who for years envisioned such a publication as an effective means of spreading the preservation gospel.

Several individuals assisted in the selection of candidates for the book and deserve credit for opening many doors. Staff members, past and present, of Historic Landmarks Foundation were most helpful: Mary Burger, Adrian Fine, Dana Groves, Todd Zeiger, Jane Cassady, Mark Dollase, Scott Zimmerman, Sherry Johnson, Jena Roy, Amy Kotzbauer, Michele James Thompson, Joshua Sutton, and Andrew Halter. Preservation leaders from all regions of the state were instrumental as well in the identification and selection of homes: Sandy Tonsoni, Patsy Powell, Joseph Kitchell, Kent Schuette, Pamela Schmidt, Carol Karst Wasson, Jeff Baker, Paul Myers, Allan Cornelius, Rob Shilts, Joanne Stuttgen, Christine Wiltberger, Ruth Berline, John Martin Smith, Suzanne Skaggs, Kurt Meyer, David Buchanan, and Judy Cowling.

I wish to extend personal gratitude to people who provided guidance and support through the years of this project: to Darryl Jones, Indiana's photographer laureate, for friendly advice and encouragement; to Tom Mason, vice president of publications for the Indiana Historical Society, for his seasoned guidance; to Henry Glassie, who informs us better than anyone else that homes don't need to be big and fancy to be richly imbued with history and culture and art; to my colleagues at Historic Landmarks Foundation, especially Suzanne Stanis, Tina Connor, and Mary Anna Hunt for valued association; and to Bill Shaw, esteemed collaborator, defender of what really matters in our culture, and enemy of all things suburban.

Most importantly, my thanks and appreciation to the people who shared their time and homes with us. To see the marvelous work and dedication of these homeowners and preservationists over the past few years has been a rare and rewarding experience, something I sincerely hope is conveyed by the images in this book.

Lastly, I wish to note that preserved homes and the people who dwell in them are not immune to change and loss. Five of those whose homes are featured in this book have passed away: Jim Hughes, to whose memory this book is dedicated; Opal Boring, artist and historian who helped save the covered bridges of Rush County and who chronicled the history of her community; Kenneth Russell, a delightful, gentle man, who operated what was arguably the best antiques shop in Indiana; Bob Beckmann, civic leader, friend of the arts, and champion of a preserved and revitalized downtown Indianapolis; and Dotti Reindollar, a dear friend who gave endlessly for the good of her community, who died as her magnificent home, Maywood, was consumed by fire.

All of these extraordinary people were a joy to know. I hope that, in a small way, this book will add to their legacies.

ACKNOWLEDGMENTS

Historic Landmarks Foundation of Indiana gratefully acknowledges the following sponsors:

Alice Cole and Joanne and Sid Kubesch
William and Gayle Cook
Jerry and Carolyn Fuhs
W. C. Griffith Foundation Trust
The James E. Hughes Family
J. Irwin and Xenia Miller
Sommer & Barnard, in memory of James E. Hughes

Anonymous (2)
Robert Beardsley
John Cottrell
Richard E. Ford
Bob and Ellie Haan
Ron and Sonja Halbauer
In honor of Paulita and William Justice
Michael and Judy Kanne
Greg and Judy Rust
Randall T. Shepard and Amy MacDonell

Anonymous (2)
Ron and Ruth Berline
Linda K. Christian Davis and John E. Christian
Tina Connor
Lynn Corson and Janet Ayres
Marsh and Grace Davis
David and Sarah Finkel
Marilyn Fischer and Mary Burger
Brent and Marina Gill
Olen R. Gowens, in memory of Harley Reeder
Joe and Betty Pogue Hadley
Vic and Karen Cochran Hasler
Phyllis Igleheart
Ray and Lou Marr
Walt and June Prosser
John Martin Smith and Barbara Clark Smith
John Watson
J. Reid Williamson, Jr.
The Board of Directors of Historic Landmarks Foundation
    of Indiana, in memory of James E. Hughes

Anonymous
Lori Efroymson, in memory of James E. Hughes
Sanford and Marjut Garner
Norman and Rosemary Hunt
Fred and Sandy Koss
Joe and Judy Rohleder
Associates at Sommer & Barnard, in memory of James E. Hughes

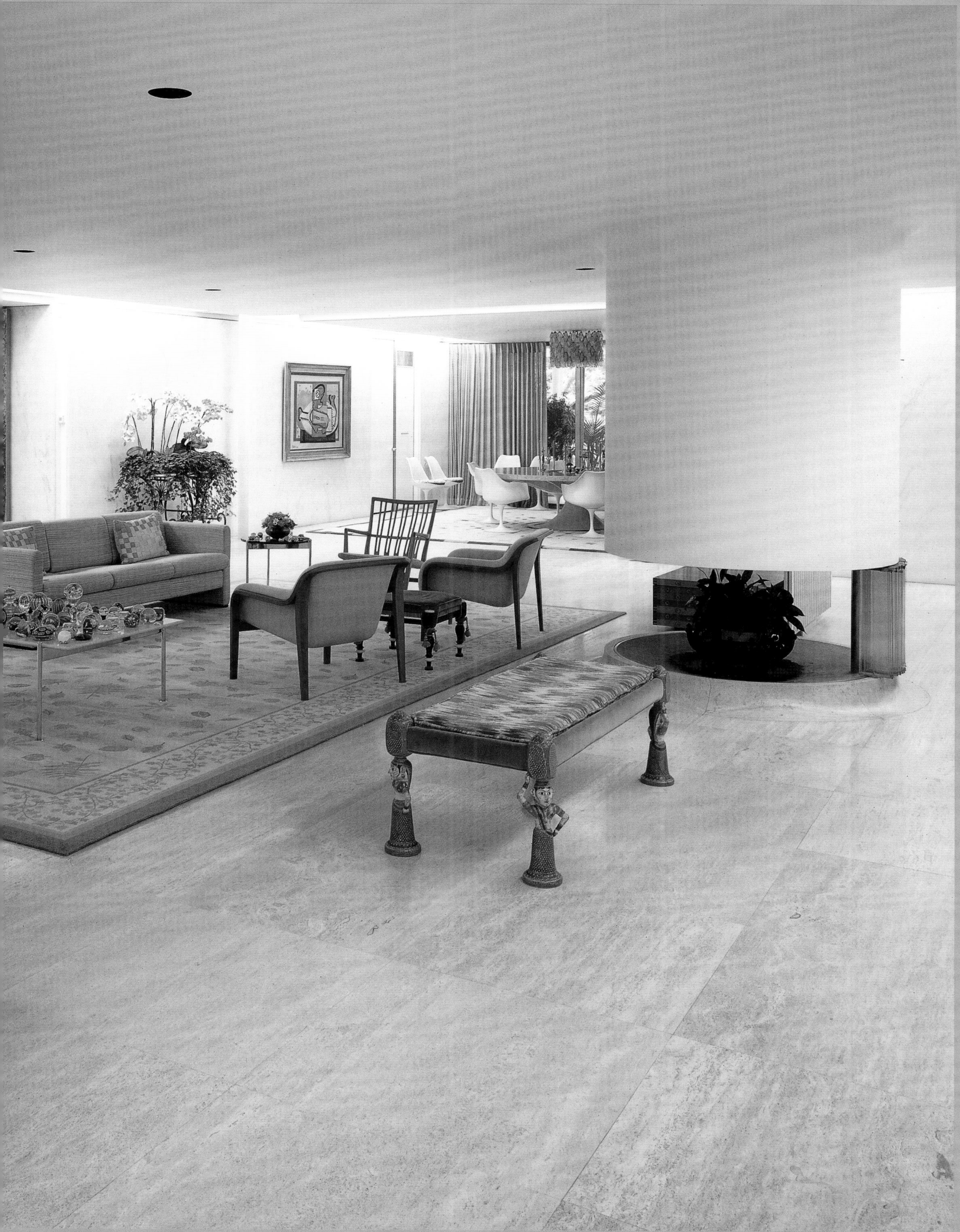

Clarence (Jake) and Eleanor Arnold

Historic Name: DR. JOHN ARNOLD HOUSE

County: RUSH

Date of Construction: 1853

Architectural Style: GOTHIC REVIVAL

LISTED IN THE NATIONAL REGISTER OF HISTORIC PLACES

In the Arnold family, it's accepted that each new generation living in the farmhouse will care for their ancestors' personal mementos. For example, Dr. John Arnold's saddlebag full of medicine bottles sits on the table where he left it around 1875. His stovepipe hat hangs on a hall peg. His books on dueling with pistols line the shelves. The desk where he counseled patients remains in the parlor, used today by his great-grandson, farmer Jake Arnold, and Jake's wife, Eleanor, current custodians of the family legacy.

"My dad died in that room," says Jake, nodding toward the bedroom.

Alice Arnold made her final donut in 1900 and her daughter, Josie, sealed it in a jar with a note that read, "The last donut my dear mother baked for me." Eleanor examined the donut in 2001 and said it looked pretty good. "The Arnolds just keep everything."

The family's American experience began in 1820 when John Arnold and his family immigrated to Rush County from the Isle of Wight in England. He bought 160 acres along Ben Davis Creek, site of a Delaware Indian village. Panthers screamed in the night and bison trudged through the forest, but John Arnold built a cabin near the creek and broke the fertile virgin soil. The cabin, which also served as Rush County's first post office, exists today, rebuilt by Jake with the original logs.

The gabled Gothic Revival farmhouse was built across the creek from the cabin by Dr. John in 1853 and has been occupied by Arnolds ever since. They've scrupulously maintained the house, cabin, barn, chicken coop, smokehouse, milk house, buggy shed, granary, corncrib, privy, and precious items, including Grandma Alice's last donut, hundreds of Indian stone points, and a bison skull found generations

ago. The farm contains a hillside burial vault built in 1820 and dozens of massive, towering sycamore and walnut trees that once shaded the Delaware Indian village. The sycamores are some of the oldest trees in Indiana.

Jake and Eleanor met at Indiana University and married in 1948. They had three children: Barbara is the Rush County Circuit Court Judge; Mary lives to the east, across the Arnold family fields; and John, a Purdue University graduate, farmed with his father until he was killed in a farming accident in 1991. He was thirty-six, a father of four. In his memory, Historic Landmarks Foundation of Indiana established the annual John Arnold Rural Preservation Award, honoring a farm family that incorporates their historic buildings into a modern-day agricultural operation.

The Arnolds are also involved in the preservation of history beyond their own property lines. They and others battled to save Rush County's six covered bridges. In the 1980s Eleanor compiled four hundred oral interviews with early-twentieth-century farm women for the Indiana Extension Homemakers Association because she wanted to preserve their valuable stories. She then edited seven volumes based on the interviews, producing an immensely valuable account of a vanishing rural America. In 1991 the Smithso-

nian Institution selected the Arnold family to represent Indiana farmers during its American Folklife Festival.

Preservation for the Arnolds is not a social activity or a newly adopted cause. It's a way of life. You don't throw away the donut, sell the valuable trees or arrowheads, paint the walnut woodwork, carpet the floors, vinyl-side the house, or allow the county commissioners to destroy the covered bridges your ancestors crossed.

"We've had a good long run here, caring for this land for 181 straight years. We just believed in taking care of things that were taken care of for us," says Eleanor.

"We did our best," adds Jake.

Janet Ayres and Lynn Corson

Historic Name: BAUM-SHAEFFER HOUSE

County: CARROLL

Date of Construction: 1855

Architectural Style: ITALIANATE

LISTED IN THE NATIONAL REGISTER OF HISTORIC PLACES

It took a year and a half driving country roads nearly every weekend before Janet Ayres exclaimed, "This is it," when she first beheld the Baum-Shaeffer house south of Delphi. Then it took sixteen more years for Janet and her husband, Lynn Corson, to renovate the house that was built in 1855 by Carroll County pioneers David and Eliza Baum.

Janet and Lynn now direct their energy and passion to renovating the barn, granary, and smokehouse. "We're obsessed," says Janet, a longtime Purdue University professor in the Agricultural Economics Department who grew up on a dairy farm thirteen miles from her obsession. Lynn, a New Hampshire native, is the director of a Purdue environmental institute. They married in 1985 and began their search for a quiet place in the country within a thirty-minute commute of the West Lafayette Purdue campus.

Janet's "this is it" reaction is easy to understand. The farmhouse is down a winding lane, about a third of a mile off a quiet county road. It's tucked in a grove of walnut trees overlooking a peaceful valley where deer, fox, and coyotes roam and time stands still. The only sounds in the little valley are the summer wind rippling through the trees and the squawking and honking of the couple's pet geese and chickens. Turkey buzzards circle overhead. When they bought the house in 1986, it came with one, inadequate acre. Over the years, they have purchased thirty-one additional acres as a buffer against twenty-first–century noise and development, a threat even in rural Carroll County.

Descendants of the Baum family gave Lynn and Janet turn-of-the-twentieth-century photographs of the farm that show a white picket fence around the house. In his brick woodshop, which was once the summer kitchen, Lynn designed and cut 434 pickets and replicated the fence. The wood rotted, so now he's doing it all over again.

"We want to maintain the integrity of the place," Janet

notes. The house and the Baum family are a fundamental part of the history of Carroll County. The Baums and four other intrepid families left Chillicothe, Ohio, in 1825. They traveled down the Ohio River in a flatboat loaded with children and household goods to the Wabash River in south-western Indiana. At the confluence of the rivers, they bought a keelboat that they then polled up the Wabash and across Deer Creek, settling just south of what is now the town of Delphi. The journey took seven weeks. The Baums and the other families were among the first white residents of the area, which three years later became Carroll County.

The first meeting of the newly organized Carroll County commissioners was held in Daniel Baum's log house. The Baum family built the county's first brick kiln. It was about one mile south of the house David and Eliza built in 1855, the one that Janet and Lynn now own.

Photographs of the Baum family and their descendants the Shaeffers hang on the walls, not far from Janet's collection of folk dolls from fifty-five countries and Lynn's father's old desk from New Hampshire. In the barn where David Baum stacked hay is Janet's grandfather's 1880 farm wagon.

Janet and Lynn plan to get two pet cows to complement their chickens and geese. They don't eat the chicken eggs and they won't butcher or milk the cows. They believe that grazing cows will add to the tranquility of their little valley.

"We just want to sit on the porch and watch them," says Lynn. "It's really too bad we have to work."

Roger and Pam Bailey

Historic Name: WILLIAM & GRACE CRAIG HOUSE

City: LINTON

County: GREENE

Date of Construction: CIRCA 1900

Architectural Style: QUEEN ANNE

After graduating from The University of Texas Medical School at San Antonio, Roger Bailey came home to Linton. "There is just something about coming home," explains Roger. "You can't bring back people but you can recreate an illusion of a person, of a time that remains near and dear to your heart."

The person Roger remembers so fondly is his beloved grandfather Dr. Edwin Bailey, a revered Linton physician who treated generations of families and was often paid in sweet corn or a basket of fruit. The times that remain near and dear to Roger are childhood days spent with Grandpa. "He was the greatest inspiration in my life and the reason I became a doctor," says Roger, an anesthesiologist and pain

management specialist. Dr. E. Bailey often took his grandson with him on house calls and hospital rounds.

In 1971, Roger's father, an English professor at Indiana State University, was named chairman of the English department at San Antonio College and the family moved to Texas. Throughout high school, college, and medical school, Roger returned to Linton each summer to visit his grandparents. On one trip, he met Pam, whom he married in 1987. They have two teenage children.

In June 1991 Roger and Pam bought a wreck of a house on Northeast A Street, or Indiana Highway 54, the main thoroughfare through Linton. It's just west of Roger's childhood home and a few doors from his grandparents' home.

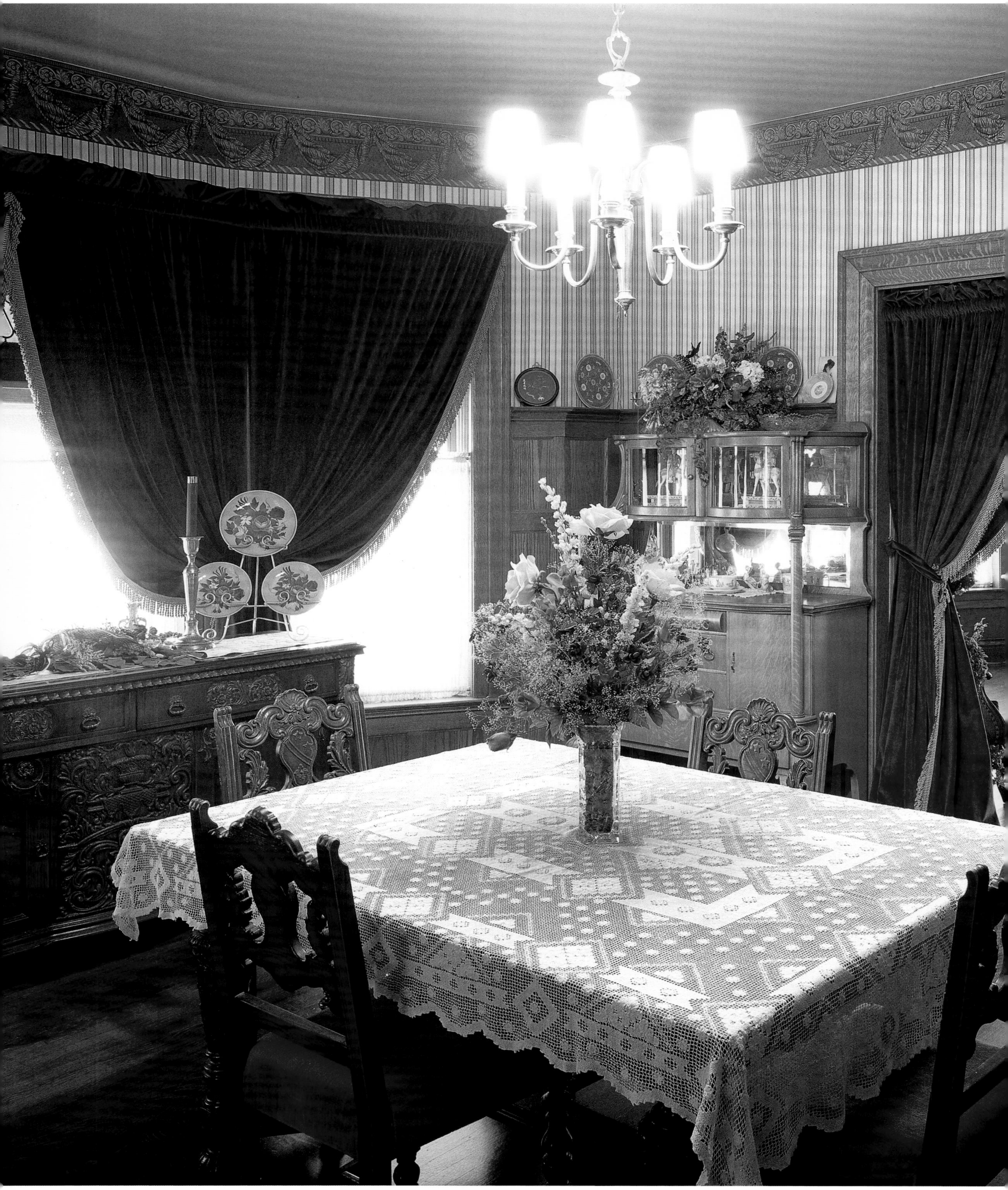

It was built around 1900 by coal-mine owner Job Freeman for his daughter, Grace, and her husband, William Craig. Job lived across the street in a massive nineteenth-century Victorian home, which he later donated to Greene County for a hospital. The Freeman-Greene Hospital was where Dr. Edwin Bailey practiced for decades and where Roger was born in 1960.

In 1974, the county built a new hospital, demolished the magnificent building that had housed the Freeman-Greene Hospital, and later sold the land to a franchise hamburger joint. Paper wrappings now litter Roger's front yard. "I was born in what is now the salad bar," says Roger. Then the city widened Northeast A Street and installed a stoplight in front of the Baileys' home, generating more traffic, noise, and litter. A neighbor hoisted up his Victorian home and moved it to the country to escape the blight. A fast food chicken place moved onto the vacant lot.

Roger remembers walking by the Craig house as a child with his grandfather. When he returned home in 1991, it was a music store and in deplorable condition. "We looked beyond the mess and decided it could be a good home," he says. "I liked the house and the neighborhood because it held so many good memories from my childhood."

Saving and restoring an old home was a learning experience beyond measure. Roger notes, "The fights with contractors were beyond belief because I wanted a faithful restoration and they didn't. I came back after twenty years with uniform good memories of house calls with Grandpa. I was determined to save this house because of what this neighborhood meant to me and my family."

"I'm proud of what we did," he adds.

7

Evelyn Ball

Historic Name: JUDGE CYRUS BALL HOUSE

City: LAFAYETTE

County: TIPPECANOE

Date of Construction: 1869

Architectural Style: SECOND EMPIRE

LISTED IN THE NATIONAL REGISTER OF HISTORIC PLACES, *Ninth Street Hill Neighborhood Historic District*

Shortly after their two sons returned safely from the Civil War, Judge Cyrus Ball and his wife, Rebecca, built a new hilltop home along a cow path two miles south of the Tippecanoe County Courthouse in Lafayette.

At the dawn of the twenty-first century, Judge Ball's glass photographs of Abraham Lincoln and General Ulysses S. Grant still hang in his library above his desk. His porcelain slop jar remains in his upstairs bedroom and a Ball family member still sleeps in his bed. The two-story Second Empire house with its tower pavilion and mansard roof has never been sold and has remained largely unchanged since it was built in 1869.

"Oh, dear, everything in this home has a story," says the charming Evelyn Ball, who moved into the family home in 1928 after marrying Cyrus Ball's great-grandson Cable Ball, a prominent Lafayette lawyer. "Let's have tea before the fireplace," she suggests. "It makes for friendlier conversation, and I'll tell you about the house, dear."

Her husband, Cable, grew up and lived in the house, which his great-grandfather built, for his entire life, dying in 1981. His other great-grandfather was the mid-nineteenth-century painter George Winter. Dozens of stunning original portraits of the Potawatomi and Miami Indians, which Winter painted in the early 1800s, still hang in Mrs. Ball's home. Several years ago a family member suggested she sell a treasured Winter painting to pay for needed roof repairs.

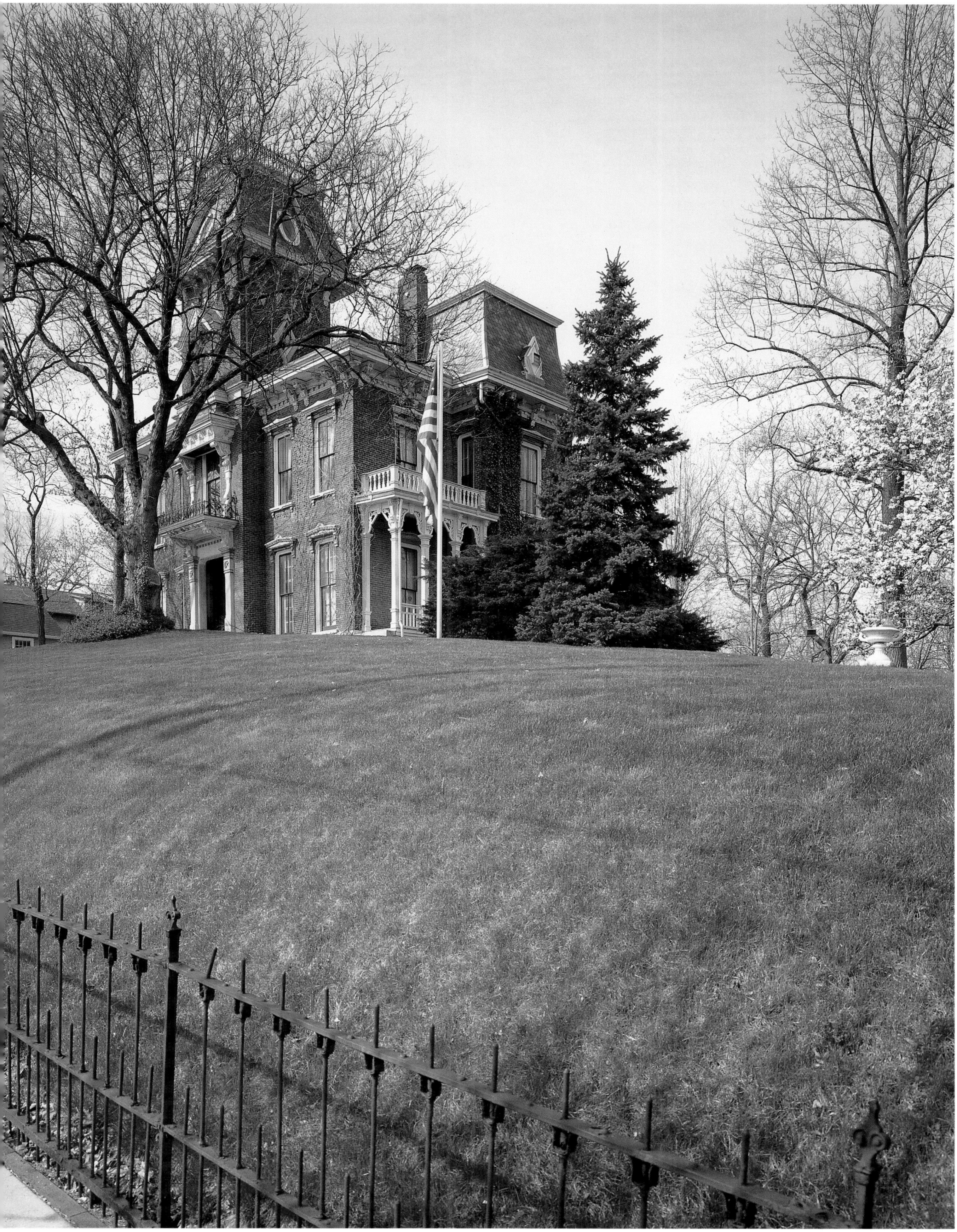

She flatly rejected the blasphemous suggestion. "It would be like selling your ancestors' body parts," she snapped. "Selling something would besmirch the family name which I must continue to honor. I have certain ideas about the value of the past, and how you must be careful not to besmirch the good names of the people who preceded you," she explains over tea and cookies.

The honorable house is within the National Register–listed Ninth Street Hill Neighborhood Historic District which includes ninety-four homes. "Many of the old Civil War–era homes have been knocked down," laments Mrs. Ball. "Many of the beautiful, kindly things I remember are gone. People have forgotten the importance of honoring scholarship and courtesy. Is there any greater insult to scholarship and courtesy than knocking down a historic home?"

Mrs. Ball grew up in Elizabeth, New Jersey, daughter of the president of the American Gas Furnace Company. She met the dashing Cable Ball in 1925 at a dance at Princeton University where he was a student. He later graduated from the University of Michigan Law School and they settled into the home on the hill and a life of courtesy and scholarship.

The house and its remarkable collection of Winter paintings and original furniture at first glance looks like a museum. But it's a *home,* as Mrs. Ball pointedly notes. "I live here and use everything," she explains. "Everything in here speaks to me. I feel like I was put on this earth to introduce people to beautiful and kindly things and hopefully remind others that if you have no past you have nothing to live up to."

Despite living in elegant nineteenth-century surroundings, Mrs. Ball learned to work a computer in her ninety-fifth year and spends several hours a day doing historical research on the Internet in Judge Ball's upstairs study. "It's a lovely instrument of learning," she says, wheeling the tea set back into the kitchen on Rebecca Ball's serving cart.

"Now, allow me to show you my new party outfit," she says, holding up a pretty, new dress and reciting a lengthy list of upcoming activities.

"I hope to die here in my home after attending some very nice party," she continues.

"Would you like a sip of brandy?"

Robert Beardsley

County: ELKHART

Date of Construction: CIRCA 1835

Architectural Style: GOTHIC REVIVAL

In 1938, Walter and Marjory Beardsley adopted a 4$\frac{1}{2}$-year-old boy from an Iowa orphanage and brought him home to Elkhart. Walter was a top executive with the Elkhart-based Miles Laboratories, the family pharmaceutical business that achieved worldwide fame when his father, Andrew H. Beardsley, invented Alka-Seltzer in 1931. The Beardsley family's enormous presence in Elkhart reaches back further, to 1834, when Robert's great-great-great-uncle, Dr. Havilah Beardsley, founded the town along the St. Joseph River. A bronze-and-marble statue of Dr. Beardsley now stands at the corner of Riverside Drive and Beardsley Avenue in Elkhart.

Robert Beardsley, Walter and Marjory's adopted son and only child, grew up in Elkhart, attended Phillips Academy in Andover, Massachusetts, graduated from Princeton University in 1955, and served three years in the U.S. Air Force. In 1958, while living in Boston and working as a salesman for a textbook publisher, he bought an old Elkhart County farmhouse in an area known as the Bristol Fruit Hills because of its once-abundant apple orchards.

"I had learned how to drive in the Bristol Fruit Hills. I love the beauty of the place and the quiet rural life," says Robert. During frequent visits home, he restored and built an addition to the 1835 Carpenter Gothic–style farmhouse and planted hundreds of apple and cherry trees on the 207 acres of rolling hills and verdant valleys. "I'm very fond of trees and I go to great lengths to preserve them," he says.

In 1965, Robert moved home to the little farmhouse in the Bristol Fruit Hills to serve as administrative assistant to his father, who was chairman of the board of Miles Laboratories. In 1978, Miles Laboratories was sold to the Bayer Aspirin Company. Robert's father died in 1980 and was followed by Robert's mother twelve years later.

As chairman of the Beardsley Foundation, Robert directed the purchase of a deteriorated three-story limestone mansion in downtown Elkhart built in 1910 by his great-great-uncle Albert R. Beardsley. It was called Ruthmere, in honor of Albert and Elizabeth's only child, Ruth, who died in infancy. Robert guided the restoration of Ruthmere, filling it with Louis XV–style furnishings and Beardsley family memorabilia. "The house needed a lot of work when we took over," Robert recalls. "Fortunately, the family living there had saved everything, which made our restoration a lot easier." It is now the Ruthmere Museum, is listed in the National Register of Historic Places, and was featured on the popular cable television program "America's Castles."

Following the death of his father and the sale of Miles Laboratories, Robert bought a home in Normandy, France, where he now lives in the winter. He spends summers at his ninety-acre estate along the Kennebunk River in Maine, but returns to the old farmhouse in the Bristol Fruit Hills each spring and autumn to walk among the trees. "This is my base," he says, looking toward the autumn hills and a lone heron wading in the pond. "It provides me the continuum and satisfies the agrarian in me.

"I've known these views my whole life. I've walked these fields, picked apples, and planted trees here for over forty years. This was my dream as a young man, the place where all my dreams began." He pauses and looks toward the hills, struggling to explain why he leaves Maine in the autumn and France in the spring to return to an Indiana farmhouse and walk among apple trees and marvel at the grace and beauty of a heron.

"This is home and I'm the last Beardsley in Elkhart County," he says. "Being adopted, I've always felt very fortunate."

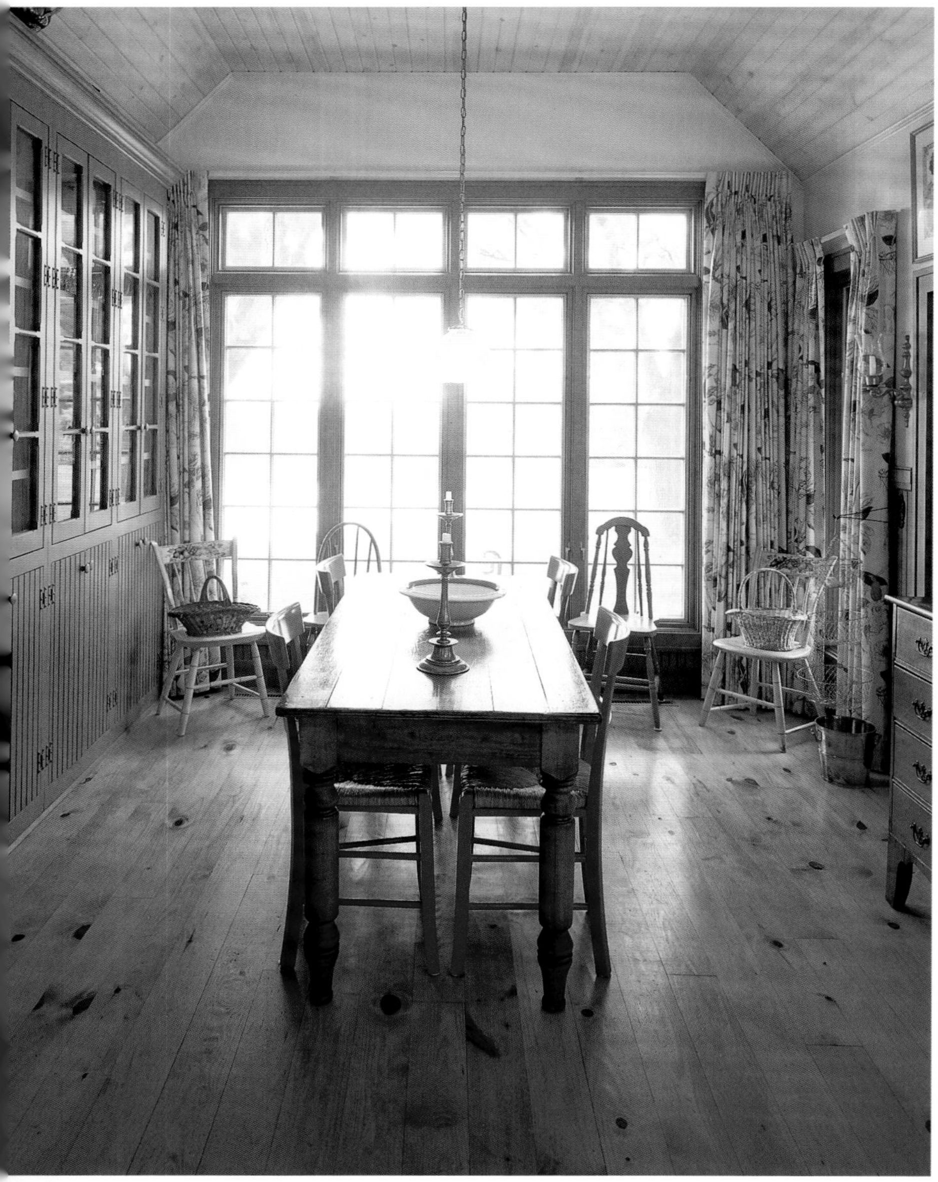

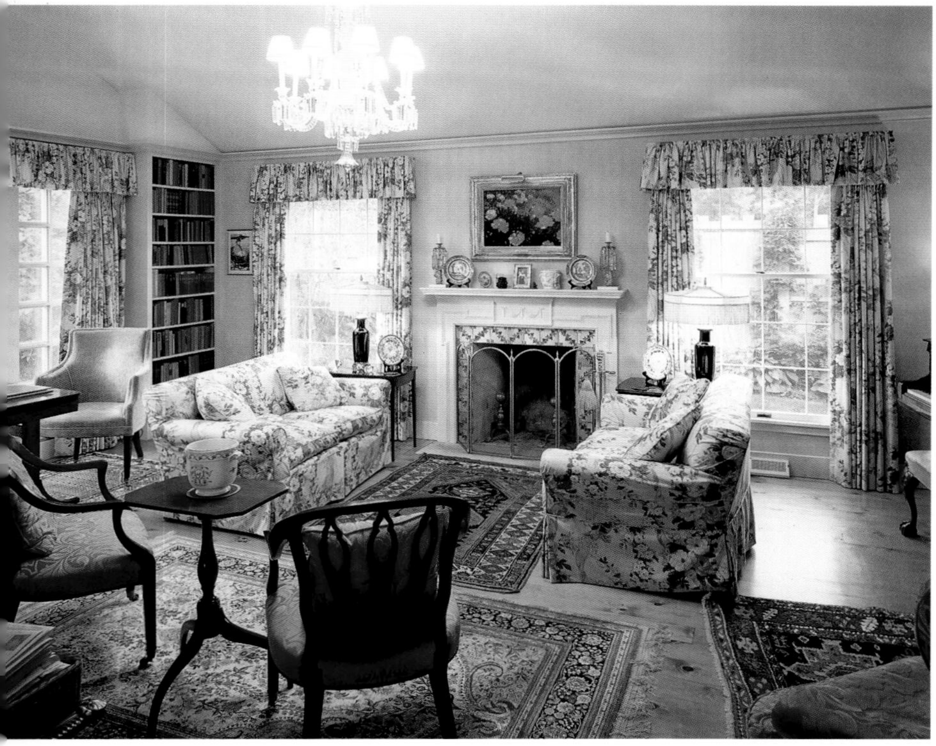

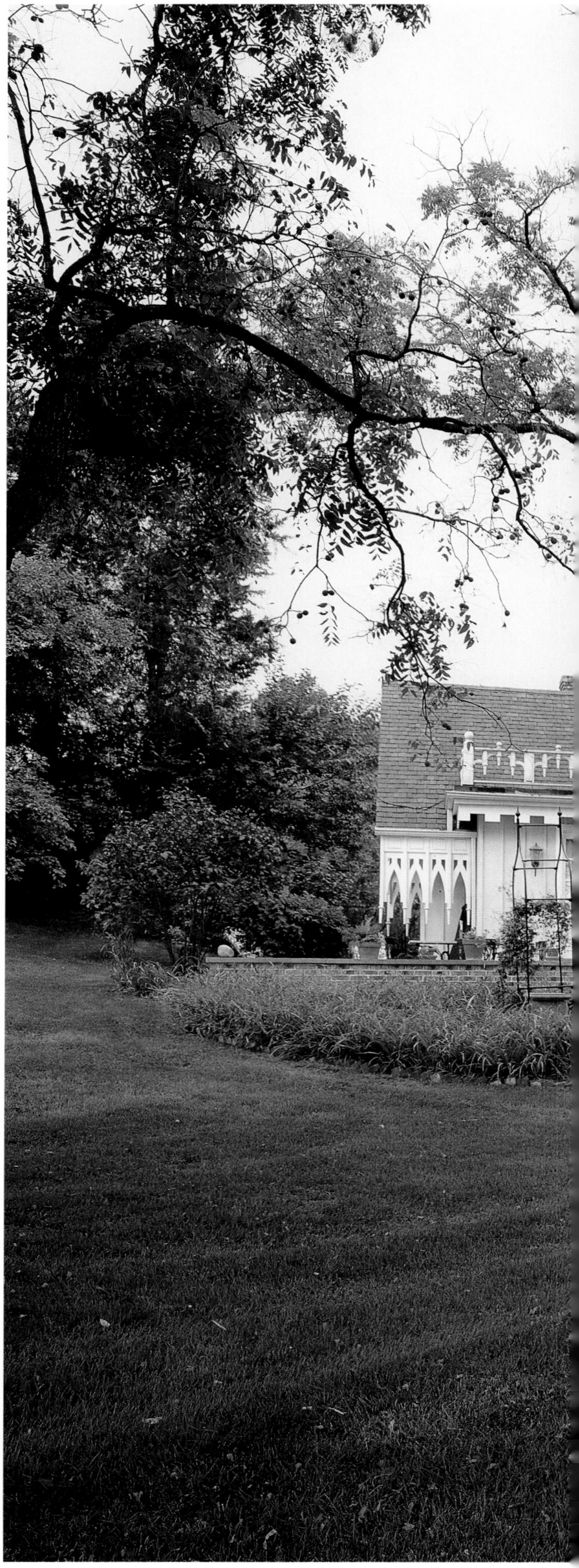

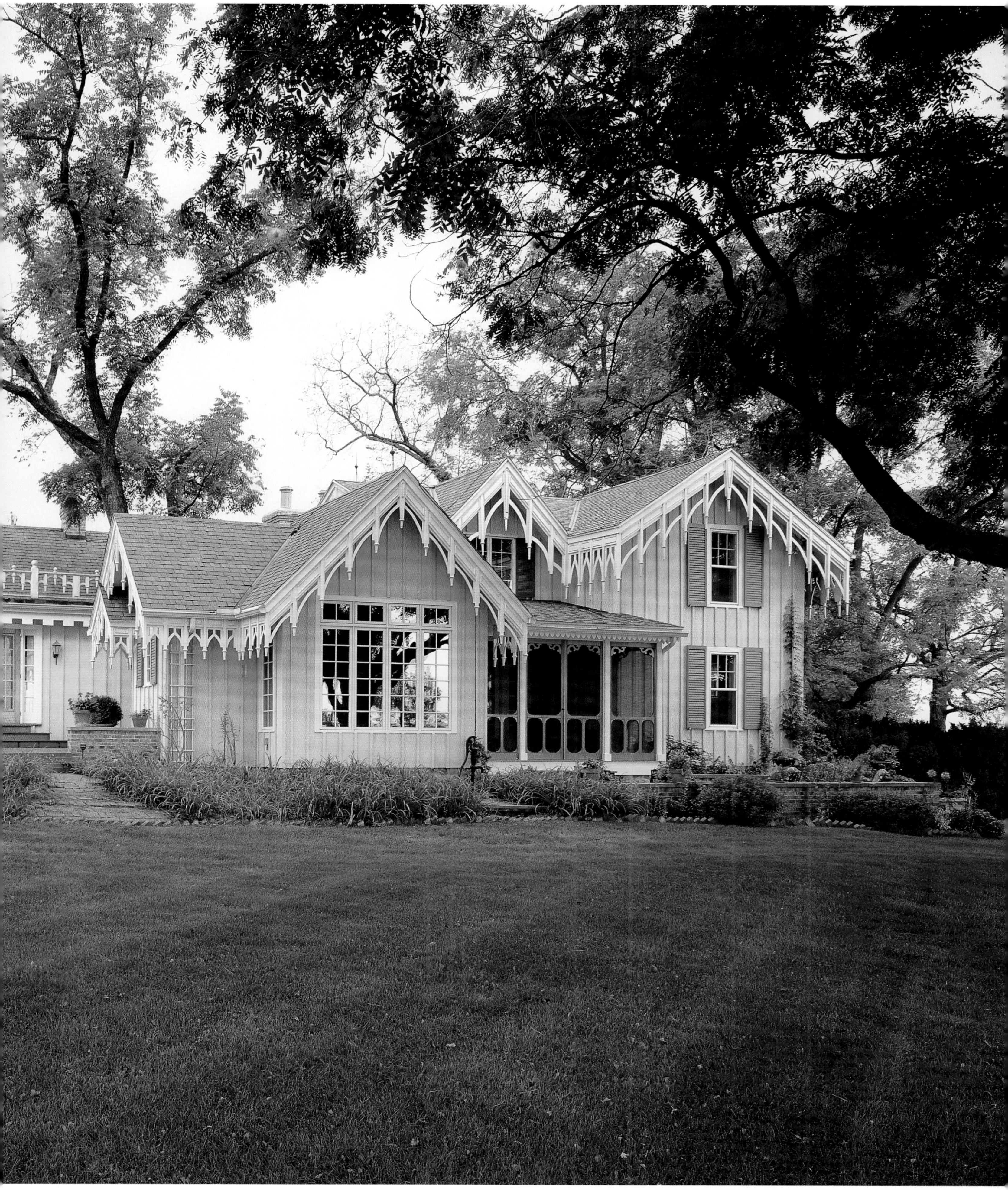

Robert (Bob) Beckmann

Historic Name: BREATHARD PAINT & WALLPAPER COMPANY BUILDING

City: INDIANAPOLIS

County: MARION

Date of Construction: 1903

LISTED IN THE NATIONAL REGISTER OF HISTORIC PLACES, *Massachusetts Avenue Commercial Historic District*

In 1985 Bob Beckmann, sensing the sweep of urban history, bought the old fifteen-thousand-square-foot Sears, Roebuck and Company "scratch and dent" commercial building in downtown Indianapolis. He converted it to a spacious loft residence. His friends thought him nuts, especially his mother. However, he had visited loft residences in historic commercial buildings in Chicago and New York and wondered, why not Indianapolis?

"When you live in a historic building in the city, you can't help but feel the sweep of history," says Beckmann, a retired real estate broker who specialized in historic commercial buildings. From 1968 to 1973, the Indianapolis native and Hanover College graduate served as a top aide to former Indianapolis mayor Richard Lugar. Beckmann directed the Lugar administration's successful effort to save the 1887 Union Station from the wrecking ball.

"That beautiful piece of railroad architecture triggered my interest in historic buildings," he says. "They are part of our heritage. Tear them down, we have nothing to remember how we were."

Beckmann's steel-reinforced, three-story concrete structure on Massachusetts Avenue was built in 1903 for the Breathard Paint & Wallpaper Company. "I'd always dreamed of living in a commercial building with big open spaces, few walls, and exposed heat pipes," he explains. He spent a year renovating the second floor, tearing out part of a concrete ceiling to create a soaring atrium and roof garden for his five-thousand-square-foot loft. The remaining space he leased to an architectural firm. Then he invited his mother over for dinner.

"It's very nice dear, but when are you going to finish it?" wondered Mother, noting the concrete floors, exposed pipes, and modern track lighting in the twelve-foot ceilings. Well, it was finished, an open expanse of light and greenery that he filled with a vast array of enormous plants; a fireplace; a huge chunk of Lake Michigan driftwood; a pink flamingo; toy dirigibles; wooden giraffes; classic, modern-design chrome-and-leather furniture; oil and acrylic modern art; sculpture; and theater memorabilia.

"There is great satisfaction living here with all the things I've accumulated. I'm not a collector and there's no organization to it, but it's great to look at these things from my travels or artists I've known," he explains. "My roots are here."

He helped found the Indiana Repertory Theater and is a frequent performer in the five theaters along the six-block Massachusetts Avenue Historic District. When he bought his building, gunshots rang out nightly among the smattering of topless bars and abandoned buildings that lined the avenue.

"I put my money where my mouth is and did my part," he says of the neighborhood resurgence in which he played a pioneering role. "Bringing back an old building in a neighborhood triggers good things."

Beckmann's favorite piece of art is an alabaster sculpture by Georgia Strange of an upside-down human head with its tongue sticking out. It's called "Do Not Go Gentle," from the Dylan Thomas poem "Do Not Go Gentle Into That Good Night." The upside-down head sticking its tongue out at conventional wisdom will eventually become his tombstone when he dies and is buried in the beautiful Crown Hill Cemetery in Indianapolis.

"My whole life has been about what that sculpture symbolizes and I like the message about not going easily."

Bob Beckmann passed away in September 2001.

Ron and Ruth Berline

Historic Name: GREY GOOSE INN

City: PENDLETON

County: MADISON

Date of Construction: 1820

Architectural Style: FEDERAL

LISTED IN THE NATIONAL REGISTER OF HISTORIC PLACES, *Pendleton Historic District*

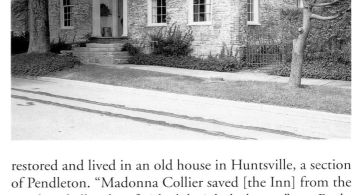

Before Ron and Ruth Berline bought, in 1980, the rooming house in Pendleton known as the Grey Goose Inn, they envisioned renovating it to be the town museum. But nobody in town was interested, so they decided to live in it, but feared the fourteen-inch brick walls would collapse in the next gust of wind. "You could have pushed the kitchen walls over," says Ron, longtime owner of the Berline Construction Company. He took a year off work to renovate the house, which was built in 1820, three years before Madison County was formed. Ron replaced the leaking roof and stripped the rotten, cracked plaster and removed each brick, one at a time, and rebuilt the walls. He had new window sashes built and spent three months cutting the original wavy glass to fit the new frames.

"I was obsessed. This kind of work is important to me," he explains. "Somebody made that glass. This whole house is handmade by craftsmen who liked what they did and did it well. It was hammer, chisel, pin, and maul and every pin and peg fit tight. That is worth preserving."

Prior to buying the Grey Goose from boardinghouse proprietor Madonna Wellington Collier, the Berlines had restored and lived in an old house in Huntsville, a section of Pendleton. "Madonna Collier saved [the Inn] from the wrecking ball and we finished the job she began," says Ruth.

Ron, Ruth, and their three children moved into the Grey Goose a year later and spent six more years finishing the enormous restoration job. The Inn was believed to have been built by James Grey and named for the flocks of geese that nested in the swamps along nearby Fall Creek. It is now reputed to be the oldest home in Pendleton, which was the first Madison County Seat.

In 1988, Ruth formed the preservation group that spent eight years performing the necessary research to have much of downtown Pendleton listed in the National Register of Historic Places. "I figured, why save one house? We wanted to save the whole town," recalls Ruth, who married Ron in 1956 after he proposed on a blind date. Like Ron, Ruth is obsessed with detail and awed by the history of old buildings and the craftsmen who made everything fit tight. Several years ago she started her own company, B.E.R. Enterprises, which buys crumbling historic homes in Pendleton, then restores and resells them.

The Grey Goose predates the platting of Pendleton by three years and was built to serve travelers along the old, dirt trail known as the Shelbyville–Fort Wayne Road and farmers hauling grain to the gristmills clustered near the waterfall on Fall Creek. A tavern was added to the back of the Grey Goose around 1832 to serve the needs of the growing town. Located two hundred yards south of the only bridge over Fall Creek, it did a brisk business as wagon traffic backed up during the wait to cross the creek.

The Berlines raised their children in the house and ran the construction business from a back room where Ron sits in a two-hundred-year-old Irish chair. Upstairs, his grandchildren jump on a two-hundred-year-old rope bed that belonged to his grandmother.

In another upstairs bedroom, Ron exposed the big oak beams that were cut with an axe, squared with an adz, and pinned and pegged together nearly two centuries ago when east central Indiana was still a vast, unpopulated hardwood forest.

"This craftsmanship is so important," he says, tracing a finger over the axe marks in an oak beam. "Someone did this almost two hundred years ago—some guy like me. That's why it's important."

Terry and Brenda Blackburn

Historic Name: WILLIAM HODGE LOG HOUSE

County: GRANT

Dates of Construction: 1849 / 1998

The Back Creek Cabin is a piece of Appalachian history transplanted from the hollows of eastern Kentucky to the flat farm country of Grant County. The eighteen by thirty-seven–foot simple oak log cabin was built near Upton, Kentucky, in 1849 by farmer William Hodge. It was barely standing in the summer of 1997 when Terry and Brenda Blackburn of Fairmount saw it. Trees grew from the dirt floor and through the top of the cabin, which had no roof. The perfect home. They paid $8,000 for the log-pile fixer-upper and had it hauled 210 miles to their five acres along Back Creek north of Fairmount.

They learned of the cabin from a friend who told them of Tony Vance, a man who scours the Kentucky hills for old cabins to buy, relocate, and resell to people like the Blackburns. A log cabin broker, in other words. "Tony, he just hates to see old cabins lost," says Terry, a retired Kokomo autoworker.

With help from Terry's father, Claude, the Blackburns reassembled the numbered logs, added a kitchen, a galvanized roof, a stone fireplace, and a second-story bedroom and moved into the cabin on Christmas Eve, 1998.

This has been a dream come true for Brenda, who grew up in the hills of eastern Kentucky. Her father and grandfather were coal miners and generations of her family lived in log cabins. "It's just something I always wanted because I never forgot it from my childhood. We were poor and primitive and I grew up visiting relatives in old cabins. Mom cooked on a wood stove, we had fireplaces for heat, and

dipped drinking water from a spring, and I went to a one-room schoolhouse," says Brenda, a registered nurse at Marion General Hospital.

Terry chinked and daubed the exterior logs while Brenda applied interior mortar, carefully following instructions from a book called *Building and Restoring the Hewn Log House.* Poplar siding from an old barn near Knightstown was milled and used for the floor. They searched antique stores and found an old-fashioned sink, a claw-foot bathtub, a 1926 refrigerator, benches from a Mennonite meeting-house, wooden bowls, an 1850 Amish dry sink, and a 1926 Roper stove, among other old items.

Their son, Terry, built a nine-foot-long dining room table

for them. They keep the unsightly television in a cabinet when they aren't watching it, and refuse to install a dish-washer or mar the aesthetics of the stark kitchen with a microwave. For six peaceful months they lived quite hap-pily without a phone, but their children and Brenda's employer complained until they relented. "I hate having a phone," says Terry. "It rings."

They did such a superb job restoring the cabin and furnishing it with primitive tables and chairs that it was featured in the February 2001 issue of *Country Home* magazine. "I want it to look like 1850 in here," says Brenda. It does.

Outside, Terry built a summer kitchen where Brenda

dries beans, herbs, and flowers. He built himself a plank garage where he's rebuilding a 1949 Farmall tractor. Six Rhode Island Red laying hens peck around the yard, providing fresh brown eggs daily. Border collies, Mack and Molly, patrol the five acres, protecting the Rhode Island Reds from hungry coyotes, fox, and raccoons.

"It's a piece of the past we saved. We went to Disney World recently with the grandkids and couldn't wait to get home to our cabin," says Brenda.

"It turned out exactly like I wanted it to," she adds. "I finally got my cabin and it's home now."

Lee M. Bowers III

Historic Name: LOUGHRIDGE-GRAYSTON HOUSE

City: HUNTINGTON

County: HUNTINGTON

Date of Construction: 1853

Architectural Style: ITALIANATE

In his 1988 address to the graduating class of Washington and Lee University School of Law in Lexington, Virginia, U.S. Supreme Court Justice Lewis F. Powell Jr. emphasized the importance of returning home and using newly acquired legal skills for the common good. Forsake the big Wall Street Law firms, Justice Powell advised the new lawyers. Your friends back home will need you more.

Magna cum laude graduate Lee M. Bowers III heeded the great man's advice. "I already felt that way but Justice Powell reinforced my decision," says Bowers, who returned home to Huntington to join the family law firm started in 1899 by his great-grandfather Fred H. Bowers. He also became a board member of Huntington Alert, the local preservation organization, applying his considerable legal skills in the ongoing battle against demolition.

Lee grew up in downtown Huntington, walking eight blocks to Central Elementary School, daily passing the imposing Loughridge-Grayston house on historically and architecturally rich North Jefferson Street. The house was built in 1853 by Wilson B. Loughridge, an eminent lawyer and the first judge of the Huntington County Court of Common Pleas. In 1860 the house was sold to Dr. Frederick S. C. Grayston when Judge Loughridge moved to Peru to assume ownership of the *Miami County Sentinel,* his family's newspaper.

The house remained in the Grayston family until the

late 1950s. It was serving as a flower shop and an art studio in 1987 when Lee's mother learned it was for sale and notified him in Virginia. Despite being in his final year of law school, he bought the house from Flower Mill proprietor Harriet DeWald. "I still didn't know if I was coming home to Huntington, but I didn't want the house to slip away," he says. "Walking past it on my way to school every day, I always wanted to grow up and live in that house." He rented it to his sister and her husband until he returned home, a fourth-generation lawyer. He began a room-by-room restoration, tearing up shag carpet and linoleum and displaying his burgeoning collection of stuffed wild-animal heads, beer bottles from Indiana breweries, and other curios.

"I don't know where it started or why," he says of the beer bottles and wall-mounted fish, moose, deer, duck, mountain lion, skunk, bear, raccoon, boar, turtle, and pheasant. "I don't even hunt or fish." It is a wildly eclectic assembly of unusual items and period antique furniture that Lee

and his partner, Huntington antiques dealer Ray PeGan, display throughout the house that William B. Loughridge built so long ago: Grandpa Lee Bowers's 1911 Huntington High School football team photograph; vintage tobacco cans and cigar boxes; Dr. Frederick S. C. Grayston's walnut medicine cabinet, which he used in the house 130 years ago while administering to the eyes, ears, noses, and throats of Huntington residents; Lee's great-aunt's cello; a plaster bust of Abraham Lincoln; an antique print of President Warren G. Harding; and a life-sized plaster statue of a Greek discus thrower salvaged from the old Huntington High School before it was torn down for a city park. In the front yard are pieces of iron and stone that Lee and Ray salvaged from long-since-demolished historic Huntington buildings.

Lee's alma mater Central Elementary School is still standing across the street. He's heard rumors that a chain drugstore is eyeing the building.

"I'm glad I came home to fight these battles," he says.

John Buhler

Historic Name: JESSE DAVIES HOUSE

City: HUNTINGTON

County: HUNTINGTON

Date of Construction: 1868

Architectural Style: ITALIAN VILLA

"The finest private mansion in the city," gushed the *Huntington Democrat* on October 7, 1868, as Jesse Davies' great house on the hill was being completed. The awestruck newspaper reporter predicted migrating flocks of geese would alter their flight plans to avoid hitting the mansion's soaring tower.

Dry-goods store proprietor Jesse Davies built the imposing fourteen-room, hilltop Italian villa a few blocks northwest of the Huntington County Courthouse. It provided a commanding 360-degree view of passing geese, the Little Wabash River Valley, and the entire city of Huntington. It took a German craftsman two years to build Jesse's open, walnut staircase that spirals up three stories into the tower.

In the latter half of the twentieth century, the magnificent villa entered a period of decline.

Oral surgeon Dr. John Buhler first noticed the deterior-

ating house in 1974 when he returned from Africa. John served as a dentist in the U.S. Army for two years at Kagnew Station in Ethiopia, where one of his patients was Emperor Haile Selassie.

By 1983, the bank had foreclosed on the house, which was in deplorable condition. Only the tower of the once magnificent dwelling was visible through the overgrown brush. The two rotten wooden porches were propped up with telephone poles.

"I recognized the house's grandeur and potential," says John, who practices dentistry in Fort Wayne. He bought the forlorn villa and happily went to work.

"I started from scratch," recalls Dr. Buhler, a wiry, athletic man of considerable energy. He's a triathlete, often runs forty miles a week, bicycles a hundred miles a week, and competes in marathons, including the Boston, where he

finished in an impressive three hours and twenty minutes in 2001. Once a year, Dr. Buhler spends a week in different locations building houses for Habitat for Humanity. So, he was well trained and conditioned for the monumental task of renovating a big, old house. Among other things, he dug out and hauled away two dump trucks full of brush and vines from the overgrown yard, had the bulging brick walls of the carriage house repaired, rebuilt two porches, and painted the whole place, which took two years.

After those two years of extensive restoration, John and his family moved into the big house in 1985. John's proudest achievement is the hand-printed Bradbury and Bradbury–esque wallpaper, which he selected and painstakingly hung on the twelve-foot-tall walls and ceilings in six of the home's fourteen rooms. Each room is a different design: Greco Roman in one; Neo-classical in another; and on and on through the fifty-three-hundred-square-foot house. John learned wall-papering by watching "This Old House" on public television. "I trimmed every inch of it," he says. "It took months just to trim it."

He also created a stencil of the design in the red glass windows on the front door, which he then duplicated along both the walls of the winding, three-story stairway. This required lying on his back on a scaffold he constructed in the stairway.

"I just like the house," says the inexhaustible Dr. Buhler. "The project was fun."

Kitty Burkhart

Historic Name: THE OLD STONE HOUSE / DANIEL STOUT HOUSE

County: MONROE

Date of Construction: CIRCA 1828

Architectural Style: FEDERAL

LISTED IN THE NATIONAL REGISTER OF HISTORIC PLACES

In 1943 when Hubert and Carol Brown bought the Old Stone House north of Bloomington in the Monroe County hills, it had no heat, running water, or electricity, and Maple Grove Road was a narrow, gravel path. It did have an outhouse and rags stuffed in the upstairs windows to thwart nesting birds and raccoons.

"It spoke to us," Carol Brown told Kitty, her skeptical daughter. The house was built of fieldstone around 1828 by Daniel Stout, a friend of William Henry Harrison, governor of the old Indiana Territory. On January 23, 1818, Stout received a 160-acre land grant in the Monroe County wilderness from President James Monroe.

The intrepid Stout first built a temporary log cabin on the site. He then chopped down massive poplar trees and dislodged stone from the creek for a permanent home. He hauled the stones a quarter mile uphill, pounded and chiseled each one into shape, and fit them together into a house, supported by the enormous logs. The walls of this pioneer masterpiece are two feet thick. When the four-room, two-story fortress was complete, the inexhaustible Daniel Stout built a gristmill on the creek, which he named for himself, Stout's Creek.

It is the oldest home in Monroe County, a tribute to early Hoosier pioneers and to Hubert and Carol Brown, who saved the crumbling stone pile from ruination when it was being used as a grain bin in 1943. "My parents were very ahead of their time. Mother's mind went in an aesthetic direction," says Kitty of her mother's far-sighted preser-

Hubert worked in the limestone business and possessed a craftsman's love of soft stone. The Browns added a kitchen, bathroom, hallway, and bedroom to the house, carefully following Daniel Stout's original pattern of stone placement.

In 1945, Kitty married Wayne Burkhart in the front yard of her parents' stone house. Their son, Garrett, was also married in the front yard in 1968. After her parents died, Kitty and Wayne moved into the house in 1986, continuing the tradition of caring for the Stout, Brown, and Burkhart family legacies. Wayne died a year later.

Kitty worked in the Foreign Studies office at Indiana University for twenty-eight years before retiring in 1995 to redirect her considerable passion and energy into local preservation efforts. In 1998, about eight square miles surrounding the Old Stone House was declared the Maple Grove Road Rural Historic District and listed in the National Register of Historic Places. It is presently Indiana's only rural historic district.

"Mother always had an interest in a house of years," says Kitty, who has lined the stairway with pictures of Stout, Brown, and Burkhart family members. "Now I understand why because this house speaks to me."

From the front porch where she was married, Kitty looks out on land that remains remarkably unchanged. The road is paved but there are few houses and the surrounding woods remain lovely, dark, and deep.

"I breathe this house," she says.

vation efforts. From Stout family descendants, the Browns received the original land grant certificate and a china saucer that Governor Harrison gave Daniel and Sarah to commemorate the birth of their daughter, Cynthia, in 1805. The items were framed and hung in the living room, along with Cynthia's childhood bonnet and portraits of Daniel Stout II and his daughter, Kiturah.

Clifford and Louise Cain

Historic Name: AUGUST ZEPPENFELD HOUSE

City: FRANKLIN

County: JOHNSON

Date of Construction: 1872

Architectural Style: ITALIANATE

LISTED IN THE NATIONAL REGISTER OF HISTORIC PLACES

It's funny how things sometimes work out. Take the case of Cliff and Louise Cain of Franklin. After receiving an advanced degree in theology from Vanderbilt University, Cliff, an ordained minister, was named dean of the Franklin College Chapel and professor of philosophy and religion in July 1981.

The Cains moved to Franklin and rented a place while looking for a house to buy. Louise, who grew up in New

Jersey suburbs, wanted an old house, but not on Jefferson Street. They had a one-year-old daughter and so Louise feared the heavy Jefferson Street traffic. Cliff, who grew up in old homes in Zanesville, Ohio, had other, unpopular, ideas.

"The symbol of success for me was a new house," he recalls. "But then Louise got me reassessing." Being selective people, they looked for four years at dozens of old houses, most of which had been "modernized" with shag carpets, linoleum, and dropped ceilings, or had been chopped up into apartments. "We didn't want to pay the money for all that and then take it apart," says Cliff, who has long since abandoned his notion of defining success with a new house.

Finally, in 1985, they bought a house that hadn't been modernized—on busy Jefferson Street. Their two children, eight dogs, and two cats have survived the traffic. The house was built in 1872 by German immigrant August Zeppenfeld, a tanner of animal hides and a bridle- and saddle-maker. High-energy Cliff undertook an extensive reassessment, launching an enthusiastic study of the home's history and eventually getting it listed in the National Register. His research uncovered some interesting information about the previous occupants, such as the fact that Jeanette Zeppenfeld, who lived in the house her uncle built from 1932 until her death in 1936, retired as head of the Franklin College German Department in 1920 when she went deaf. "She possessed a fine mind and was a keen, diligent, painstaking research worker," the Franklin newspaper noted in Jeanette Zeppenfeld's obituary.

"I like stuff like that," says Cliff, who often rides his 1975 Dutch bicycle the eight blocks to Franklin College, which was founded in 1834 by the American Baptist Church. (In 1841 it became the first college in Indiana to admit women.) "I know the names of all the people who've lived in this house," Cliff continues. "I've moved around a lot but when you live in an old house with a history you feel rooted."

Cliff met Louise when they were students at Muskingum College in New Concord, Ohio. They married in 1975 and lived in The Hague in the Netherlands for a couple of years, where Cliff studied and preached, bought a bicycle, and learned how to wear wooden shoes. The house that tanner and bridle- and saddle-maker August Zeppenfeld built three blocks west of the Johnson County Courthouse now contains the Cains' collection of Dutch windmill art, furniture, and several pairs of wooden shoes, which Cliff says are surprisingly comfortable. On his school-related international journeys, Cliff has accumulated a collection of tribal ritual masks from Guatemala, Yucatan, Belize, and Capetown, South Africa, which provides an interesting contrast to the Dutch windmill art.

"You could take every stick of furniture out of this house and it would still have a personality," says Louise, who works at the Franklin Animal Clinic. When she was a child living in generic subdivisions, her parents talked continually about one day buying an old house.

"I just wanted to do something my parents always wanted to do but never did," she says.

Merrill and Pat Carrigan

Historic Name: JAMES F. HARCOURT HOUSE

County: RUSH

Date of Construction: 1880–1881

Architectural Style: ITALIANATE / SECOND EMPIRE

LISTED IN THE NATIONAL REGISTER OF HISTORIC PLACES

Were it not for Opal Boring's splendid 624-page history of Orange Township, who would remember that world middleweight boxing champion Norman Selby was born in 1873 in nearby Moscow, a tiny Rush County town on the Flatrock River? Or that Norman, known as Kid McCoy, married ten times, served eight years in a California prison for killing his lover Thelma Mors, and finally committed suicide in April 1940 in Michigan? Opal believed that no bit of Orange Township history should be ignored or forgotten.

Opal was born and died in Orange Township, devoting most of her ninety-six years to painting and studying the beautiful landscapes and rich history of her beloved southwestern Rush County. She lived most of her glorious life

in a big house on a hill built around 1880 by her grandfather James F. Harcourt. In 1866 he invented, patented, and began manufacturing "The Young Hoosier," a mechanical device to plant wheat between rows of standing corn. Opal was born in the house on April 28, 1904, went to college, returned home, married farmer Bonnel H. Boring, and had three children. In 1960 she moved back into the house to care for her mother, Adeline, who had moved into the house in 1900 when she married farmer Ira, son of "The Young Hoosier" inventor.

Moving into the house on the hill to care for ailing parents is an unquestioned family tradition. In 1997, Opal's daughter, Pat Carrigan, and Pat's husband, Merrill, moved into the big house to care for Opal. "We always knew we'd

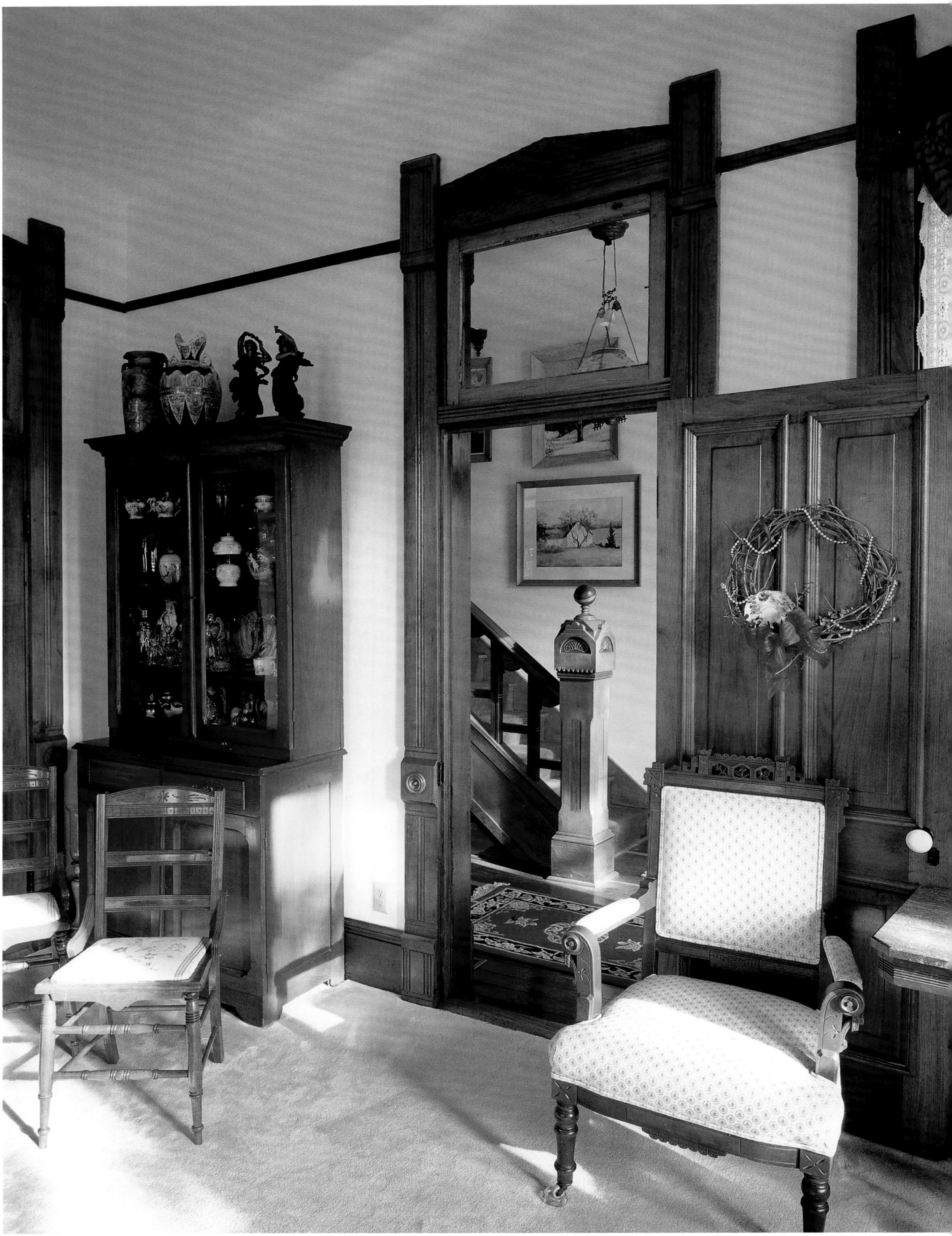

keep the tradition going of moving in to care for parents. It's an important part of my family history," says Pat.

Pat and Merrill met at Earlham College, married in 1957, and returned to Orange Township to farm and raise five children in a house one mile from Opal's. Merrill taught biology at Rushville High School for thirty-two years before retiring in 1990.

"This house has never been out of the family and hasn't changed much," says Pat. Merrill did add a downstairs bathroom for Opal, so she didn't have to climb stairs. Opal died on November 11, 2000, four days after voting in the U.S. presidential election, something she never missed. Death could wait.

The Harcourt house is surely one of the most picturesque homes in east central Indiana, located in a Hoosier still life of gently rolling hills, soaring hawks, and the green valley of Big Flatrock River, where Pat and Merrill often canoe on lazy summer days. The only sound heard on the large front porch where Opal wrote about Kid McCoy is the

occasional, rhythmic clop, clop, clop of an Amish horse-and-buggy trotting down the quiet road.

A few years before her death, Opal painted the house light pink, its original color. In her research into family history, she found that her grandfather had visited New Orleans in the 1870s, admired the light pink houses in the French Quarter and their wrought-iron balcony railings, and duplicated the look with his new house.

Pat and Merrill's devotion to preserving the grand house and Opal's legacy extends to 104 acres of surrounding farm-land, which is planted in ground cover for wild birds and animals. Merrill, a member of the Big Flatrock River Restoration Project, helped remove trash and repair twenty-eight miles of eroded riverbank. Pat is secretary of Rush County Heritage, the local preservation organization founded in 1986 to save the county's covered bridges.

"One day our kids will inherit the house and land and hopefully maintain the family tradition and care for us when we get old," says Pat. "It's how we do it in this family."

John E. Christian

Historic Name: SAMARA / JOHN E. AND CATHERINE E. CHRISTIAN HOUSE

City: WEST LAFAYETTE

County: TIPPECANOE

Date of Construction: 1956

Architect: FRANK LLOYD WRIGHT

Architectural Style: USONIAN

LISTED IN THE NATIONAL REGISTER OF HISTORIC PLACES

Before John Christian reveals the secret location of his hidden living room television, you must sit and say, "Open Sesame." Loudly.

"Louder," demands the animated John Christian, delighting in the intriguing details of his Frank Lloyd Wright–designed house. Like where the great architect hid the damnable television contraption back in 1956. It rises from a wall cabinet with the push of a remote-control button and descends with another button-push. "Mr. Wright knew every home would have a television, but he didn't want it cluttering up his design," says John, retired head of the Purdue University bionucleonics department.

In 1950, John and his wife, Catherine, boldly phoned the aging Wright at Taliesin, his Spring Green, Wisconsin, home. Amazingly, he invited the young couple to Taliesin to discuss designing the home they wished to build on a sloping one-acre lot in West Lafayette.

"Mr. Wright agreed to do the house, even though we had no money," explains John. Five years later, Wright completed plans for the house he named Samara, after the winged seed of a pinecone. It was one of his last Usonian designs, a contemporary, glass-enclosed, middle-class, low-maintenance home. "Usonian" was Wright's euphemistic name for the United States of America.

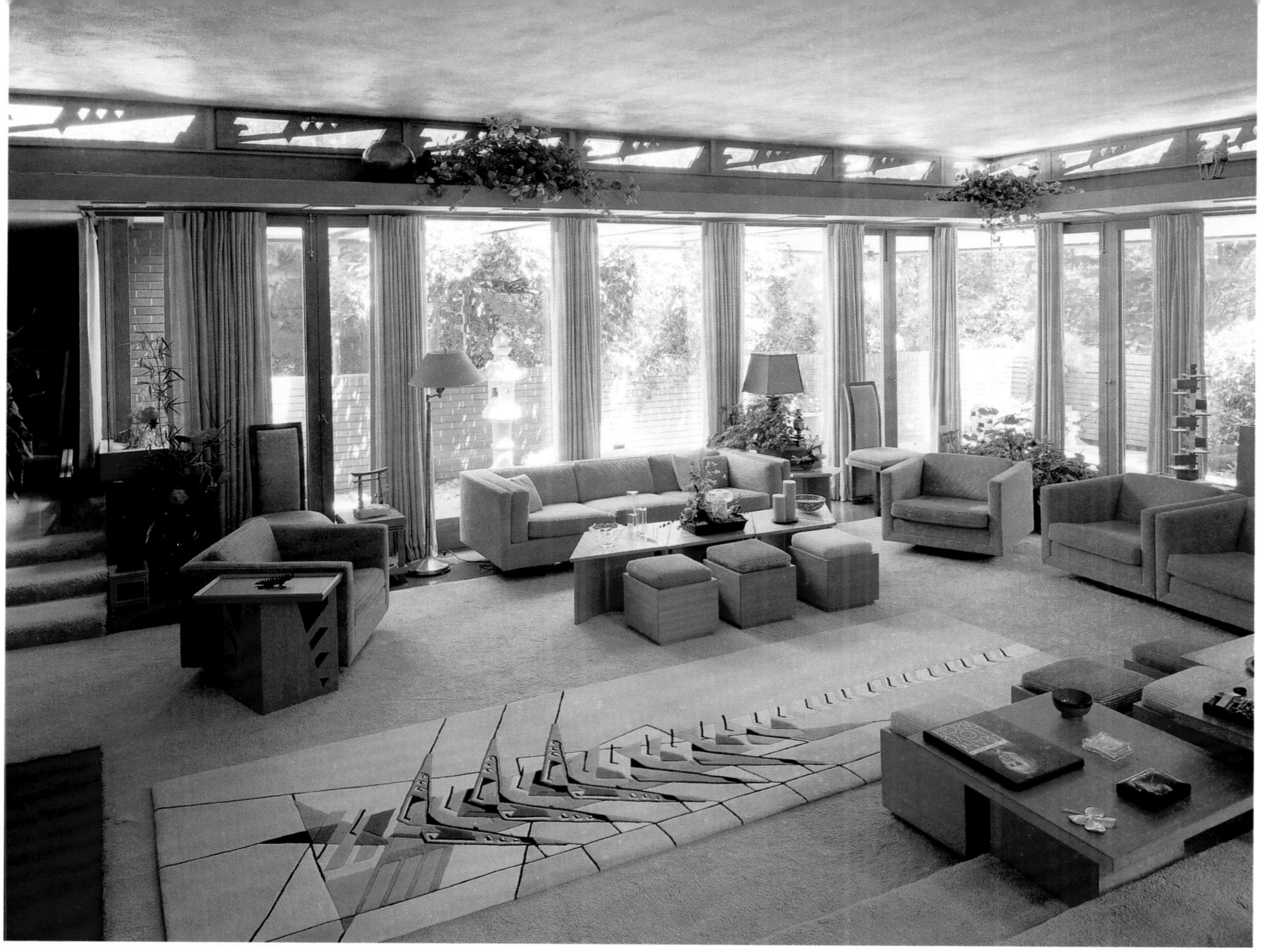

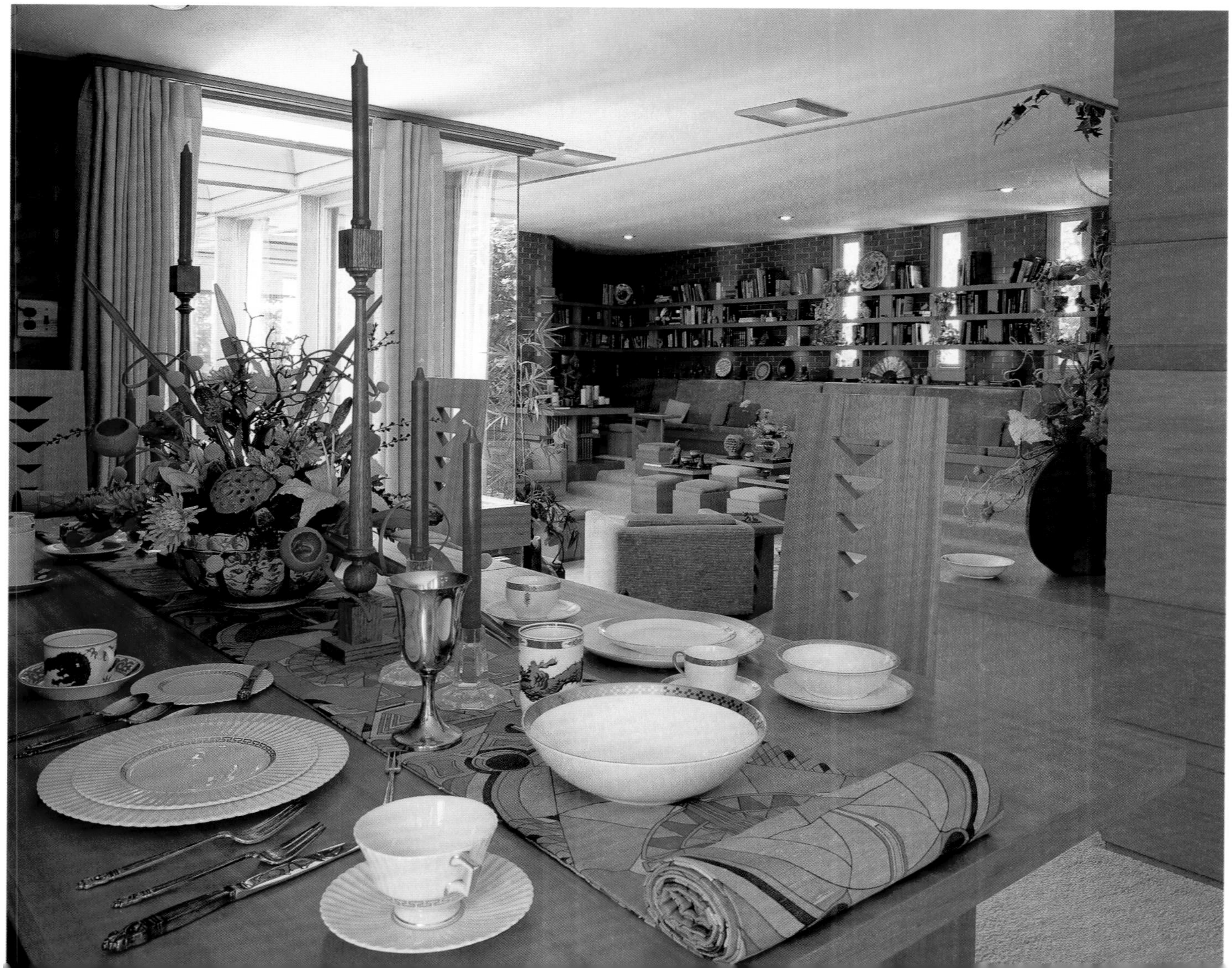

The Christians exchanged numerous letters with Wright during the design process and visited Taliesin several times through the years. At one point in the extended design process, Wright directed the Christians to bring him brick samples from twelve foundries within fifty miles of the home site. Wright selected bricks from Attica, Indiana, for the exterior. Interior and exterior wood is Philippine mahogany, although Mr. Wright didn't order the Christians to the Philippine Islands to collect samples.

Wright also designed the furniture, specifying the wood, colors, and fabric, as well as where each chair, table, couch, lamp, and bed should be placed. He designed the carpets, rugs, and drapes, candlestick holders, picture frames, bedspreads, shower curtains, towels, wastebaskets, and the toilet-paper holder. He specified the china and silverware and told them what indoor plants to put where. He also designed the landscaping, specifying over seventy species of trees and shrubs, mostly pines, juniper, and yews, and told the Christians where to plant them.

"We did everything Mr. Wright said," explains John.

Mr. Wright did everything but tell them where to sit while watching the television. When the house was complete in 1956, the eighty-eight-year-old genius, who favored pork pie hats, declined John's invitation to visit the magnificent house he designed amid the pine trees.

"I don't need to visit your house," he told John. "I know what it looks like." Catherine died in 1986. John retired in 1988 and now conducts tours of the twenty-two-hundred-square-foot, three-bedroom National Register home. Nothing has been changed or altered in the house. John scrupulously adheres to the original drawings.

The house is a monument to Wright's enduring architectural genius and the Christians' admirable commitment to maintaining the rare Usonian dwelling.

John has established the John E. Christian Family Memorial Trust with his daughter, Linda Davis of Houston, and Historic Landmarks Foundation of Indiana. The house will be maintained as a Frank Lloyd Wright educational center.

"I'm as much a purist on Mr. Wright's design as is humanly possible," says John. "Nothing here will ever change. I've arranged for that."

Mrs. James O. (Alice) Cole

Historic Name: WESTLEIGH / SAMUEL AND KATE PORTER HOUSE

County: MIAMI

Date of Construction: 1913

Architectural Style: COLONIAL REVIVAL

By the late nineteenth century, James Omar Cole of Peru was one of the richest men in America, presiding over a financial empire that included land in the California gold fields, the timber-rich hills of West Virginia, and places in-between. He also owned expanses of bottomland near the confluence of the Wabash and Mississinewa Rivers in Miami County. The Miami Indians called the area "the land between the rivers."

In 1913, nearing the end of his life, he built a great brick home along the Frances Slocum Trail, southeast of Peru, Indiana, for his daughter, Kate, and her husband, Samuel Porter. Cole named the gift house Westleigh. Sam and Kate Porter's only child, Cole, was studying at Yale University and writing songs. James Omar Cole, who had

made millions in the forest and coal mining industries and by selling supplies to miners during the California gold rush, beseeched his grandson to forego his frivolous song-writing obsession. Grandpa once loaded Cole into a buggy and trotted over to the Miami County Poor Farm. "That's where you'll end up if you don't quit writing music and get a real job," he told his grandson. Cole ignored the advice and in 1928 wrote *Paris,* the first of many successful Broadway musicals, and hit songs like "Begin the Beguine" and "Anything Goes."

Sam Porter died in 1927, but Kate continued to live on the eight-hundred-acre Westleigh estate. In the 1930s and '40s, Cole Porter, by now an internationally acclaimed songwriter, was an occasional visitor to Westleigh. When

his mother died in 1952, Cole asked his first cousin, attorney James O. Cole and his wife, Alice, of Washington, D.C., to take over Westleigh.

They brought their four children to the house, including Joey (Joanne), who in 1962 married Lieutenant Colonel Sid Kubesch, a pilot stationed at the Bunker Hill Air Force Base near Peru. A year later, Sid and his crew established a world speed record by flying a B-58 jet bomber 8,028 miles from Tokyo to London in eight hours and thirty-five minutes. Since 1974, Joey and Sid have lived down the road from Westleigh on another of the Cole family farms known as the Good Enough farm.

Joey's father died in 1997, but her mother, Alice, remains in Westleigh, which contains several of Cole Porter's possessions: his baby pictures, his desk, a full-length mirror, a painted vase. Alice recalls Porter's periodic returns to Indiana and to Westleigh up to his death in 1964. She and her children remember his piercing eyes and unwavering attention.

Through the years James and Alice maintained and added to the understated grandeur of Westleigh. "You stay in a place long enough and you grow increasingly attached to it," says Alice, who has lived there for half a century.

Down the winding road, Sid and Joey raise Black Angus cattle on the Good Enough farm, check in with Alice, and manage Westleigh and other Cole family holdings in Illinois and West Virginia. "Caring for the farms requires much work," notes Sid, who is encouraged by the assistance of his son and son-in-law.

"There's a lot of history here," says Sid of the house James Omar Cole built on the land between the rivers. "We hope this will always be a farm and remain in the family."

William and Gayle Cook

Historic Name: CEDAR FARM / KINTNER-WITHERS HOUSE

County: HARRISON

Date of Construction: 1837

Architectural Style: GREEK REVIVAL

LISTED IN THE NATIONAL REGISTER OF HISTORIC PLACES

The magnificent twenty-five-hundred-acre Cedar Farm, located along a broad, scenic stretch of the Ohio River in Harrison County is the only antebellum plantation–style complex in Indiana. The sprawling estate provides sanctuary to many rare species of birds, plants, animals, glades, waterfalls, and caves because it has remained largely undisturbed since it was established in 1837. Isolated in one of the most remote places in Indiana, Cedar Farm is gated,

not visible from the road, and not open to the public—so don't stop by, advise the current owners, Bill and Gayle Cook of Bloomington, who ask that their privacy be respected.

The Cooks bought the antebellum mansion, tobacco barns, milk houses, tenant houses, cookhouse, schoolhouse, and icehouse in 1984 from the three sons of Julia Kintner Withers, granddaughter of Jacob and Elizabeth Kintner, who built Cedar Farm. Julia Kintner was born in the house in 1888 and lived in it until her death in 1980. It had never been remodeled or modernized and had no heat. The Kintners were the only family to live in the house until the Cooks bought it and began a massive, meticulous restoration project.

The Cooks, who own the Bloomington-based Cook Group, a manufacturer and worldwide distributor of medical devices, have restored over fifty historic buildings throughout southern Indiana, most notably Cedar Farm, the West Baden Springs Hotel, and much of the Monroe County Courthouse Square.

"Preservation is good business," says Gayle, who grew up on a farm near Evansville and graduated from Indiana University in 1956 with a degree in fine arts. "Besides, we enjoy it. My husband likes the bricks and mortar and I like the history and research."

The Cooks first heard of Cedar Farm in 1968 from Gayle's brother, who bought and sold corn with one of Julia's sons. When Julia died, the family contacted the Cooks, knowing they had the means and desire to properly renovate and care for the home.

Before the Cooks began renovating, the buildings were photographed and measured and new blueprints were drawn. Old photographs, paintings, diaries, official records, and family descendants were consulted for historic accuracy. The house was painted yellow with white trim and green shutters, based on an 1898 William Forsyth painting of Cedar Farm. Thousands of personal Kintner household items that were left behind when Julia died were photographed, catalogued, and stored in the attic.

"Everything that was left meant something to the history of this house. The evidence is there for someone in the future," says Gayle. "We owe a lot to the Kintners. The family has given us a lot of personal items for the house."

The Cooks split their time between Bloomington and Cedar Farm. They often allow researchers and scientists from The Nature Conservancy, Indiana Department of Natural Resources, and various universities to stay in the cabins and study the natural wonders of the unique, undisturbed landscape that includes a south-facing glade featuring rare cactus and a butterfly species once thought to be extinct in Indiana.

When Jacob and Elizabeth built their grand home, they planted a double row of cedar trees leading six hundred feet down to the riverbank. It served as a familiar landmark to boats passing up and down the river and docking at Cedar Farm to conduct commerce with Jacob Kintner.

"It was the beauty of the river, the history of the place, and the peace and quiet that drew us here," says Gayle. "We couldn't let it go."

Allan Cornelius

Historic Name: ACORN HALL / WILLIAM P. SQUIBB HOUSE

City: LAWRENCEBURG

County: DEARBORN

Date of Construction: 1883

Architectural Style: ITALIANATE / SECOND EMPIRE

In the early 1970s Allan Cornelius was stationed at a U.S. Army base in the Bavarian region of Germany. Munich still bore grim reminders of World War II, most notably in razed blocks, which had yet to be rebuilt after bombing. Years later, after living in Paris, New York, and Charleston, South Carolina, Allan moved home to Lawrenceburg in southeastern Indiana and was reminded of Germany.

"Downtown Lawrenceburg looked as if it had been bombed," he says, referring to the methodic destruction of many of its magnificent nineteenth-century buildings.

Weed lots replaced historic buildings in Indiana's fourth-oldest city, founded in 1804 during the heyday of steamboats on the Ohio River.

"The urge of American towns is to become a strip mall and Lawrenceburg is leading the way," he moans. Allan is a passionate preservationist, locked in a long and difficult battle with politicians and developers. In 1989 he founded the Historic Lawrenceburg Foundation to help preserve the town's architectural heritage, which dates to Indiana's pioneer era.

Allan grew up in Lawrenceburg and graduated from Transylvania University in Lexington, Kentucky, with a degree in French. In 1974, after his army tour of duty, he lived in Paris and taught English to Chrysler Corporation employees. He moved to New York City in 1976 and started a firm that designed and remodeled apartments and shops. In 1985 he moved to Charleston and bought and restored four historic houses.

During a Christmas trip home to Lawrenceburg to visit his parents, he noticed the abandoned Squibb house on Ridge Avenue with an open front door and a snowdrift in the parlor. "We called it the wicked witch's house when I was a kid because it was so spooky," says Allan. He bought the spooky house, which was built in 1883 by William P. Squibb, a distiller of rye whiskey. Lawrenceburg has been a whiskey-making town since 1809. The Joseph E. Seagram and Sons distillery down the street from Allan's house remains a world leader in whiskey production.

After three years of renovation, Allan converted the seventeen-room house into a bed-and-breakfast, which he operated for five years before exhausting himself.

"I wanted my house back," he says. "I got tired of fixing breakfast for seventeen people, seven days a week." Now he lives alone in the house and sleeps in an 11½-foot-tall, king-sized bed with curtains. He built the monstrous bed with woodwork salvaged from a New York brownstone apartment. "The bed should have its own zip code," he jokes. William Squibb's dining area is now a replica of Allan's New York City apartment, with seventeenth-century gothic furniture, 1579 medieval stained-glass windows, and a 1480 Italian Renaissance marble mantle.

Allan says his undiminished passion and relentless defense of Lawrenceburg's architecture and rich heritage are rooted in his family's long history in the once majestic river valley. In 1793 his ancestors rafted down the river and settled near what is now Lawrenceburg, just upstream from where the Argosy Casino stands today.

"It's in my blood to care about this place. I inherited the passion," he explains.

John Cottrell

Historic Name: RICHARD CLAYPOOL HOUSE

City: WILLIAMSPORT

County: WARREN

Date of Construction: 1852

Architectural Style: GREEK REVIVAL / ITALIANATE

It's a safe bet that John Cottrell is the only resident of Los Angeles who maintains a second home in the sleepy, picturesque western Indiana town of Williamsport. The obvious question is, why? Why does John leave his lavish high-rise downtown L.A. condo and fly to Williamsport once or twice a month?

"Because I collect houses and I love this one," he says of the house that dry-goods merchant and lawyer Richard Claypool and his wife, Elizabeth, built in 1852 a few blocks east of the Warren County Courthouse. John grew up in

Crown Point and moved to Fountain County across the Wabash River from Williamsport in 1954 when his father took a job selling Chevrolets in an Attica dealership.

After graduating from Attica High School in 1956, John drove to Los Angeles, for no particular reason, with $55 in his pockets and a girlfriend. He got a job driving a furniture delivery truck around Los Angeles to support himself while wondering what to do next. He began designing furniture display windows and discovered he was quite good at it. He is now one of the top one hundred interior designers in the world, so proclaimed by the prestigious *Architectural Digest* magazine. The John Cottrell Company, which he started when he was twenty-eight years old, designs homes around the world in the $25 to $50 million range.

"I have an instinctive, practical sense about design," he modestly notes. He owns a twenty-seven-acre estate in Gloucester, Massachusetts, and ten other historic homes scattered from Culver on Lake Maxinkuckee in northern Indiana to Warren and Fountain Counties, including the Claypool house.

He first spotted the Claypool house when he was in high school, daydreaming through Spanish class, wondering what it would be like to one day live in such a magnificent place. He sketched the house on a notepad, designing new wings, porches, and an elaborate landscape. In 1988, his mother, Ruth, phoned from Attica to tell him that the Claypool house and fifteen surrounding acres were for sale. He bought it, pulled out his old sketches and doodles and redesigned much of the house, just like he daydreamed of doing while in high school.

"It's one of the most beautiful houses in the area, a magical house," he says. He added three bedrooms, two porches, a three-car garage. "It's not appropriate for the house, but it's comfortable, and my house and I don't care." The renovated and remodeled house and its magnificent, showcase furnishings were featured in the February 1993 issue of *Architectural Digest*.

When John and his partner and business associate, John Nelson, return to Williamsport, they also oversee a square block of historic homes and an 1848 church they bought and restored across the river in Attica. John established the John Cottrell Foundation to purchase, renovate, and furnish the mid–nineteenth-century homes, cabins, and church, which he loans to various civic and arts organizations for

special events. John played organ in the old church when he was in high school. When it was threatened with demolition, he bought it. "I like saving things and seeing people enjoy them," he says. "That church was an important part of my childhood. I couldn't lose it."

John plans one day to retire in Indiana and devote his considerable energy to full-time restoration of homes in the Attica and Williamsport area. "We don't have wonderful old homes in Los Angeles," he explains on one of his weekend trips to Williamsport.

"It's terrific to take an old thing that's falling apart and give it new life."

Kevin Cox

Historic Name: R. G. WATSON BUILDING / THE WOODMEN'S LODGE

Town: FARMLAND

County: RANDOLPH

Date of Construction: 1908

LISTED IN THE NATIONAL REGISTER OF HISTORIC PLACES, *Downtown Farmland Historic District*

You don't often see egg cartons glued to the ceiling of a historic building, but Kevin Cox has a good explanation. Kevin lives in a former buggy factory in picturesque downtown Farmland. The egg cartons are glued to his second-floor music-room ceiling for acoustic purposes.

"I didn't want to carpet this beautiful wood floor, but egg cartons on the ceiling produce the same three-dimensional sound field," he explains. Kevin listens to his rock-and-roll CDs in the acoustically perfected room while suspended on a porch swing hanging from the egg-carton

ceiling. The music room also contains two 20 mm cannon shells and ten trophies that his grandfather's 1929 Packard won at car shows around the country in the 1950s.

It's possible that buggy maker R. G. Watson hadn't heard the word "automobile" when he built his buggy factory in 1908. Or maybe he didn't think the automobile would ever replace the horse-and-buggy in rural Randolph County. Within a couple of years, however, Model T's were bouncing around Farmland streets and throughout east central Indiana and R. G. Watson was out of business.

The building, which also served as headquarters to a secret fraternal lodge called The Woodmen, was later converted to a coal-storage facility and then a feed-and-grain store, among other things, over the next couple of decades.

In 1945 it became a chicken hatchery and egg grading and distribution center, which everyone in town called "the egg plant." Kevin bought the eight-thousand-square-foot brick building in 1997, installed his egg-carton ceiling and porch-swing music room, and set up a woodworking shop in the former hatchery section of the second floor, where The Woodmen once met.

"Guy said to me 'egg plant's for sale'; so I bought it. I've been working on it ever since," says Kevin. "It was pretty rough." He lives in the five rooms on the second floor and rents the street-level storefront to retail businesses.

Kevin grew up on a Randolph County farm, graduated from Monroe Central High School in 1977, attended Purdue University for two years, and then joined his father's auto parts business in Farmland. The business, Farmland Auto Parts, was started in 1957 by his grandfather Roe Miller. Kevin and his brother, Kristin, assumed ownership

of the auto parts store when their father, Jack Cox, retired.

"We have no computer, no cash register, and we hand-write everything," explains Kevin, who is also the vice president of Historic Farmland USA, the local preservation organization. "We do everything the same as in 1957 when Grandpa started the business. We aren't rich, but we aren't going crazy, because we live in Farmland, which is paradise. No crime. No traffic. No Wal-Marts, malls, or subdivisions."

Farmland is an authentic, intact small town, an increasing rarity in Indiana. The downtown isn't abandoned. It has well-maintained sidewalks, a bank, an independently owned grocery, hardware store, liquor store, drug store, restaurant, dry cleaners, and Kevin and Kristin's auto parts store. None of its original twenty-one brick masonry buildings have been knocked down, including the 1919 Goodrich Brothers grain elevator with its 125-foot tower.

The only minor problem is the mile-long CSX freight trains that roar through town sixty times a day, every day, around the clock.

"You get used to it," Kevin shrugs. "We prefer to think of it as adding charm to our little town."

Samuel O. Crane

Historic Name: THOMAS MOUNT HOUSE
County: SHELBY
Date of Construction: 1843
Architectural Style: I-HOUSE

When Samuel O. Crane bought the deserted pre–Civil War farmhouse atop a low hill in rural Shelby County, the walls sagged, the roof leaked, the floors buckled, there was no plumbing or electricity, and birds flew in and out of the broken windows.

"My life has always been pointed backwards, so I liked it," says Sam, who was born in Shelbyville and quit school in the tenth grade to join the navy and see the world, which he did. He later worked on crab-processing ships in Alaska and oil fields throughout the West. In 1988, divorced and

feeling defeated at age fifty-three, he returned home and bought the brick house, which was basically unchanged since farmer Thomas Mount built it in 1843.

He slowly repaired the sagging, two-story structure using nineteenth-century hand tools out of respect for its history and character. He worked alone for years, avoiding people, talking only to Tommy the turtle and Robert the parakeet. He cooked on a wood stove, drew water from an outside well, read Greek mythology by oil lamp, and filled the house with old furniture, a bust of Mozart, portraits of George

Washington and Abraham Lincoln, and hundreds of books ranging from Dutch, Japanese, and American history to physics and clock-making.

After living in the nineteenth century for years, he decided to stay. "The longer I lived without running water and electricity, the more I realized I didn't need it," he says. "I'd gotten used to going outside to the outhouse, so why change?"

Sam lives a nearly pure 1843 existence, independent of modern society with its gadgets and complications. He sews clothes on a foot-powered sewing machine, splits thirty ricks of wood a year for heat, washes clothes on a scrub board, bathes in a galvanized tub in water heated on the wood stove, and lives on a meager $200 a month.

Once a month he drives a 1977 truck to town for canned food and dried meat. He bakes bread, makes soup, drinks evaporated milk, bakes light, fluffy piecrusts in his old-fashioned wood stove, and strangles a chicken for special-occasion meals. He writes with a goose quill pen. He couldn't be happier.

"To get warm, I must haul wood, so I really appreciate the warmth; I can't just push a button to make coffee, I have to heat the water and wait—so I'm always looking forward to something," he explains with his usual gusto.

He has no bank account or credit cards. His daughter paid to have a phone installed in case of any emergencies but he never answers it. He doesn't even know the number. He pulls his own teeth when they come loose, holds his silver eyeglasses together with packing tape, and wakes up before dawn to behold every sunrise.

"Living like I do keeps me in tune with everything around me," he says.

He keeps a detailed diary of each day's events, noting the times of sunrise and sunset, the weather, wind direction, what he ate, baked, sewed, and read, and how many eggs the six hens laid. He illustrates his diary by drawing pictures of himself doing things, like hanging laundry on the line.

"This house is exactly like it was 160 years ago and I live exactly like people did 160 years ago. Why should I change the house to suit me? I've suited myself to the house," he says, while removing a peach pie from the Florence Hot Blast wood stove.

"I live here because I have seen the light," he adds. "Would you like a piece of pie?"

Theresa Crawford

City: INDIANAPOLIS

County: MARION

Date of Construction: CIRCA 1890

Architectural Style: QUEEN ANNE COTTAGE

LISTED IN THE NATIONAL REGISTER OF HISTORIC PLACES, *Ransom Place Historic District*

In 1990, plans were underway to revitalize downtown Indianapolis by building a shopping mall and food court, now known as Circle Centre Mall. It was designed to attract shoppers back to the downtown area.

Meanwhile, eight blocks northwest of the rising eight-hundred-thousand-square-foot shopping mall, Ransom Place, one of the oldest African American neighborhoods in Indianapolis, was emerging from years of crime, neglect, and minimal city services. Drug dealers had taken over condemned and abandoned homes. Sidewalks had crumbled.

During the 1970s much of the beleaguered neighborhood was demolished by Indiana University–Purdue University to expand its massive complex of parking lots and new office buildings. Longtime elderly residents, mostly poor blacks, were evicted from neighborhoods and homes built by their nineteenth-century ancestors.

Due largely to the efforts of longtime residents, the Ransom Place Neighborhood Association, and Historic Landmarks Foundation of Indiana, Ransom Place, now a National Register–listed historic district, began a long, slow turnaround. Historic Landmarks Foundation's revolving fund, the Fund for Landmark Indianapolis Properties (FLIP), began buying condemned homes and rehabilitating them for resale.

Theresa Crawford, a U.S. government budget analyst, drove through Ransom Place in 1992. Living in a generic

far-eastside subdivision, she hoped to move downtown. The condemned house she spotted had been vacant for fifteen years and served as the neighborhood crack cocaine headquarters.

"It was a rough-looking house but had good bones," says Theresa, who grew up in Cincinnati, graduated from Central State University in Wilberforce, Ohio, in 1982, and moved to Indianapolis to work for the federal government. "My friends thought I'd lost my mind. The whole neighborhood looked like it was on the way down. People were sleeping in their cars. It was a mess, but I wanted to live in a real neighborhood, not a subdivision where all the people and houses look alike."

The house, believed to have been built by Irish immigrants around 1890, was renovated with the aid of Historic Landmarks Foundation, and Theresa bought it in 1994. She was among the new homeowners to gamble on the venerable neighborhood, which is now roughly six square blocks containing about 110 homes.

As a member of the Ransom Place Neighborhood Association, she hounded city officials to clean and repair the streets and sidewalks, pick up the garbage, and enforce the drug laws.

The neighborhood was named for local resident Freeman B. Ransom, an attorney and general manager for the Madam C. J. Walker Company, an early-twentieth-century manufacturer of hair care products for African Americans. By 1925 the neighborhood of mostly small, one-story frame houses was home to many of Indianapolis's prominent African American residents.

The long decline began in the early 1930s during the Depression. White slumlords bought Ransom Place homes, allowed them to deteriorate, and doubled the rents for hard-pressed black tenants. But somehow, the proud little neighborhood has survived racism, poverty, slumlords, university expansions, crack dealers, and official indifference, largely because of pioneers like Theresa Crawford, who were willing to take a chance on rough-looking houses with good bones.

Tim and Sue Crowley

Historic Name: WATKINS NISBET HOUSE

City: EVANSVILLE

County: VANDERBURGH

Date of Construction: 1880

Architects: ROBERT BOYD AND HENRY BRICKLEY

Architectural Style: SECOND EMPIRE

LISTED IN THE NATIONAL REGISTER OF HISTORIC PLACES, *Riverside Historic District*

The cotton trade and wholesale dry-goods business along the Ohio River were very good to Watkins Fuqua Nisbet, so in 1880 he built the largest Victorian house in Evansville for his wife and ten children. It had twenty-three rooms, including one for the live-in seamstress, fifteen fireplaces, a basement, and a walnut staircase spiraling up to a fourth-floor tower overlooking the city.

"The most perfect specimen of first class residences that have been erected in our city for several years," an *Evansville Journal* reporter wrote of the lavish brick home. Yet soon

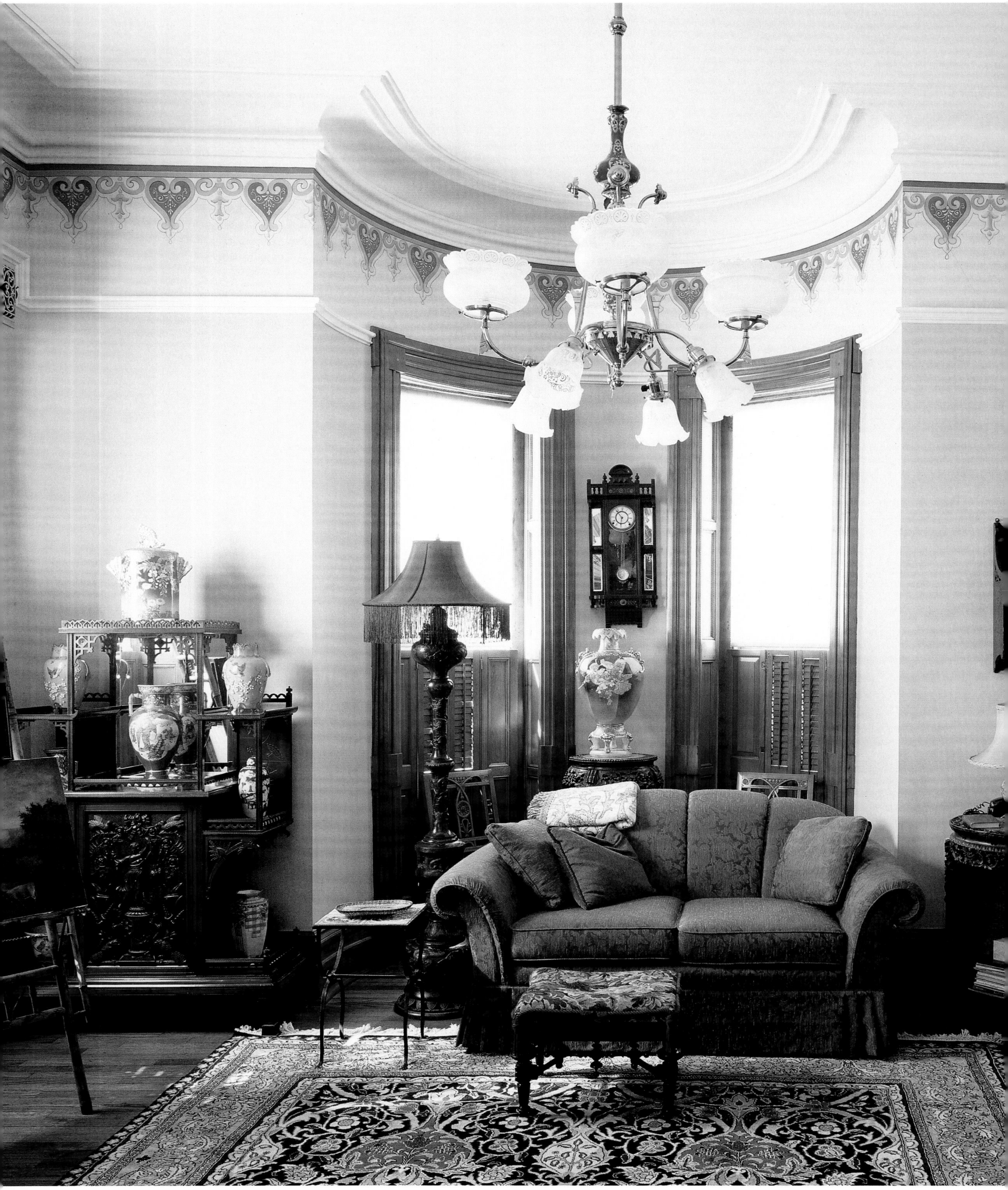

after that, things fell apart for the Nisbet family. Watkins died six years later. Wife Fanny died in 1896 and the children scattered. By 1900 the perfect specimen of a first-class residence was a boardinghouse. By the early 1930s, vagrants slept in the abandoned house and then a Mrs. Teichiner bought it and converted it to twenty-three sleeping rooms for shipyard workers. By 1960 it was empty again, slated for demolition and stripped of the original light fixtures, doorknobs, woodwork, fireplace mantles, and anything else that could be torn from the walls and ceilings. In the early 1960s it was rescued once again, this time by Gwen Koch, who converted it into a ten-unit, low-rent apartment building.

Tim and Sue Crowley were living in Evanston, Illinois, in 1983. Tim was finishing his ophthalmology medical residency at Northwestern University Hospital, specializing in eye surgery. He grew up in Evansville and was planning to move home and open a practice. Sue, a nurse, grew up in Chicago and had never heard of Evansville until she met Tim. One day he was flipping through a book on Evansville local architecture and spotted the Nisbet house.

"I fell in love with the house from a picture," recalls Tim. "I'd always had an interest in old stuff and collecting things like coins and tropical fish." They bought the house, removed twenty-three mailboxes from the front hall and slept in the kitchen for a year during the early renovation process. Sue and the three children moved out when the water in the tray of the Christmas tree froze. They returned once a new furnace was installed.

Their first monthly utility bill was $1,200. "Our first taste of old-house living," says Tim.

"We figured it would take twenty years to completely restore it and we're still working on it nearly twenty years later, although we're up to the third floor," says Tim, a stickler for accuracy and precision—desirable qualities in an eye surgeon. He hired local artists to recreate original wall stencils and ceiling paintings, and searched auctions for historically accurate Victorian-era doorknobs, woodwork, molding, and fireplace mantles.

The Victorian furnishings are all from 1870 to 1880. It took Tim and Sue's teenage son, Evan, and a friend two years to scrape and repaint the intricate exterior trim on the massive house. They first had to remove the rusty bean and coffee cans that someone had painted white and placed on the cornice years ago.

The unrenovated third-floor rooms still have apartment numbers on the doors but are now crammed with Tim's extensive collection of antique lamps and chandeliers, which have replaced his once extensive collection of coins and tropical fish. "We have more lamps than we'll ever need," moans Sue.

"I'm a hobbyist and getting it historically perfect is my hobby," says Tim enthusiastically. "If I won the lottery I'd give up my medical practice and work on this full time."

Jim and Mary Davidson

Historic Name: A. D. BOOTH HOUSE
City: NOBLESVILLE
County: HAMILTON
Date of Construction: 1887
Architectural Style: QUEEN ANNE

While abundant money is obviously a major advantage in accurately and quickly restoring a historic home, enormous amounts of time, hard work, and dedication to a noble goal help make up for an anemic bankroll.

Jim and Mary Davidson achieved their goal in Noblesville with their Queen Anne–style home. They didn't have money to hire a contractor, so they tore up the carpets and removed fifteen coats of lead-based paint from the hickory floors and walnut woodwork—and probably cooked a few brain cells during the toxic project, they figure. One contractor estimated it would cost $60,000 to strip layers of paint from the exterior cedar clapboards, repair the damage, reseal the wood, and paint it. So they did it themselves. It took four backbreaking years.

The Davidsons also re-plastered, scrubbed, scraped, sanded, painted, and stripped, blistering their hands and often working with little sleep on the weekends to complete other household projects after buying the house in 1993. They used reproduction wallpaper throughout the house to duplicate as nearly as possible what it may have looked like in the late 1880s.

"We basically did it all ourselves by sacrificing some brain cells," says Mary, a Noblesville attorney who had a couple of noble goals in mind after graduating from law school in 1992. She wanted to walk to work, which she does. The courthouse and her two-person law firm are only four blocks away. And she and Jim, an accountant, wanted to live in an old home in a genuine neighborhood where people wave and talk to each other while strolling down the sidewalk after supper.

Interestingly enough, this old tradition is returning to the courthouse square in Noblesville as more and more people move into old downtown homes. On lazy summer evenings, neighbors often stroll to the square, buy an ice cream cone, and sit on the benches and visit. Precisely the atmosphere the Davidsons sought after living in a sterile Indianapolis condominium complex while Mary attended law school.

They looked at eighty to a hundred homes, some in subdivisions where the atmosphere was depressingly similar to the sterile condominium, poorly constructed and with neighbors who didn't know each other, much less eat ice cream together in the evenings. "We didn't see anything good for our daughter, Emma, in those subdivision environments. Tract home after tract home," says Mary. "What if the suburban value system rubbed off on her?"

The modest eight-room, two-story house with the left-handed walnut stair rails was built in 1887 for A. D. Booth, a young physician. Dr. Booth, who was apparently left-

handed, had just graduated from medical school and opened his first practice in the house where he also lived.

"We're not hobbyists," says Mary. "We wanted a large, spacious old place with tall ceilings and some craftsmanship worth preserving. We're here for the long haul and we wanted to raise our daughter in a livable, middle-class neighborhood with a good mix of people."

The message: "You don't have to be rich to live in an old house," says Jim. "Just work hard. It's worth keeping neighborhoods that people can afford to live in."

Travis and Helen Disler

City: LAPORTE

County: LAPORTE

Date of Construction: 1925

Architectural Style: CRAFTSMAN BUNGALOW

Between 1908 and 1940, Sears, Roebuck and Company sold nearly a hundred thousand homes through its mail-order catalogue. It's true. You could order underwear and a new house from the same place. Sears offered over four hundred different floor plans ranging from $600 modest bungalows to $6,000 mansions.

Some assembly was required, however. The house arrived by railroad in a kit containing up to thirty thousand pieces, including screws, nails, doorknobs, and windows. The pieces were precut so no sawing was required. Each piece and part was keyed by number to an easy-to-follow blue-print. Plumbing and wiring were not included.

"All you need is a hammer," promised the catalogue. Not quite. Most people hired contractors to piece the puzzle together.

It's not known how many of these mail-order houses remain intact around the country, but a fine example now belongs to Travis and Helen Disler of LaPorte. It was assembled in 1925 on Michigan Avenue, twelve blocks east of the LaPorte County Courthouse. It's a sturdy, one-story,

one-bathroom, two-bedroom, fifteen-hundred-square-foot bungalow model called The Ashmore and the original kit sold for about $2,000.

It has built-in bookcases, a cobblestone chimney, French doors that were put on backwards, a screened-in side porch, cedar shake siding, and magnificent hardwood floors.

"Too bad you can't see the beautiful floors," says Helen. "We put carpet over them because I didn't want to clean hardwood floors because I'm lazy." In a small sitting room off the living room hang several Norman Rockwell prints.

"Got 'em at the Salvation Army for $1 each," she says.

Helen and Travis grew up in small towns in northern Allen County. Travis's father knitted ladies silk hosiery at the old Fort Wayne Knitting Mill Company. The couple met at Leo High School and married in 1944 and had two children. Travis, who flew reconnaissance airplanes in the South Pacific during World War II later worked as a salesman for General Telephone Company in Fort Wayne. At one point, he was transferred to LaPorte for five years before being transferred back to Fort Wayne.

When he retired in 1985, Helen announced she wanted to move back to LaPorte because she liked its small-town atmosphere, smiling neighbors, tree-lined streets, and the Sears house she admired on her bicycle rides.

"In Fort Wayne you had to drive ten miles to buy a stamp. If I smiled at someone on the street they looked at me like I'd forgotten my skirt," says Helen. In Fort Wayne they lived in a large two-story house. Travis often climbed on the steep roof for periodic shingle inspections and gutter cleanings.

"I wanted a one-story house, so it wasn't such a long drop if Travis fell off the roof," says Helen. Travis had no opinion.

"I didn't care where we lived, but we did what she wanted," explains Travis. "You do that when you get older." They knocked on the door of the Sears house and asked if it was for sale. The owner said sure, the Dislers bought it, and now they walk a few blocks downtown to buy a stamp or go to the library.

The house is so unique, sturdy, and well kept that people often knock on the door offering to buy it, just like the Dislers did in 1985. Helen placed it on her sorority house tour to satisfy the curious.

"We enjoy sitting on the porch waving and smiling at people," says Helen. "It's a good house for that."

Tim and Jaya Dodd

Historic Name: BENJAMIN BOSSE HOUSE

City: EVANSVILLE

County: VANDERBURGH

Date of Construction: 1917

Architect: CLIFFORD SHOPBELL

Architectural Style: ARTS AND CRAFTS

LISTED IN THE NATIONAL REGISTER OF HISTORIC PLACES, *Riverside Historic District*

"The neighborhood was the pits, but the house was a bargain. We knew we'd buy it when we walked up the sidewalk," recalls Evansville attorney Tim Dodd. "We liked the Oriental look of the house."

It was 1971 and Tim had recently returned home to practice law after a tour of duty with the U.S. Army in Pusan, South Korea. He also met his future wife, Jaya, in South Korea. She was the assistant branch manager at the Bank of America in Pusan, where Tim cashed his checks. Jaya is a graduate of Yonsei University in Seoul.

Shortly after moving in, Tim was named City Attorney by Evansville mayor Russell Lloyd. In 1974 Tim wrote the preservation ordinance creating the Riverside Historic District, which helped transform the crumbling, crime-ridden area in which he lived into the city's finest neighborhood.

"Now you've got to get permission to paint your house purple, and that protection gives people confidence to spend money fixing up their homes," says Tim.

In 1980 Jaya opened a Korean restaurant that has flourished despite being in nearly vacant downtown Evansville.

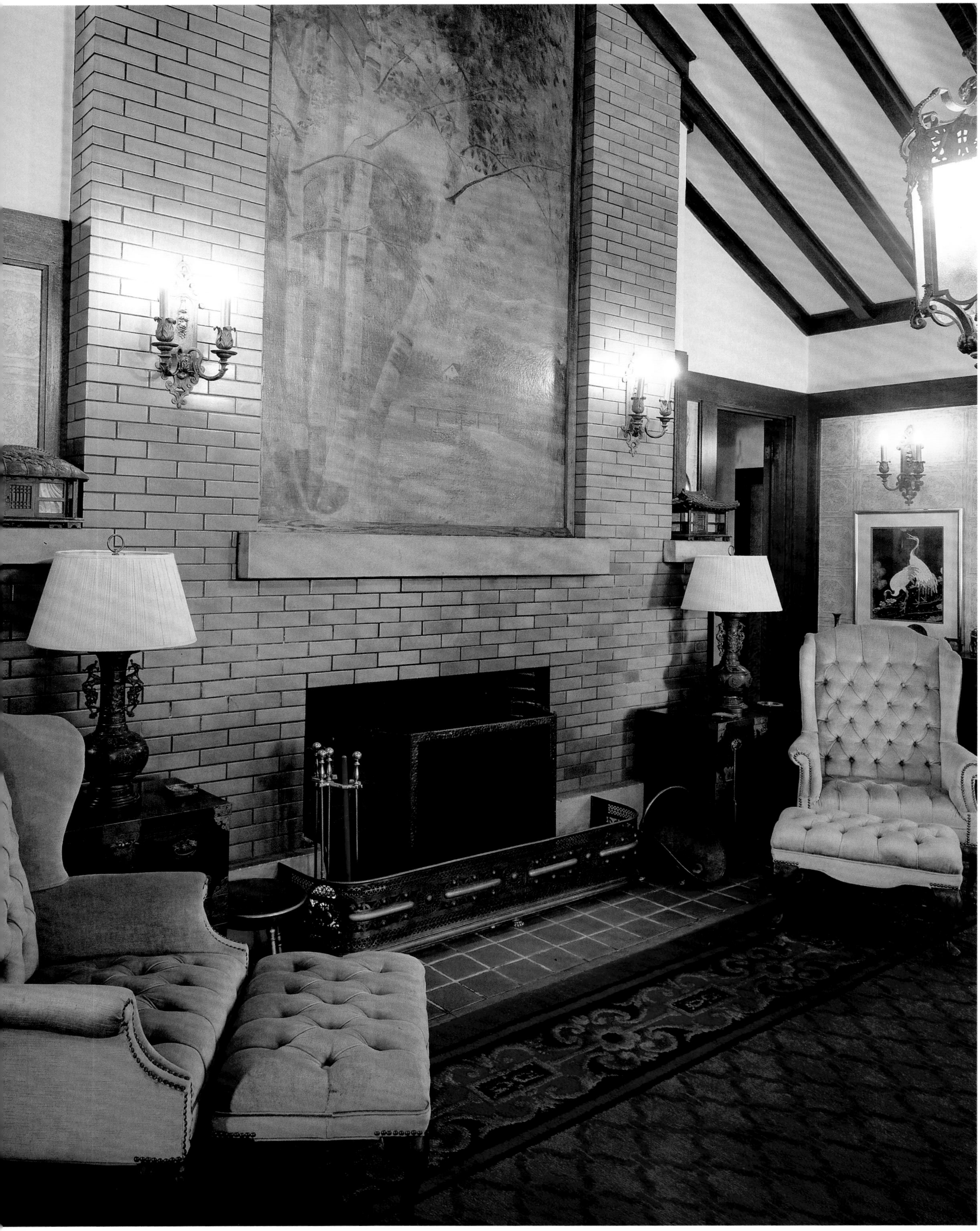

It's called Jaya's, and is one of Evansville's finest. "Not too many Orientals live here, but I wanted to introduce native Korean food and hospitality to Evansville," explains Jaya, who greets customers by their first names and cooks on an open grill at one end of the sparkling dining room. "Downtown Evansville was going down the hill when I opened and this is a meat-and-potatoes town but the people like my food. I have very loyal customers."

The house in which they raised Christopher, their only child, was built in 1917 for Benjamin Bosse, the city's popular three-term Democratic mayor and wealthy furniture-company owner. Unfortunately, Bosse died young, at age fifty, while in office.

Over the living room fireplace is a mural that Mayor Bosse commissioned of his boyhood farm in northern Vanderburgh County. "He was a big, rotund man, a fat guy," explains Tim, pointing out the mayor's enormous shower stall, which is roomy enough to hose down a horse. The mayor, known for his weekly poker parties with the boys, hid his liquor during Prohibition in a secret basement-wall compartment.

The distinctive Indiana-limestone house is striking in many ways. The low-slung, Prairie-style architecture stands in sharp contrast to the large Victorian homes in the near-downtown neighborhood. Many of the Oriental rice-paper lithographs and most of the Korean teak furniture with inlaid pearl design belonged to Jaya's grandparents. The house never fell into disrepair, was never altered or remodeled, and looks much as it did that sad day in 1922 when it was draped in black wreaths for the mayor's funeral.

"It was in excellent shape when we bought it and still is," says Tim, who received his undergraduate degree from Dartmouth College in New Hampshire and graduated from the Indiana University School of Law in 1966.

It was a chance encounter with a Republican precinct committeeman that led the Dodds to Mayor Bosse's house. Tim was standing outside his Evansville apartment one day when the committeeman asked to register him to vote. Tim told him, no, they were looking for a house and would be moving soon to another precinct.

"I know a house for sale," the committeeman told him.

"Next thing you know, we're buying Mayor Bosse's house," says Tim, who later became the Republican precinct committeeman in his new neighborhood, which led to the City Attorney job with Mayor Lloyd, which allowed him to write the historic preservation ordinance creating the Riverside Historic District.

Max and Renee Ellison

Historic Name: E. W. ANSTED HOUSE

City: CONNERSVILLE

County: FAYETTE

Date of Construction: 1898

Architectural Style: ROMANESQUE REVIVAL

During the first quarter of the twentieth century, there were at least ten automobile manufacturers in Connersville, including the Lexington-Howard Motor Car Company owned by E. W. Ansted. In 1898, Ansted built a magnificent twenty-two-room home on busy Central Avenue a few blocks north of the Fayette County Courthouse.

It was Connersville's premier residence, a striking eighty-two-hundred-square-foot showplace with a third-floor ballroom, six fireplaces, curved stained-glass bay windows, and carved mahogany staircases intricately inlaid with tiger oak.

Max Ellison grew up ten blocks from the Ansted mansion. "I was fascinated and scared by it," he recalls. The house remained in the Ansted family long after E.W. died.

The Lexington-Howard Motor Car Company and all the Connersville automobile manufacturers went out of business in the late 1920s. They couldn't compete with the speed and efficiency of Henry Ford's Detroit automobile-assembly lines.

Max and Renee Ellison married in 1973, the same year the Ansted mansion and all its contents were put on the auction block by E.W.'s aging descendants, the Huston family. Max worked in a factory and dabbled in photography. His dabbling was pretty good and in 1980 he opened a photography studio on Grand Avenue, specializing in high school and wedding portraits.

By 1994, Max had just about cornered the portrait

photography business in Connersville and needed a bigger studio and home. A real-estate friend told Max that the Ansted mansion was for sale. He bought it, applied 187 gallons of fresh interior paint, and relocated his home and photography studio, wife and two children into the house that had scared and fascinated him as a child. His wife, Renee, is a surgical nurse at the Fayette County Memorial Hospital, which was built on land donated by E. W. Ansted in 1916.

The Ellisons are only the fifth family to live in the house. Other than peeling paint, the house was in superb condition, a tribute to the previous owners, who recognized its place in Connersville history. The servants' sitting room is now Max's office and the studio is in the old third-floor ballroom. "The house has adapted perfectly to our busi-

ness. People go up the back servants' stairs to the ballroom and don't intrude on our living space," says Max, who is also president of the seven-member Connersville City Council. He's perhaps Indiana's only Republican city council president with a long ponytail and earrings. And he opposes tax abatements for suburban industrial development. "I want to use tax breaks to encourage local, independent merchants to return to downtown Connersville," he says.

A photographic portrait of E. W. Ansted hangs over the parlor fireplace as a tribute to the builder of the house, along with a watercolor painting of a 1911 Lexington automobile called The Minuteman. In the 1920 Pike's Peak Hill Climb, E.W.'s Lexington roadsters placed first and second.

"Part of the fun of this house is people are very interested in it. Little old ladies stop by to tell us stories about E.W.'s wild parties in the ballroom. People in Connersville feel very strongly about this house, so we feel very protective of it," says Max.

"We wake up every day still saying we can't believe we live in this great house," he adds. "I've had offers to sell it, but I tell people they don't have enough money."

Mark and Rebecca Ewing

Historic Name: MONTCLAIR FARM

County: KNOX

Dates of Construction: CIRCA 1809 / 1911

Architectural Style: FEDERAL / NEOCLASSICAL

Around 1804, President Thomas Jefferson appointed Pennsylvanian Nathaniel Ewing "receiver of public land" and dispatched him to Vincennes in the Northwest Territory. The French, British, and various Indian tribes had been driven out of what is now Knox County, Indiana. Jefferson directed Nathaniel to divide the land and issue official deeds to Americans who were pouring into the Wabash River Valley.

Nathaniel deeded himself two thousand acres north of the territorial capital of Vincennes and built himself a house and a life of prominence. He was elected to the state legislature after Indiana became a state in 1816 and founded the Bank of Vincennes, among other achievements. Even more impressive is the fact that the house is still in the Ewing family, having been owned and occupied in an unbroken line stretching over seven generations and nearly two centuries. The house is older than the state of Indiana and contains many of Nathaniel's books, diaries, correspondence, and French furniture dating back to the 1700s, including the bed in which he died.

Nathaniel's great-great-great-great-great-grandson Mark, a Vincennes tax attorney, and his wife, Becca, now live in

the Ewing house. Mark grew up in the house, graduated from Syracuse University in 1973, and married Becca, a classmate from Erie, Pennsylvania. Her father was president of the Welch's Grape Juice Company. Mark later graduated from law schools at Willamette University in Oregon and New York University. They thought about living in New York City or Portland, Oregon, but Mark was offered a job with a Vincennes law firm and his thoughts turned home. His father, Nathaniel Ewing, a surgeon, was ill and still living in the family home, but was worried about its future.

"I think Dad orchestrated the job offer because he wanted me back here in this house," Mark says. In 1977 Mark and Becca moved home and lived in the old tenant farmer's house on the property which sheltered ex-slaves after the Civil War. When Dr. Ewing died in 1985, Mark and Becca and their two children moved into the house, the sixth and seventh generations.

"I get to live in my childhood playground," says Mark, referring to the five hundred acres of woods, creeks, ponds, and farm fields. "I also get to see my kids grow up where I did."

The house, built in 1809, is an extraordinary repository of Ewing family memorabilia, artwork, and photographs from every generation. For example, William L. Ewing, Mark's great-grandfather, grew up in the house and later moved to St. Louis, where he was elected mayor in the 1880s. He later returned to the Vincennes home, where he died.

The family donated the mayor's papers to the St. Louis Historical Society, but kept his top hat, waistcoat, pencil case, and silk ties. "We've got something from everyone," says Mark.

In the late 1800s Mark's great-grandmother Molly Ewing planted hundreds of oak trees along the long, winding driveway leading to the house. She watered the trees from a horse-drawn water wagon. Grandma, a tough and determined Ewing, tearfully sold fifteen hundred of the original two thousand acres in order to save the farm during the Depression. Mark recently planted over a thousand hard maple trees among the great oaks, insuring the Ewing trees live on a few more centuries.

Whether Mark and Becca's teenagers will one day live in the family house remains to be seen. Mark is philosophical about an eighth generation residing in the house.

"If my son comes back to live here, I'd be tickled. But if his life is somewhere else, that's fine, too," he says. "We've done our best for almost two hundred years."

David and Sarah Finkel

Historic Name: T. DORSEY AND HELEN JONES HOUSE

City: SHELBYVILLE

County: SHELBY

Date of Construction: 1930

Architects: MCGUIRE AND SHOOK

Architectural Style: SPANISH ECLECTIC

LISTED IN THE NATIONAL REGISTER OF HISTORIC PLACES, *Shelbyville West Side Historic District*

When prominent furniture-factory owner and civic leader T. Dorsey Jones and his wife, Helen, built their unique limestone Shelbyville home in 1930, they ordered a hinged panel cut into the heavy, arched front door.

"Mrs. Jones didn't like to open the big door for the newspaper boy," explains the home's current owner, David Finkel, who appreciates those little insights into the people who preceded him. Because of this same appreciation, he chose not to remove T. Dorsey's wheelchair marks on the woodwork.

David and his wife, Sarah, bought the house in 1992 from Charlotte Jones, daughter of T. Dorsey and Helen.

She had lived in her parents' house her entire life before moving to a retirement community. She left for the Finkels some mementos of her parents' lives. T. Dorsey Jones's 1901 Spencer High School diploma, his 1907 Indiana University diploma signed by William L. Bryan, and Helen's 1907 Shelbyville High School diploma still hang in the home. "It was important to Charlotte that her parents' spirit lived on in this house and we've honored that," says David, who framed the diplomas and hung them in the hall.

T. Dorsey Jones owned the Spiegel Furniture Factory. In the 1920s there were at least nineteen furniture factories in Shelbyville, most of which date to the mid–nineteenth

century when southeast Indiana was shrouded with ancient white oak and walnut trees. With the Great Depression of the 1930s and the foolish clear-cutting of the vast forests, the furniture factories began closing.

T. Dorsey Jones, however, prospered, producing low-cost bedroom furniture. In the 1920s he spent vacation time in Florida and admired the Spanish eclectic–style beachfront homes. In 1911 he'd bought three homes on Broadway Street three blocks west of the Shelby County Courthouse and in 1930 he knocked them down to build a Palm Beach–style house of Bedford limestone and arched doorways. It is one of the most distinctive homes in Shelbyville, a touch of Florida in small-town Indiana.

David and Sarah grew up in Shelbyville, met while playing in the community band, married in 1990, and had just finished restoring a 1917 home when they heard that Charlotte was selling her family home.

"She felt we were the right people to care for her parents' house. It was providence," says Purdue University graduate Sarah, a kindergarten teacher and an expert in American antique needlework. Her great-grandfather emigrated from Germany to work in the furniture factories. The Finkels

remodeled the house to accommodate their little girl, Elizabeth, as well as David's interest in music, art, and high-tech gadgets. They converted a shower room into a stereo closet containing sixteen hundred classical music CDs, a VCR, a DVD player, and a PC, which are wired to every room in the house on digital cable.

"Just because a house is old, it doesn't have to act old," explains David, who played alto horn in the Indiana University marching band, majored in theater set design, and now runs the family-owned automotive parts distributorship with his brother, Ken. He plans to build an addi-

tion to the back of the house to accommodate a massive theater pipe organ.

"You won't be able to tell it's an addition," he cautions. He plans to take great care not to disturb the roots of a huge backyard silver maple tree that is probably more than two hundred years old and measures fifteen feet, nine inches in circumference.

"This is a working house," says David. "It's a house we live in. We have a toddler and two dogs that run all over the place. Charlotte chose us and we won't let her down, but I think she'd appreciate what we're doing here."

Marilyn Fischer

Historic Name: GEORGE AND MARY INSKEEP HOUSE

County: WHITE

Date of Construction: 1901

Architectural Style: QUEEN ANNE

Sometime in the late nineteenth century, farmer George T. Inskeep inherited $67 from his grandfather's estate, a Virginia plantation operated with slave labor. The inheritance earned George the unique distinction in local history books as "the only living resident of White County who ever inherited anything from slavery."

George was born near Romney in Tippecanoe County in 1852 before the great forests were cut, the sweeping prairies plowed, and the tangled swamps drained and planted in grain. He moved to White County as a young man, hauled logs five miles over a foot of snow in the frozen winter of 1875, built a house, and married Mary F. Davisson. They prospered and produced five children, moved to a 263-acre farm two miles west of Monticello, and built a grand Queen Anne–style home in 1901, establishing themselves as one of White County's preeminent families.

"His fellow citizens have complete confidence in his integrity, his competence as a businessman, and in all the relations of an active life he has measured up to the best standards of citizenship," a 1915 county history book wrote of George Inskeep.

One of George T.'s sons, George A., remained on the farm working with his father. He married Flossie Harrison and they built a small house down the hill from his father's. They had two children, Marilyn and William. Marilyn still remembers her grandfather in his later, ailing years, sitting before the big bay window looking wistfully toward the gently rolling farm fields he once plowed and harvested. She also remembers her grandmother, a former school-teacher, sitting in a rocking chair, reading book after book. Grandmother believed in knowledge.

"I named my daughter, Mary Frances, after Grand-mother," says Marilyn, who left the farm in 1941, graduated with a biology degree from Western College at Oxford, Ohio, and moved to Indianapolis to work as a microbiologist testing vitamins at Eli Lilly and Company. In 1957, she married John Fischer, who designed advertisements for an appliance store. They had three daughters. The big Monticello family farmhouse was at that time occupied by Marilyn's two elderly aunts and a brain-damaged uncle disabled from childhood by severe sun-stroke.

By 1973, the two aunts and the uncle were dead. Marilyn, John, and the girls returned home to the house Grand-father built. "At first we just moved in to clean it out because my aunts never, ever threw anything away," recalls Marilyn. "We never did get it cleaned out so we just kept staying. It seemed like a good deal."

And it was. The house once again served a new genera-tion. John worked for a heating supply company. Marilyn was a substitute teacher. The three girls helped raise sheep, chickens, ducks, geese, and guineas. "We had the security of the house," says Marilyn. "Our friends in Indianapolis always asked why we moved away and I said, 'Because it's our home and it had always been ours.'"

John died in 1989 from a stroke. He was sixty-four years old. The girls went to college, married, and moved away. Marilyn stayed in the house where Grandmother read and Grandfather, who'd inherited slavery money, sat by the bay window surveying his beloved fields. It was, after all, the house where her father grew up and spent his life, and the farm where she was raised, and where her daughters raised sheep, chickens, ducks, geese, and guineas.

"I knew all these people, going back to Granddad," says Marilyn, explaining why she chose to remain in the house. "It's always been ours and it's always been home."

Richard E. Ford

Historic Name: EDWIN FORD HOUSE

City: WABASH

County: WABASH

Date of Construction: 1901

Architectural Style: COLONIAL REVIVAL

LISTED IN THE NATIONAL REGISTER OF HISTORIC PLACES

Richard E. Ford lives in the house his parents, Wilbur and Florence Ford, bought in 1928. When Richard's two brothers died suddenly in the late 1970s, he left Washington, D.C., where he worked for the United States Environmental Protection Agency, to return home to Wabash to help his parents through the difficult ordeal. He now lives in his boyhood home, from which he coordinates a wide range of philanthropic and cultural endeavors devoted to, among other things, classical music and historic preservation.

Immediately to the south of Richard's house is the 1901 Colonial Revival home which Richard's grandparents Edwin and Elizabeth Neff Ford had occupied since 1926.

In 1898, Edwin Ford founded the Ford Meter Box Company, which remains headquartered in Wabash. It manufactures water-meter setting and testing equipment and brass fittings for the water industry. Ford Meter Box Company products are sold throughout the world.

Richard maintains his grandparents' house, in addition to his own adjacent residence, on six splendidly landscaped acres that slope down to Charley Creek and beyond. He is developing the acreage's gardens as an educational and aesthetic experience for visitors to the Wabash area.

"It's a privilege to live in Wabash," he says of his city, which, incidentally, was the first electrically lighted city in the world. (In 1880, arc lights were lit on top of the court-

house dome, drawing thousands of spectators.) "I certainly enjoyed growing up here and I want to now focus my energy on helping the city restore its downtown."

The 1901 Edwin Ford house presently serves as a living repository of memorabilia, including furnishings and archival materials, of the Ford and Neff families. Among these are the epaulets worn by Edwin's father, Dr. James Ford, as part of his Civil War surgeon's uniform, and his medicine box. Another great-grandfather, John Neff, walked to California in 1882 and returned with enough gold to buy a large farm in Wabash County.

Richard, a board member of the Indianapolis Museum of Art and the Indianapolis Symphony Orchestra, and past president of the American Pianists Association, also puts his grandparents' home to good use as a guesthouse for visiting performing musical artists. "I try to further good music in Wabash," he says in his typical, understated fashion. "Music festivals and workshops are wholesome things for any community."

Richard Ford has extended the devotion he feels for his parents and for his family's heritage into a major community asset, enhancing the cultural life of Wabash and encouraging the preservation of its historic architecture. "I hope my parents would be pleased that these family houses and memorabilia remain intact, and that music and preservation activities are being supported in the community they loved so much."

Malcolm and Faith Fraser

Historic Name: BILLINGSLEY HOUSE

County: OHIO

Date of Construction: 1846

Architect / Builder: TIMOTHY NEWMAN

Architectural Style: GREEK REVIVAL

"This is our little piece of America," British-born Malcolm Fraser says of the handsome farmhouse he and his wife, Faith, bought in 1993 in a remote valley along Laughery Creek in tiny Ohio County.

Since 1987, Malcolm has held the J. Ralph Corbett Distinguished Chair of Opera at the University of Cincinnati Conservatory of Music, one of America's leading opera training programs, which has launched some of this country's finest operatic talent. Faith is a freelance set and

costume designer. They have directed and designed opera productions throughout the world.

Their farmhouse was built in 1846 and the property includes sixty-two hilly acres in one of the most secluded spots in Indiana. "It's a fifty-minute commute to Cincinnati, but who cares," says Malcolm. "The great thing about America is you can achieve your dreams. This place is our dream, something we could never afford in Europe."

They both grew up in London and met while working

at Sadler's Wells Theatre. In 1993, the Frasers were living in Cincinnati near the university campus with their four boys and hoping to one day live in rural America. They'd been considering buying and converting an old theater building in Aurora, Indiana, into an opera house.

The opera house deal didn't work out, but on a drive through the Indiana countryside they spotted their future piece of America. It was owned by Lawrence Elliott, a direct descendant of Billingsley, who homesteaded the land and built the house in 1846. Lawrence was a reluctant seller, saddened that the stately house on the hillside would finally leave the family after more than 150 continuous years. "The property was dearly loved by Lawrence and his wife, Rosella, who had taken good care of the house and the land," recalls Faith.

From the second-floor porch, they have a commanding view of the valley, the steep hills of far southeastern Indiana, and the flocks of wild turkey that roam the flatlands.

There is not another house or building in sight. The only sign of the twenty-first century is the lightly traveled, unmarked Hartford Pike, which passes before their house.

"We knew nothing about tractors and floods and barns until we bought this place," adds Malcolm, referring to the unpredictable Laughery Creek and its history of dangerous flash floods. They've since learned about tractors, flash floods, and especially the original barn that remains in perfect condition, a massive structure of hand-hewn timbers. Malcolm marvels at the craftsmanship and backbreaking work required to build such a structure.

"The house represents such civilized values, such a brave home place in what must have been a very rough environment when it was built," he says, running his fingers over adze marks in a timber beam. "American pioneers were tough, determined people."

The Frasers have combined their fascination for music, theater, and design with their rural setting. Christmas visi-

tors to the Tower Place Mall in downtown Cincinnati would be surprised to know that the huge and colorful toy soldiers, one of Faith's many projects, were painted and decorated in the barn.

Shortly after moving into the house, Malcolm and Faith saw potential in the great big barn. Now each autumn they host an opera concert there. Students, professors, and Conservatory patrons sit on hay bales, swat flies, and listen to Italian opera.

"This isn't just our house," says Malcolm. "It is living our dream in America, where we can combine our love of the arts with this wonderful opportunity to live in a beautiful house in the countryside."

Warner and Carol Freese

Historic Name: W. C. B. SEWELL HOUSE

City: COVINGTON

County: FOUNTAIN

Date of Construction: 1867

Architectural Style: GREEK REVIVAL / ITALIANATE

LISTED IN THE NATIONAL REGISTER OF HISTORIC PLACES

In 1972 when the Quaker Oats Company transferred engineer Warner Freese to its Danville, Illinois, oatmeal plant, Carol Freese was not pleased. "I never thought I'd be happy again," she says. She grew up in Maryland, had met Warner at Duke University in 1963, and they had just renovated an old German farmhouse in the mountains of western Pennsylvania.

"I'm an easterner and the Midwest is very different," says Carol, who was a public health nurse in Pennsylvania. They made the best of their Midwest exile and looked across the Wabash River for an old home in Covington in west central Indiana. They bought "The House with the Lions," as it was known locally, an 1867 brick Victorian built by

businessman W. C. B. Sewell. He placed two enormous metal statues of resting lions by the front porch and a black wrought-iron fence around the yard, both of which remain. The Freeses bought the house from Sewell descendants, the Mayer family.

"The house had problems. It was empty and smelled of cats," says Carol. "It looked like a haunted house, but it was pure, with very few changes over the years, and we had two baby girls and needed a place to live." The chandeliers are all original to the house and they still use a 1906 bathtub.

It took two years to get the house in shape and fill it with Victorian furniture. "I'm a purist. You have a Victorian house, you put Victorian furniture in it and yet make it

livable for a family with two kids," says Carol. She continued buying antiques long after the house was filled and Warner wondered why.

"He said, 'You gotta quit buying all this stuff' and I said, 'It needs to be saved,'" says Carol, who then opened the House with the Lions antique shop in the maid's quarters in the rear of their home. Business was so good that she recently moved her shop downtown across from the Fountain County Courthouse.

As a child, Carol watched her father refinish old furniture. In high school, following in her father's footsteps, she was a tour guide for the U.S. Park Service at the Antietam National Battlefield near Sharpsburg, Maryland. The September 17, 1862, battle on this site resulted in twenty-six thousand casualties, the single bloodiest day of the Civil War. Her father's devotion to these activities made a deep impression on her.

"You can't understand yourself if you don't understand the past," Carol explains. She recently bought an 1840s house on Fourth Street, which she plans to renovate and donate to the Fountain County Arts Council to use as a museum. "I want to save it. Not enough people appreciate what they have. If I don't do it maybe nobody will. It's part of our heritage," she continues.

The Freeses placed "The House with the Lions" in the National Register of Historic Places in 1984, a time when Covington's older homes were being bulldozed at an alarming rate. "We lost ten historic buildings during a short period of time, including a wonderful Victorian home that CVS pharmacy knocked down. We wanted to protect our house," explains Carol, who has changed her mind about the Midwest.

"In 1972 when we got here I thought I'd never be happy again, but now I'll never leave 'The House with the Lions,'" she declares.

Jerry and Carolyn Fuhs

Historic Name: MT. AIRIE

County: ORANGE

Date of Construction: 1928

Architectural Style: COLONIAL REVIVAL

Given its rich and colorful history, it's probably fitting that dynamic businessman Jerry Fuhs would eventually live in the great Orange County mansion on the hill known as Mt. Airie. The house once hosted such celebrated and diverse visitors as murderous gangster Al Capone and New York governor Franklin D. Roosevelt, who were drawn to the nearby French Lick and West Baden gambling casinos and mineral spas.

Jerry, a college dropout, owns several businesses throughout southern Indiana, ranging from hotels, restaurants, and an Amish theme park to a fuel tax recovery operation. He and his wife, Carolyn, recently bought and renovated the Hillside Hotel in Madison and purchased the 120,000-square-foot, 1864 Old Cotton Mill on the Ohio River. In the early 1980s, while living in Jasper, he booked hundreds of concerts for country-and-western singers George Jones,

Merle Haggard, and Hank Williams Jr., among others. Jerry's interests are extensive and varied, not unlike business wheeler-dealer and political strongman Thomas Taggart, who built the house in 1928.

"It was fate I guess that led me to Mt. Airie," Jerry explains. The house was probably named Mt. Airie because it's surrounded by air, perched on an enormous, windy hilltop with a spectacular thirty-mile, 360-degree view of the southeastern Indiana hills. At about twelve hundred feet above sea level, it is believed to be the second-highest point in Indiana.

The twenty-eight-room, V-shaped Taggart mansion contains a secret china cabinet and two hidden staircases. Taggart was a turn-of-the-century Indianapolis mayor, national Democratic Party chairman, and an influential businessman who apparently needed hiding places. In 1901, he

organized the business syndicate that acquired and rebuilt the French Lick Hotel into an elegant twenty-five-hundred-acre resort, known throughout the world for its mineral spring spas and nearby gambling activities, which mysteriously flourished for decades despite being illegal.

In 1997, Jerry and Carolyn, a French Lick native, bought Mt. Airie and fifty surrounding acres and began an extensive restoration project. They were living in Christmas Lake Village in Spencer County at the time. "We decided the only place we'd ever move to in Orange County was Mt. Airie," he recalls.

"We want to return Mt. Airie to its glory days," says Jerry. He and Carolyn have immersed themselves in the history of the Taggart house and French Lick's early years as a gambling hotspot. In the 1920s French Lick and adjacent West Baden contained at least twelve gambling casinos, which were presumably protected from the law by Taggart's powerful political allies. Carolyn has filled an upstairs room in the mansion with old photographs, poker tables, and roulette wheels, mementos of French Lick's previous existence.

"Local people weren't allowed in the casinos. They were reserved for proper, high-end people from out of town. It was part of the culture," Jerry explains.

"Look at this," he says, removing two wooden walking sticks from a glass-topped display table. One belonged to Taggart, who modestly had his image engraved on the handle. The other cane was brought to Mt. Airie by Franklin Roosevelt during one of two political visits he made to French Lick to confer with Taggart. Roosevelt gave his cane to Auty Shipman, who worked for the Taggart family for thirty years. Shipman gave both canes to Jerry, who clearly values their history. Fuhs also acquired two torch lamps that are original to the house.

"The history of the house appealed to me," Jerry says. "Plus on foggy days we're above the clouds and the valley below looks like an ocean."

Sanford and Marjut Garner

City: INDIANAPOLIS

County: MARION

Date of Construction: 1887

Architectural Style: QUEEN ANNE

LISTED IN THE NATIONAL REGISTER OF HISTORIC PLACES, *Herron-Morton Place Historic District*

Living in the Herron-Morton Place Historic District near downtown Indianapolis has several distinct advantages for Sanford Garner. He can walk, bike, jog, or roller-blade the short distance to his architectural firm. Walking, in fact, is how Sanford and his Finnish-born wife, Marjut, found their house in 1995.

Sanford grew up in the Broad Ripple neighborhood of Indianapolis and graduated from Howard University in Washington, D.C., in 1993. His father, Dr. LaForrest Garner, is the retired dean of the Orthodontics Department at the Indiana University School of Dentistry in Indiana-

polis. Dr. Garner traveled extensively lecturing on his dental specialty, the cleft palate.

"Dad took us all over the world and I took pictures of buildings and noticed the amazing effect architecture can have on people," says Sanford, explaining his early interest in design.

He met Marjut in an art gallery while studying architecture at the University of Helsinki. They married and returned to Indianapolis, and lived in and renovated a duplex owned by Sanford's mother, Alfreida, in the Fall Creek Place neighborhood.

In the spring of 1995, on walks to several Indiana Pacer NBA playoff basketball games, they admired a modest 1887 frame house with interesting gable work that appealed to Sanford's sense of style and proportion. They bought it, ignoring their friends' advice to move to the suburbs.

"An architecture professor of mine had this theory which I share, that when you throw a subdivision together in a cornfield, you simply have a mass of homes with no history, no innate sense of energy, no nothing; essentially a sterile, generic environment," says Sanford. "We wanted to live in a real neighborhood with a sense of history and purpose where people knew each other."

The neighborhood is rich in Hoosier history. Prior to the Civil War, the area was home to the Indiana State Fair. When war broke out, Governor Oliver P. Morton turned it into an induction and training center for Union soldiers. Later in the long war, it served as a prison camp for Confederate soldiers. By war's end, more than fifteen thousand Confederate soldiers had been confined in the prison, many of whom died in the wretched place.

At the turn of the twentieth century, land was platted into 280 residential lots that later became home to some of Indianapolis's leading citizens, including two U.S. senators, a governor, and Dr. Willis Gatch, who invented the first adjustable hospital bed. The John Herron Art Institute was established in the neighborhood in 1907, hence the name Herron-Morton Place.

Following World War II, as the city expanded north into cornfields, Herron-Morton Place deteriorated. Many fine homes were chopped up into low-income apartments or demolished in a series of misguided urban renewal projects. In the 1970s the neighborhood stirred to life once again, homes were restored, and the historic vibrancy of the area returned. All of which appealed to Sanford and Marjut—the history, cultural diversity, and ease of roller-blading to work and walking to Pacer games.

In 1999, Sanford and Marjut's son, Kendall, was born, adding yet another layer of diversity to the neighborhood. "We have white, black, gay, young, old, and retired people in this neighborhood of various income levels," says Sanford. "But I don't know of any other kid who speaks Finnish and English around here."

Robert (Skip) and Marta Gerometta

Historic Name: EMMETT BOYD HOUSE
City: LAPORTE
County: LAPORTE
Date of Construction: 1911
Architect: ROBERT SPENCER
Architectural Style: ARTS AND CRAFTS

When Skip and Marta Gerometta and their two little girls were house hunting in 1978, they were looking along the Lake Michigan shore in LaPorte County and who could blame them? With apologies to people along the Ohio River in southern Indiana, the LaPorte County stretch of shoreline is one of the most exceedingly beautiful places in the state. White sand beaches, dune grasses, pine trees bent from the wind, and the sheer grandeur and size of the great lake itself are compelling attractions, especially in mostly land-locked Indiana.

But Marta liked the kite-shaped leaded-glass window-panes in a house on Indiana Avenue in the city of LaPorte, fourteen blocks east of the courthouse and fifteen miles southeast of the lake. "I was a Kappa Alpha Theta at Purdue and our sorority pin was shaped like a kite," explains Marta. To compensate for lack of water, they installed a backyard swimming pool. The Arts and Crafts–style stucco house, built in 1911 for the Emmett Boyd family, was designed by Oak Park, Illinois, architect Robert Spencer, yet another in the line of Frank Lloyd Wright students, protégés, and

met Marta at Portage High School. She was born in the Republic of Panama, where her father was a surgeon. Her parents divorced when she was a toddler and her mother remarried an American engineer who was working in Panama. The family moved to Portage when Marta was twelve. Skip went to the University of Michigan and Marta to Purdue. They both graduated in 1968, lived in Norfolk, Virginia, for three years while Skip served in the U.S. Navy, and moved to LaPorte when he was offered a job with an architectural firm.

Skip later formed his own architectural firm based in Chesterton in adjacent Porter County and Marta opened LePanache, an interior design studio on Lake Michigan in New Buffalo, Michigan, fifteen miles from LaPorte. They drive a lot.

When they bought the house in 1978, they planned to raise their daughters there, then try again to find a place on Lake Michigan. Their daughters are gone now and every couple of years they think about leaving the peaceful neighborhood for a house on the lake. But they don't.

"I still like the windows," says Marta.

family members whose homes are found throughout northern Indiana.

"I've been around construction my whole life," says Skip, whose given name is Robert. "To replicate anything close to this house would be prohibitively expensive. The walls are plaster, for example. Try even finding a plasterer today. I think there's *one* in LaPorte."

Skip, an architect, was familiar with Spencer and building construction and design in general. His grandfather Marcello Gerometta, a stonemason, emigrated from Italy to Gary in 1907. Grandpa and his brothers chose Gary when they heard that U.S. Steel Corporation had purchased nine thousand acres of land in Lake County, including seven miles of Lake Michigan shoreline to build the world's largest steel mill.

Grandpa correctly predicted a building boom in the new town of Gary, which U.S. Steel chairman of the board Elbert H. Gary named after himself. Marcello and his family later formed Gerometta Construction Company, which built hundreds of houses for steel workers, the Holy Angels Cathedral, and the Hotel Gary in 1927, to name a few of his considerable achievements.

Skip's father later took over Gerometta Construction Co. Skip grew up in Ogden Dunes in Porter County, where he

Leroy and Vivian Gibbons

Historic Name: SAMUEL SMITH HOUSE

County: WAYNE

Date of Construction: 1888

Architectural Style: ITALIANATE

LISTED IN THE NATIONAL REGISTER OF HISTORIC PLACES

The death of Harold S. Smith in 1989 set off a complicated, unpleasant family situation. Who would inherit the house was a touchy topic. Harold never married and had no children. Even so, he left thirteen legal heirs, none of whom could agree on an equitable distribution of the estate, which included the magnificent house and eighty surrounding acres in the rolling hills just west of Richmond in Wayne County. The house was built in 1888 by Harold's grandfather Samuel G. Smith, a farmer.

The only solution to the touchy situation was a public auction. Sell the place and divide the proceeds thirteen ways. The subdivision disease and other signs of urban blight were moving west toward the farm, and developers were interested.

Harold's niece Vivian Gibbons and her husband, Leroy,

were determined to keep the house in the family. Growing up in nearby Fountain City, Vivian often visited the house as a little girl to pick strawberries, work in the garden, and help her meticulous grandmother Ida Smith with the annual spring cleaning.

"We weren't allowed to put soap in the water because Grandma didn't want to damage the shellac on the woodwork," says Vivian, recalling the family's dedication to maintaining the red brick house in pristine condition. It still has the original slate roof, and the woodwork gleams. When Vivian's grandfather Howard Smith died, Grandmother Ida and her daughter, Anna, continued to work the farm. Grandma was milking cows a few days before her death.

"Two women kept this place going until Harold moved

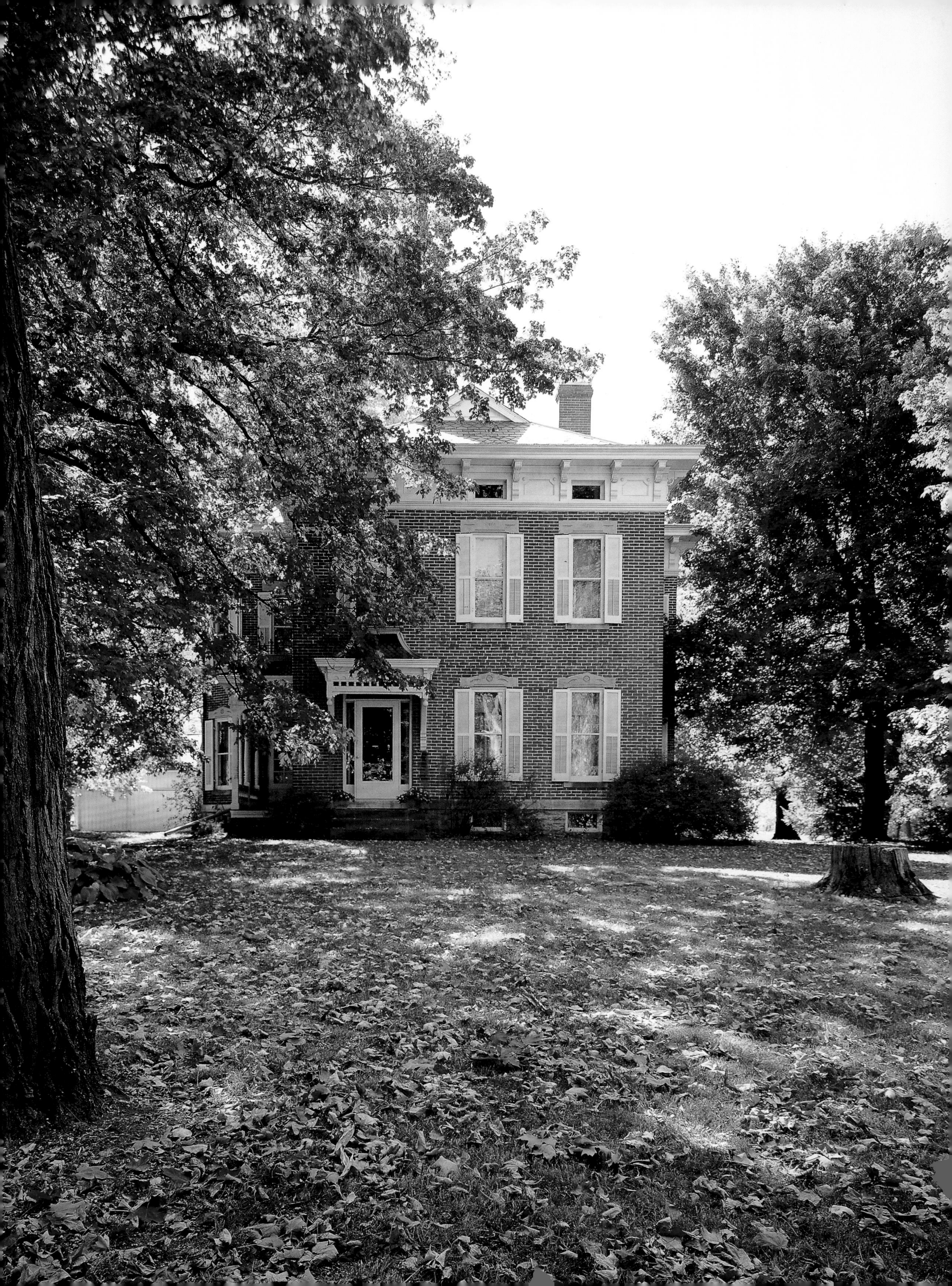

in," says Vivian. "Uncle Harold worked so hard to maintain the house and he got it listed in the National Register because he wanted it preserved forever."

Leroy and Vivian bought the farm in the public auction, ending the legal wrangling among Uncle Harold's heirs, insuring that it will remain in the family for another generation and soap won't touch the woodwork.

"The situation with the thirteen heirs was very unpleasant," says Vivian. "But Leroy agreed we had to keep the place in the family. No matter what."

Leroy, a retired air force bomber pilot, married Vivian in 1954. They lived all over the world, raised four children, and returned home to Wayne County when Leroy retired in 1975. The Gibbons are the fourth generation to live in the house, which remains in remarkable condition and contains some of the original furniture Samuel Smith bought in 1888, including a $28 hall tree and tri-corner cupboard.

Samuel G. Smith was born across the road in a log cabin in 1840. Vivian found a couple of bricks and planks from the cabin, which fell apart long ago.

Some of the largest beech trees in Indiana surround and shade the house. The Gibbons are rechinking and restoring an old cabin that Uncle Harold rescued and brought to the farm in 1934. "It will make a good playhouse for the five grandkids," says Vivian. They also restored the old two-hole outhouse, the chicken house, and the icehouse. And they've allowed the eighty acres to recover from a century of farming and return to grass, wildflowers, and trees.

Grandma Ida Smith's 1949 Buick, with a mere 49,259 miles on the odometer, is parked in the massive, two-story barn and covered with a protective tarp. And guess what? The Buick still runs. Grandma took good care of her things.

"Since my family worked so hard to keep this farm going, we couldn't let it go," says Vivian, admiring Grandma's car. "My family believed in taking care of everything from the woodwork to the cars. We're just gonna keep taking care of things."

Jeff Gibney

Historic Name: A. D. BAKER HOUSE

City: SOUTH BEND

County: ST. JOSEPH

Date of Construction: 1888

Architectural Style: QUEEN ANNE

LISTED IN THE NATIONAL REGISTER OF HISTORIC PLACES, *West Washington Street Historic District*

In the early 1970s, West Washington Street, once South Bend's most elegant, prosperous neighborhood, was in a desperate state of collapse, its great homes crumbling beneath a wave of crime, drugs, racial tension, and neglect. To cite one depressing example, an early Prairie-style Frank Lloyd Wright home had become a low-rent tavern.

Then along came social worker Jeff Gibney. He attempted to buy a Washington Street house built in 1888 by A. D. Baker, controller of the Oliver Chill Plow Works factory. South Bend banks, which had redlined the neighborhood, refused to loan Jeff the money. The house, across the street from the Frank Lloyd Wright beer hall, had been abandoned for seventeen years and was being used as a warehouse.

"This was the worst, most dangerous area in the city, but I wanted to live in a grand, old neighborhood for the fix-up challenge," he recalls. He turned to the newly organized, non-profit South Bend Heritage Foundation (SBHF), which was attempting to revitalize decaying neighborhoods by offering low-interest loans to prospective homebuyers. He got the loan, moved into the unheated, unplumbed house with his brother David, a carpenter, and restored it.

Jeff also began organizing the demoralized residents,

resurrecting block clubs and neighborhood associations. They loudly demanded better police protection and municipal services. They marched. They protested. And they succeeded. Jeff, with his social worker conscience, political savvy, and relentless drive, was a key factor in the West Washington Street neighborhood rebirth. It's now the West Washington Street Historic District, a vibrant neighborhood just west of the St. Joseph County Courthouse.

In 1978, impressed with his neighborhood work, the SBHF hired Jeff as its first executive director to apply his skills in neighborhoods throughout South Bend. "We don't believe in gentrification," Jeff says. SBHF doesn't invest in themed, "upscale" projects that exclude low- and middle-income residents and destroy the neighborhoods' historic character and charm. "We want real neighborhoods with a good mix of historic properties, apartments, and affordable housing at all economic levels," says Jeff, who grew up in South Bend, graduated from Indiana University in 1971, and spent a couple of years teaching school in Sierra Leone, Africa, and San Paulo, Brazil.

He returned home in 1975 to tend to family matters and found boarded-up neighborhoods resembling Sierra Leone and San Paulo slums. South Bend banks refused to

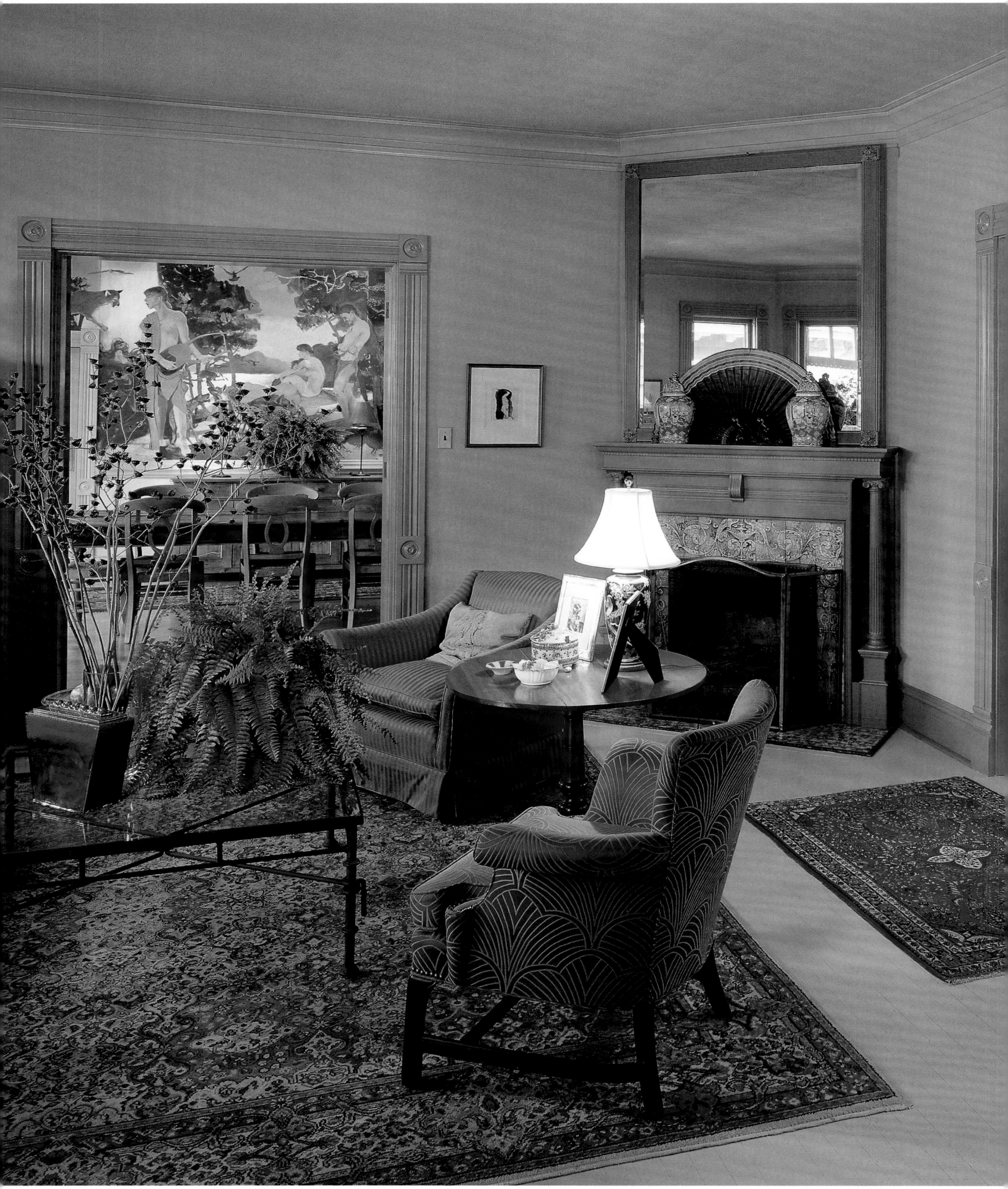

invest in crumbling neighborhoods, thereby hastening the decay. City officials simply neglected and ignored the old neighborhoods, handed out corporate welfare checks to suburban developers, and called it "economic development."

"The injustice of it hit me. Neighborhoods don't fall apart. They are purposefully pulled apart," he says, reciting the usual list of suspects: banks, corporate law firms, profiteering real estate developers, and their city hall coconspirators who approve taxpayer-subsidized infrastructure extensions into suburban areas at the expense of urban neighborhoods.

Oh, and the Frank Lloyd Wright beer hall? It is being restored by Tom Miller, a fine arts professor at the South Bend Indiana University campus.

"It's the social worker in me, I guess," says Jeff. "Somebody had to do something."

91

Brent and Marina Gill

Historic Name: GERHARDT SCHEPMANN HOUSE
County: JACKSON
Date of Construction: CIRCA 1840
Architectural Style: FEDERAL

When Brent and Marina Gill bought the Federal-style farmhouse in Jackson County in 1989, they planned to convert it to an antebellum mansion with big pillars and a sweeping forty-three-foot portico. Luckily, Marina consulted professional preservationists who expressed horror at her plan to destroy the integrity of the house. It was built around 1840 by farmer Gerhardt Schepmann for his wife and herd of seven children.

"Well, we didn't know any better at first," says Marina of the antebellum mansion idea. She is now one of the area's most passionate preservationists and a persistent critic of local officials and their pals, the corporate money-

huggers, who seem determined to strip-mall, subdivide, and pave every inch of Jackson County.

"I've ticked a lot of people off," says the fiery Marina, during a tour of the house and eight acres, which includes the original smokehouse, barn, and log building where Gerhardt Schepmann slaughtered four hundred hogs a year. The Gills bought it from the heirs of two Schepmann descendants who mopped the linoleum floors three times a day with disinfectant. Erna and Alma, the fastidious elderly sisters, didn't go out much, never went upstairs because there was no heat there, and ordered visitors to remove their shoes before entering. The house was empty for two years following their deaths.

"It smelled of death," says Marina, who married Brent, a Seymour lawyer, in 1974. "We had three boys and wanted to give it life again." During the renovation process, Marina only hired contractors over sixty-five years old, figuring seasoned craftsmen would appreciate the home's character

and share her determination not to mess it up. "I wanted their experience and respect for this kind of building, because I felt a duty and responsibility to bring it to the standard it was intended for," she says.

Marina even paid $8,000 to have utility lines to the house buried. "I didn't do all this to have utility lines in the sky and poles down the long driveway," she says.

Marina and Brent added two bedrooms, two bathrooms, and heat upstairs for their sons. They put an antique pool table in the old brick kitchen for the boys and their friends and renovated the old barn for Rosie and Megan, the horses. The Gills' sons all attended Culver Military Academy and rode in the famed Black Horse Troop.

In 1996, the Gills bought the twenty-eight-room, three-story, 1854 Walton Hotel in downtown Seymour. They bought it after city officials and the money-huggers demolished the old Lynn Hotel and replaced it with an unnecessary parking lot. They hoped to save the Walton from

a similar fate. They opened O'Gill's, a highly successful bar and dance hall on the first floor of The Walton, and continued to rent rooms to low-income residents during the renovation process. Unfortunately, a resident started a fire on Christmas Day 1998 and the hotel burned down. Two residents died. All that remains of the building is a pile of red bricks that Marina had hauled to her driveway.

Marina has since directed her considerable energy to saving the county's endangered iron bridges and the 1868, 325-foot-long Bell Ford Covered Bridge, one half of which

was blown off its foundation and toppled into the East Fork of the White River during a 1999 storm.

From the front porch, the Gills can see and hear U.S. 50 in the distance. They are working to have the house placed on the National Register of Historic Places to prevent transportation officials from one day expanding the highway through their land to accommodate the ever-encroaching suburban sprawl.

"Trying to save our architectural wealth in this county is a full-time job," Marina sighs. "I fight 'em every day."

Henry Glassie and Kathleen A. Foster

Historic Name: WILLIAM FULWIDER HOUSE
City: BLOOMINGTON
County: MONROE
Date of Construction: CIRCA 1890
Architectural Style: QUEEN ANNE

LISTED IN THE NATIONAL REGISTER OF HISTORIC PLACES, *Prospect Hill Historic District*

When Henry Glassie and Kathy Foster bought the old Fulwider home in Bloomington's Prospect Hill Historic District in 1988, they feared that their thousands of books would collapse the creaky hundred-year-old floors. Henry is a Distinguished Professor at Indiana University's internationally acclaimed Folklore Institute, a presidential appointee to the National Council of Humanities, and author of fifteen books ranging from *Vernacular Architecture* to *Art and Life in Bangladesh.* He doesn't own a television. He reads. "Our daughter Ellen was raised in a house of reading and writing," he says. Kathy is an author and curator of modern art at the IU Art Museum.

To support the books, they reinforced the floors with railroad ties. Henry built shelves in every room, designing open space to accommodate the hundreds of art objects he and Kathy collected on their world travels. "I didn't want

it to look like a library so I included passages in the shelves for decorative items," says Henry, who received a Ph.D. in folklore from the University of Pennsylvania in 1969.

The decorative items nearly outnumber the books: pottery from Bangladesh, China, Ireland, Japan, and Turkey; sacred sculpture from India and Latin America. The floors are covered with Turkish rugs, and Kathy's collection of watercolors and prints fills the walls.

The house was built by lumberman and Monroe County Bank president William A. Fulwider around 1890. When Henry and Kathy bought it a century later, it had been a day care center for elderly people and divided into a series of tiny rooms. Henry learned carpentry from his grandfather while growing up on a Virginia farm that was the site of the Battle of Bull Run during the Civil War. He removed the day care center walls with a sledgehammer and crowbars, and replumbed, rewired, and renovated the house to suit himself.

"I had no interest in restoring the house to its original state of affairs," he explains. "I wanted it to look good. I wanted it open and spacious."

Like his father, Henry was active in civil rights, working for change, and yet he wished to preserve a record of the old Southern tradition. He lived in what he calls "the dilemma of a child's soul," and feels grateful that the study of folklore has allowed him to intellectualize his heritage.

Henry speaks Turkish, spent years in villages in Ireland, Turkey, Bangladesh, and other remote places, but he resembles a gaunt Confederate soldier with his curly moustache and long, gray hair. He maintains a grueling schedule, and is often gone months at a time, crossing oceans to live with potters, artists, or intellectuals in obscure places, exploring the relationship between art and cultural history and accumulating more books and works of art.

"I like being in other places, but I like coming back to Bloomington where I can pass the time in amateur carpentry and work on behalf of historic preservation," he says.

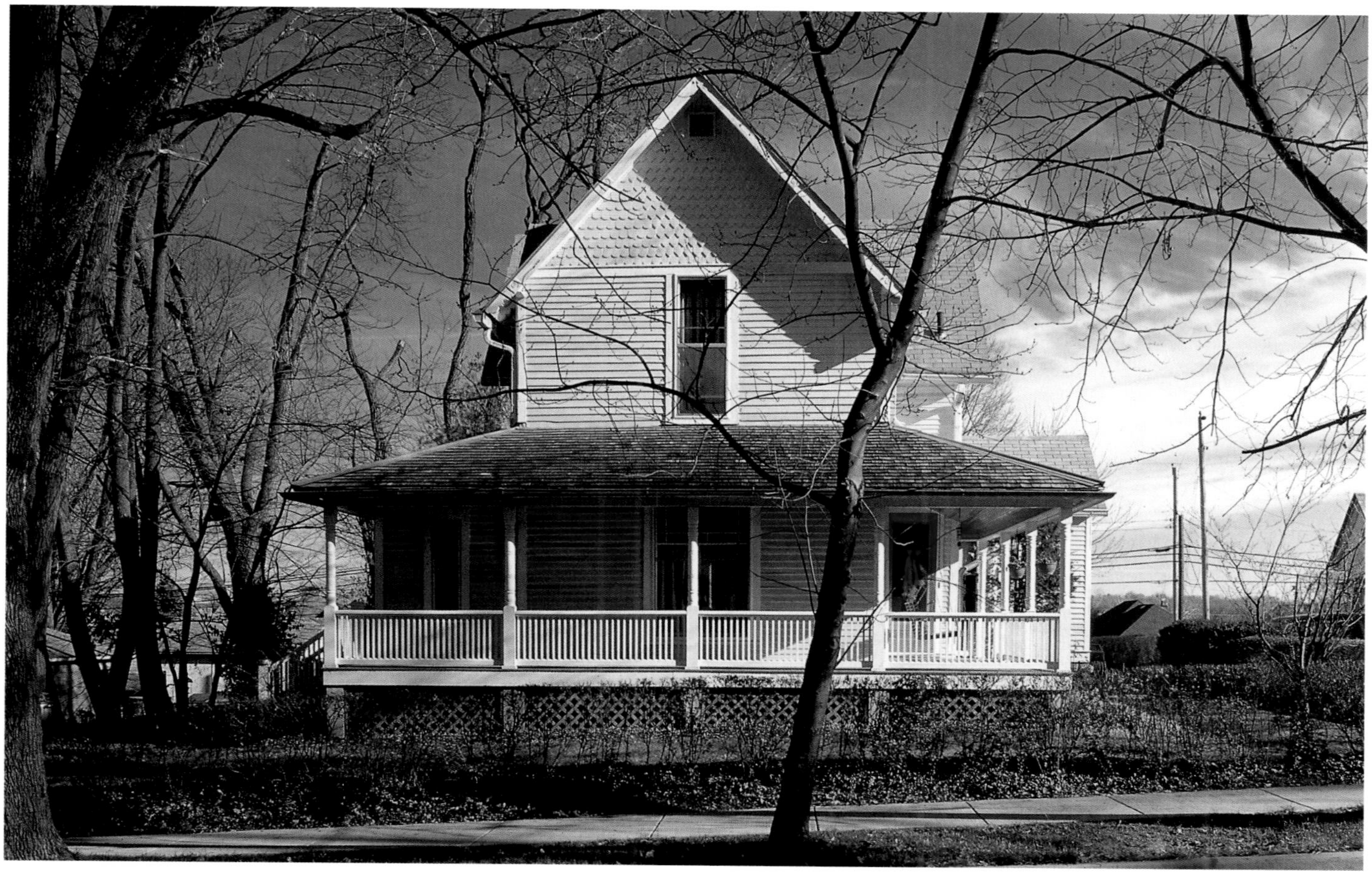

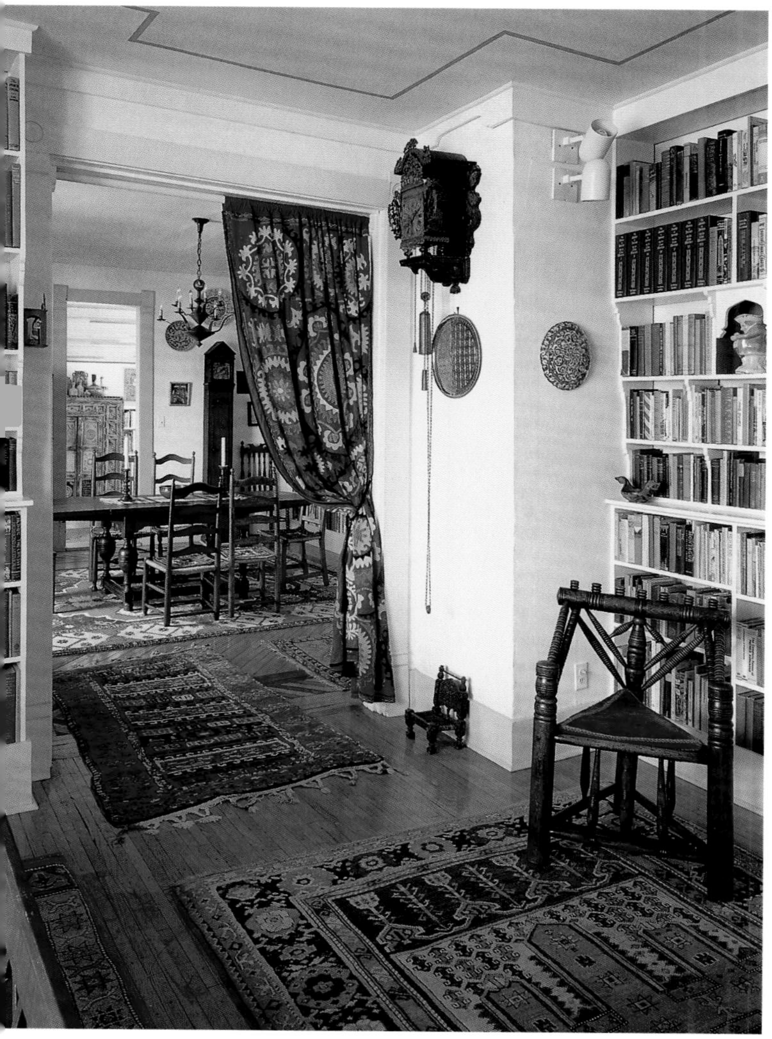

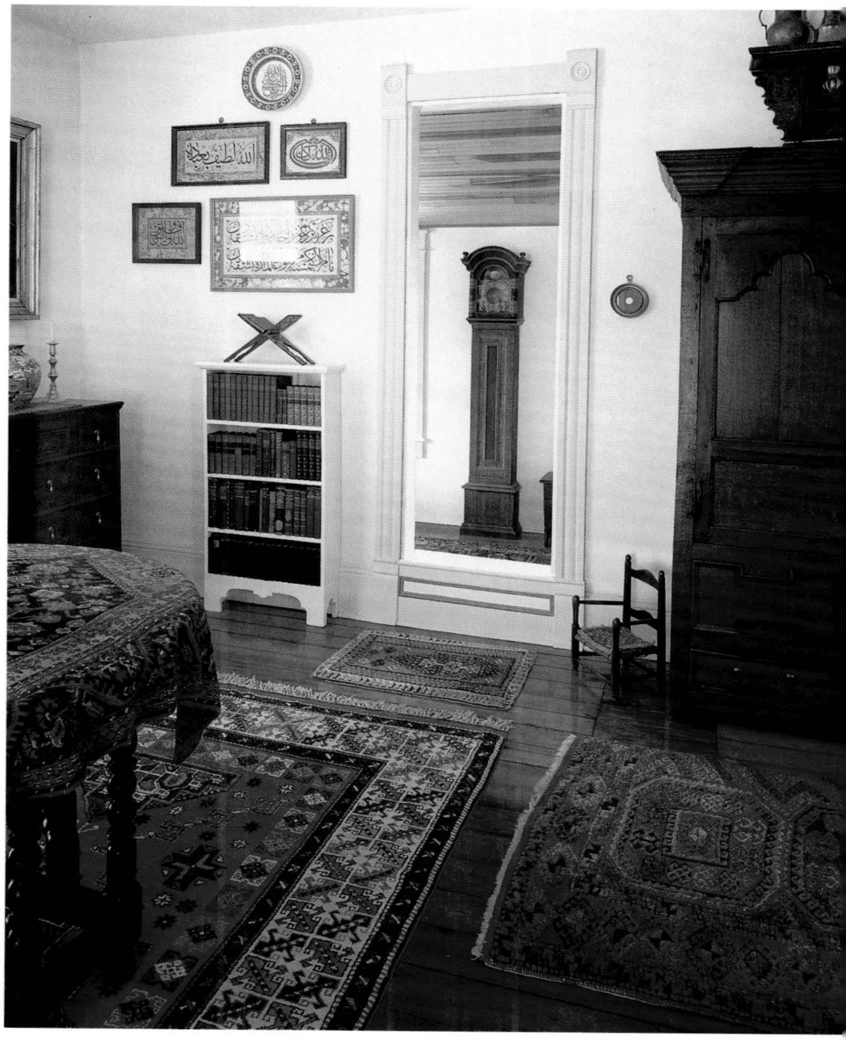

Olen Gowens

Historic Name: ASHBY PLACE

County: MONTGOMERY

Date of Construction: 1883

Architectural Style: ITALIANATE

Two pivotal events in Olen Gowens's childhood charted his life, eventually calling him from the lonesome, wind-swept wheat fields of western Kansas to a big house in the green, rolling hills of Montgomery County.

Born in 1922, Olen was the tenth of eleven children. His father was a struggling wheat farmer and his mother raised canaries for extra income. When he was eight and confined to home during a smallpox quarantine, Olen read a magazine story about the restoration of Mt. Vernon, George Washington's home. To pass the time, he used wood from an orange crate and built a scale model of Mt. Vernon, triggering a lifelong interest in American history and stately homes. About that time, as the great dust clouds rolled through Kansas, he saw a painting of a midwestern covered-bridge scene in autumn. He hoped one day to live in that painting, amid enormous trees, a winding creek, covered bridges, and green rolling hills: a place without dust.

Olen later graduated from Friends University in Wichita and moved to brown and treeless Los Angeles, hoping to become an opera singer, which didn't happen. He then

moved to treeless Phoenix and worked for the state of Arizona as a workman's compensation specialist. He also sang in the church choir, where he met Harley Reeder, a Phoenix chemist and seed analyst, who grew up in Parke County and graduated from Purdue University.

"Oh, tell me about the covered bridge festivals," Olen asked Harley during a church supper. In the autumn of 1974, Olen visited Parke County with Harley.

"I'd never seen a more beautiful autumn. I asked Harley if he'd like to move to Indiana and we could buy an old farmhouse and restore it," says Olen. "I was so happy and surprised when he said yes."

In 1977, they retired, left Phoenix, and bought what remained of the Ashby house along Cornstalk Creek outside Ladoga. Built in 1883, the two-story Italianate house with eighteen-inch double-brick and masonry walls had been unoccupied for twenty-five years and was near collapse. Harley and Olen installed heat, plumbing, and electricity, painted and wallpapered, and hand-scraped every inch of walnut, oak, cherry, and chestnut woodwork, sanding it three times and returning it to its original luster. They worked two backbreaking years to make it habitable.

"We worked so hard that we couldn't stand up at night," says Olen.

In January 1992 the grand home with its elegant and rare antiques, family heirlooms, and artwork received the Great American Home Award from the National Trust for Historic Preservation. The house, a spectacular Montgomery County landmark, is now on the National Register of Historic Places and Olen is one of the area's leading preservationists.

The twenty-four-room house was built by Robert Ashby, a prominent farmer and lumber, coal, and grain merchant. Bricks were fired in a kiln on the property and the nearby forest provided walnut and poplar for the floors and beams. Ashby's daughter, Bertha, who was born in the house in 1900, later became head librarian at Indiana University and founded libraries in Brown County and Ladoga.

Harley was diagnosed with cancer in 1994. "I'll care for you," Olen told his longtime companion, and he did. Harley died in 1996. He was eighty-seven. "I suffered a great deal with Harley," Olen recalls. Shortly before he died, Harley told Olen he had no regrets about returning to the green rolling hills and renovating the big house.

"And I told him I finally ended up in that painting I saw as a kid."

Alan and Maureen Grinsfelder

Historic Name: JOHN B. AND AMELIA FRANKE HOUSE

City: FORT WAYNE

County: ALLEN

Date of Construction: 1914

Architect: BARRY BYRNE

Architectural Style: PRAIRIE

If a house is a good indicator of the owner's personality, then John B. Franke was surely one of Fort Wayne's most innovative and colorful characters back in 1914. Franke, who founded the Perfection Biscuit Company in 1901, hired Barry Byrne, a protégé of famed architect Frank Lloyd Wright, to design a Prairie-style home in the fashionable Forest Park neighborhood.

Franke liked complicated gadgets. His new three-story, brick-room home was rigged with a Turner Inter Conversing System, an intricate intercom system complete with switchboard and headphones. Each room was wired with individual thermostats connected to the steam heat radiators. Seven self-correcting built-in wall clocks throughout the house were connected through a complex series of pneumatic hoses, pumps, and bellows to maintain accurate, down-to-the-second time. He controlled electric lights

throughout the house from a single panel. The crown jewel of this early-twentieth-century technology was a two-story, motorized pipe organ. It has four hundred pipes.

In the living room, Franke commissioned artist Alfonso Iannelli to paint a ten-foot "Tree of Life" wall mural featuring naked Adam and Eve figures. Franke's wife, Amelia, was aghast and ordered clothes painted on the naked figures.

"It's certainly an interesting house," notes the home's current owner, architect Alan Grinsfelder, who bought it in 1972 over his father-in-law's strenuous objections. "Dad said, 'Don't buy that old house. It'll be nothing but problems,'" recalls Alan's wife, Maureen. "It's been a challenge, certainly."

The pipe organ is on a second-floor balcony overlooking the living room and the curious mural. John B. Franke opened the living room windows on Sunday afternoons and invited the neighbors to picnic on the lawn while he serenaded them with organ music.

"Our boys would pile cushions on the living room floor and jump into them from the balcony," says Maureen, prov-

ing once again the functional nature of the unique house.

Mr. Franke's gadgets are still in place, none of which work, but they serve as interesting conversation pieces, especially the massive organ and the hundreds of rolls of music. The Grinsfelders bought the house from John Franke's grandson Leslie Popp Jr. Another grandson, John Popp, was the real estate agent who handled the transaction.

"I wanted the Grinsfelders to have the house because they appreciated it," recalls John Popp, who is now CEO of the family-owned Perfection Biscuit Company. "Another couple looked at it but I could tell they wanted to remodel it and mess it up, so I discouraged them." Brothers John and Leslie grew up in the great house and were determined to find new owners who would maintain its integrity and Grandpa's gadgets.

The Grinsfelders were the perfect buyers. "We had four boys and needed a bigger house and since I'm an architect I like the Prairie-style design, the lines and the light," says Alan, who studied architecture at the University of Michigan, where he met Maureen Isay. They married in 1958 and later moved to Fort Wayne when Alan was hired by a local architectural firm. He now owns his own business, Grinsfelder and Associates.

Alan's architectural firm did the restoration work on the magnificent Fort Wayne City Hall and the DeKalb and Steuben County courthouses. Maureen, who grew up in Whitley County, is executive director of the Fort Wayne Educational Foundation.

"This house has only been owned by two families," notes Maureen. "And it has served all of us very well."

John and Pam Guthrie

Historic Name: MARK AND BERTHA GUMBERTS GROSS HOUSE

City: EVANSVILLE

County: VANDERBURGH

Date of Construction: 1895

Architectural Style: QUEEN ANNE

LISTED IN THE NATIONAL REGISTER OF HISTORIC PLACES, *Riverside Historic District*

Pam Guthrie fondly remembers family trips to downtown Evansville in the late 1950s. The streets hummed with excitement and activity, the independently owned retail stores were crowded, and the smell of peanuts, popcorn, and candy filled the thick, humid air along the Ohio River.

"I still remember the peanut man," she says. "After shopping for school clothes we'd eat lunch at the Kresge's soda fountain and maybe go to a movie at the Grand Theater. The last movie I saw there was *The Parent Trap* with Haley Mills in 1960."

The Grand Theater is gone, replaced with a parking lot. Downtown Evansville today resembles one giant, deserted parking lot with plenty of spaces available. The dime store, clothing store, peanut vendor, and nearly all retail stores are gone, victims of 1970s urban renewal projects and the mass suburbanization of Evansville. The smell of peanuts, popcorn, and candy are distant memories.

"Most of downtown was bulldozed," says Pam, a member of the Evansville Preservation Commission, a city agency created in the aftermath of the bulldozer's devastation to protect the remaining historic homes.

Thankfully, what's not gone is the downtown Riverside Historic District, one of Indiana's most architecturally distinctive and diverse neighborhoods, a genuine treasure, two blocks from the Ohio River. The area was originally platted in 1814 by Hugh McGary, the founder of Evansville; the city was named after his friend, Robert M. Evans, a territorial legislator.

It never occurred to Pam and John Guthrie to live anywhere but in the Riverside District, a few blocks from the

Vanderburgh County Courthouse. The old courthouse is a metaphor for downtown Evansville. It's empty, replaced years ago by a new civic center, which houses county offices.

"I never forgot the smell of downtown," says Pam, a 1971 graduate of the University of Evansville. John grew up on a Warrick County farm, which has since been swallowed up by a massive Amax coal company strip mine. They met at Reitz High School in Evansville and married in 1971 after John graduated from Purdue University's School of Pharmacy.

He worked for a small pharmacy in nearby Chandler which he eventually bought. It's now the Guthrie Pharmacy and John offers free delivery and calls his customers by their first names. In 1972, the Guthries bought a spectacular Victorian home in the Riverside Historic District built in 1895 by "gentleman's tailor" Mark Gross and his wife, Bertha Gumberts Gross.

"I'd never seen anything like it," recalls Pam of the house that is across the street from the boyhood home of former Indiana governor Robert D. Orr. "The woodwork, the stained glass, and the light shining through the windows. Even though downtown is a deserted mess, we love our little island of protected historic homes."

Pam worked for the phone company for twenty years, raised two girls in the house of light, and now runs an antique shop in New Harmony and another in the Guthrie Pharmacy. She's a tireless advocate for her historic neighborhood and would like nothing more than to see downtown Evansville return to life.

"I want to see the peanut man and all the retail stores come back," she says. "Or at least get a grocery store downtown so we don't have to drive to the suburbs for food."

Bob and Ellie Haan

Historic Name: WILLIAM S. POTTER HOUSE

City: LAFAYETTE

County: TIPPECANOE

Date of Construction: 1904

Architectural Style: COLONIAL REVIVAL

LISTED IN THE NATIONAL REGISTER OF HISTORIC PLACES, *Ninth Street Hill Neighborhood Historic District*

Surely the most well-traveled home in Indiana belongs to Lafayette's Bob and Ellie Haan. The massive Colonial Revival–style house was built in St. Louis as the Connecticut Pavilion at the 1904 World's Fair in St. Louis, which was called the Louisiana Purchase Exposition. The house was created using the architectural components of three Colonial-era homes in Connecticut and shipped by railroad to St. Louis to be displayed at the fair, where it was spotted by visiting Lafayette attorney and land speculator William S. Potter. After the fair, Potter bought the 10,900-square-foot house as a present for his wife, Fannie. It was shipped by rail to State Street in Lafayette and put back together on a five-acre plot of land not far from the Tippecanoe County Courthouse.

Bob and Ellie Haan often strolled by the home on their walks through the Ninth Street Hill Neighborhood Historic District, always admiring the house but never imagining they could own it. An offhand comment by Ellie to a local real estate agent revealed that it might be available.

Bob grew up on a Clinton County farm and later earned an M.B.A. at Harvard University. Ellie, whose father was a factory worker, was raised in a blue-collar Muskegon, Illinois, neighborhood. Their modest, practical backgrounds triggered concerns about occupying such a grand, spacious home in one of Lafayette's premier neighborhoods. The Haans, both Purdue University graduates, own a successful business located in nearby Otterbein that manufactures sewing kits for middle schools throughout the country. They feared

appearing ostentatious by living in an enormous home with soaring front porch pillars.

"We didn't want to be known for our house and we didn't want to live in a museum," they say of their initial apprehension about buying a three-story, twenty-seven-room mansion with seven fireplaces and a twenty-two-foot ceiling in the rotunda.

After the youngest of their three sons left for college, the spirit of the house quickly consumed them, tapping the passionate side of their understated Hoosier personalities. They restored the home, replacing the heating and electrical systems without altering the house's historic integrity. They scoured northern Indiana for wavy nineteenth-century window glass to replace a multitude of broken windows.

The Haans filled the house with period furniture, including an eight-foot-tall Tiffany grandfather clock, a Rosewood grand piano, a seven-foot-tall Weller vase that won grand prize at the 1904 World's Fair, a Wooten desk, an 1878 Brunswick Rosewood pool table, and an extraordinary collection of original paintings by The Hoosier Group, late-nineteenth-century Indiana painters and early-twentieth-century Brown County artists. It is believed to be the most important privately held collection of artwork by nine-teenth-century Indiana artists in the world, part of which is made up of an extensive collection of T. C. Steele and J. Ottis Adams paintings.

Because they believe in sharing beautiful things and great art, they allow the home to be used for receptions and fundraising events by arts and preservationist organizations. They also loan their artwork to museums in Indiana and throughout the country. The joy, they believe, is not in possessing, but in sharing.

"We do that so other people can see it and appreciate the beautiful work done in Indiana. It's not fair to not share history and art with others," Bob explains. "We don't feel like we own the house, the furniture, or the artwork. We feel we're taking care of it for future generations."

Prior to buying the house and immersing himself in the study of Indiana history, art, and furnishings, Bob Haan was a fanatical Purdue basketball fan. "Now he doesn't even know when they play," says Ellie. "He's more interested in checking art and furniture auctions."

Joe and Betty Pogue Hadley

Historic Name: WILLIAM LUICK HOUSE

City: MUNCIE

County: DELAWARE

Date of Construction: 1882

Architectural Style: ITALIANATE

LISTED IN THE NATIONAL REGISTER OF HISTORIC PLACES

In the spring of 1981 Ball State University education professor Betty Pogue confronted difficult mid-life decisions following the death of her husband. Widowed, nearing the end of a long teaching career, and living alone in a cookie-cutter subdivision, she gambled.

"I was smothered in a cut-your-yard subdivision with people that were all very much alike and I asked myself what would make me happy. It was an old house that would make me happy. So I decided to commit social and economic suicide and buy one," recalls Betty.

She bought the economic black hole, a brick farmhouse called the William Luick House, on the unfashionable southeast side of Muncie, far from the northwest-side faculty members' neighborhoods.

The house had been empty for two years and was extensively vandalized. It had two feet of water in the basement, collapsed front and side porches, rabbit pellets in

the cold air ducts, burst pipes, one broken downstairs toilet, and not much else.

"Don't panic," a friend from the university's architecture department warned her. She didn't. She repaired the basics, water and heat, moved in within three months and began the slow, costly restoration process, including reconstructing the porches from old photographs. She tackled one project at a time and, like a well-prepared teacher, thoroughly researched each problem, found the proper contractor, and closely supervised the work.

"I like problem-solving and this was a problem," says Betty, who retired in 1990 after twenty-six years of teaching students to become elementary school teachers. The grand house is now considered one of the finest examples of Italianate architecture in Delaware County and Betty is pleased.

"I had to see what I could do alone," says Betty, wander-

ing through the gamble that paid off, pointing out three generations of family portraits. "I was unhappy, my husband was dead, I figured I'd always be a widow, but this house expanded me and made me amazingly happy. Who would have thought?"

In 1988 she married Joe Hadley, who had retired from GMAC, and no longer faced life alone. In the interest of marital harmony, they installed heat and a toilet upstairs.

Carriage-maker William Luick built the house in 1882 on 160 acres between the New Burlington Turnpike and the White River. Over the years Muncie closed in around it and the house now sits on only five acres, but the walnut trees are enormous and the land still runs down to the river.

When faced with spending money on antique furniture, Betty carefully weighed her options, balancing costs against intangibles like happiness. "The pleasure of this nice, old furniture gives me 20 percent interest," she explains. "In the bank the money only earned 6 percent."

Beyond the house the red brick patio is shaded by the big walnut and magnolia trees and faces the White River where the Delaware Indians once camped. It's Betty's favorite place, a solitary refuge of birds and swaying branches.

"I married this house and grew with it," she says, looking toward the river. "I learned to enjoy the process as much as the final result."

Ronald and Sonja Halbauer

Historic Name: JAMES MCLEASTER HOUSE

City: LAWRENCEBURG

County: DEARBORN

Date of Construction: 1842

Architectural Style: ITALIANATE

"It's not livable anymore. The development is tragic," says Ron Halbauer, standing in his front yard, shouting over the unceasing traffic roaring and honking along U.S. 50 in Lawrenceburg. No shouting was required in 1969 when Ron and Sonja bought the big house and twenty hilly acres above the Ohio River in Dearborn County.

They'd been living in nearby Glendale, Ohio, but needed a bigger place for Sonja to breed and train American Saddlebred horses. Ron was a research executive with The Procter & Gamble Company in Cincinnati, retiring in 1988 after thirty-two years.

In 1983, while waiting to turn in to her driveway, Sonja's Volkswagen was rear-ended at seventy-five miles per hour

by a kid rushing to the mall. Sonja's skull was fractured. She could no longer ride or train her beloved horses, something she began as a little girl. She sold the horses.

"With the accident, we about had it here, but we loved the house too much to leave," says Sonja. The house was built in 1842 by riverboat captain James McLeaster and hasn't changed much. "We never modernized. We like it this way," notes Sonja, referring to several original gas chandeliers that have never been electrified. It is a magnificent home, covered in Virginia Creeper vines and shaded by enormous walnut, catalpa, and mimosa trees, a twenty-acre island in a raucous sea of asphalt and honking horns.

After the traffic accident, the Halbauers converted the

sixteen-stall barn they had built for the horses into a storage facility for their expanding vintage Jaguar car collection, trading one passion for another.

Sonja grew up on a Kentucky horse farm, attended National Cathedral School in Washington, D.C., and graduated from Stephens College in Columbia, Missouri, in 1958. Ron grew up in Ohio, the son of a dentist. He graduated from the University of Cincinnati and married Sonja in 1966. It's a union built on a love of old cars, horses, and Victorian antiques.

"I drove a 1932 Chrysler one-half block to school," says Ron. In the foyer beside a late 1800s baby carriage is a child's 1948 Austin pedal car. "Old Jags, horses, and old houses, that's what we like," he adds. "Too bad about this."

What's too bad is that the house faces the belching smokestacks of a power plant across the road. A new power plant a quarter of a mile away will be fueled by natural gas delivered in a pipeline gouged through the Halbauers property. A snarl of overhead electric transmission lines crosses their land and more lines are planned. Next door, a 250-unit condominium project is planned. Then there's the gambling riverboat one mile away and the endless succession of strip malls, blinding array of billboards, fast food joints, tire barns, tanning spas, and other "economic develop-

ment" triumphs. U.S. 50 in front of their vine-covered house is one of the ugliest stretches of urban sprawl in Indiana. At rush hour, they must call the police to block traffic if they want to leave their driveway.

It is the only house remaining in what was once a spacious residential area. "We've had it," says Ron. "We love the house but who can live like this?" They are considering selling the property to someone who will turn the house into a restaurant or some commercial venture to save it from a developer's bulldozer.

"We'll put restrictive covenants on it, so it can't be torn down," says Ron, still shouting over the traffic. Then what? "We'd like to save another old house."

Joe and Joanna Hanshew

Historic Name: ENOS ADAMSON HOUSE
Town: HUNTSVILLE (PENDLETON)
County: MADISON
Date of Construction: CIRCA 1840
Architectural Style: GREEK REVIVAL

Bears were nearly extinct in Indiana by 1840 when Enos Adamson built a house, a sawmill, and a tannery along Fall Creek in the tiny Madison County town of Huntsville. So Joe Hanshew could hardly believe his eyes when he found the bones of a bear beneath the floor of Enos Adamson's house. He also found a perfectly preserved bird skeleton, possibly a chicken, which he left beneath the floor. He pulled out the bear bones, a poignant, stark reminder of life in Indiana before the European invasion wiped out the wild animals, not to mention the Indian tribes that lived along Fall Creek.

Joe also found a brick containing a deer hoof print, which he relaid in the hearth of the original fireplace he uncovered behind a plaster wall. A deer no doubt stepped on the brick while it was still hardening back around 1840.

"I just find this stuff fascinating," says Joe, who bought the Adamson house in 1988. At the time, Joe and his wife, Joanna, owned the Pendleton Antique Mall a few miles away. Joanna ran the mall. Joe has worked at an automotive factory in Anderson since graduating from the Wendell

Willkie High School in Elwood in 1964. They previously lived in a ranch house furnished with primitive antiques.

"We had this huge collection of antiques so we wanted an antique house," Joanna says of the decision to buy the Adamson house.

Joe has collected antiques most of his life, an interest spawned by his mother who loved Hoosier history and old stuff. When he met Joanna playing racquetball in Anderson, she hated history and old stuff.

"I didn't like antiques because they were old, but I was in love with Joe so I started learning about them," says Joanna, who married Joe in 1981. They bought the Pendleton Antique Mall in 1982 and specialized in high-quality, pre-1875 items. They owned it for sixteen years, but finally gave up when customers began demanding Beanie Babies, "collectibles," wooden ducks, cute doodads, and gourmet coffee.

"We couldn't take those people," says Joe, a good judge of character.

Joe has worked with machinery his entire adult life and

spent four hard years in the U.S. Coast Guard bouncing around the storm-tossed North Atlantic Ocean. He appreciates hard physical labor and marvels at the prodigious amount of work that went into building a house in 1840 that remains standing and functional 160 years later, long after the bears and Indians were killed or driven away.

In the root cellar, which was obviously dug by hand, he points to the massive ceiling logs that were felled with a crosscut saw, hauled to the building site, quartered with an axe, and laid in place. They remain perfectly level. The foundation is built of tons of creek stone, hauled one mile from Fall Creek and fit tightly together to hold a house.

Sand and water were mixed and fired to make bricks, including the one a deer stepped on.

"The craftsmanship is unbelievable," Joe says. "The amount of work that someone put into building this house is amazing." The second owner of the house was B. F. Aiman, a Pennsylvania immigrant who bought it from Enos Adamson in 1865 and added a second floor. B. F. Aiman served as a Madison County commissioner. His wife and child died in the house. In 1865, he signed his name on the wall of the root cellar and it's still visible.

"We own a part of history," says Joe.

Vic and Karen Cochran Hasler

Historic Name: PETER HECK HOUSE

County: JOHNSON

Date of Construction: CIRCA 1868

Architectural Style: ITALIANATE

LISTED IN THE NATIONAL REGISTER OF HISTORIC PLACES

Much of what is now Clark Township in northern Johnson County was once known as The Great Gulf, a thick, tangled, soupy mass of primeval forest, bogs, and impenetrable swampland. Then the great swamps were drained, the land farmed, and sometime around 1868 cattleman Peter Heck built a fine brick home on a slight hill just south of the tiny town of Clarksburg.

Now suburban sprawl, oozing and metastasizing southeast from Greenwood, threatens to bury Clark Township under a sea of asphalt, subdivisions, malls, CVS pharmacies, car dealerships, cul-de-sacs, and other "economic development" horrors.

Vic and Karen Hasler, who live in Peter Heck's old farmhouse, are at ground zero of the development time bomb, but take a good-natured, philosophical view of the inevitably bleak future.

"We'll be gone by then," says the optimistic Vic, who retired in 1998 after thirty-six years as a finance officer at Eli Lilly and Company in downtown Indianapolis. "Meanwhile, we're busy enjoying living in our historic home."

That's an understatement. Their enthusiasm for the elegant home and surrounding three acres of gardens and their multitude of projects is boundless. The home has been restored and refurnished to a degree of elegance that the prosperous Peter Heck, his wife, Jane, and their five children could never have imagined. Vic and Karen bought the house in 1994 after living most of their married lives eleven miles west in the Center Grove area where they raised three children. The sadly neglected Italianate house had been restored by a previous owner in 1975, and the Haslers have continued the restoration, returning the house as much as possible to the era of its construction.

The house could easily be a museum of mid–nineteenth-century life and to the family histories of Vic and Karen, both of whom grew up in Greene County. It overflows with a wide variety of magnificent antique furniture, curios, and photographs of family ancestors, including Karen's father, Hugh Cochran, who died in a southern Indiana coal mine accident when Karen was eleven years old, as well as pencil drawings of Vic's great-grandparents who emigrated from Switzerland.

The coal miner's daughter is a highly regarded maker of quilts, a collector of old toy sewing machines, a mystery book reader, and a volunteer for numerous civic and cultural organizations including Historic Landmarks Foundation of Indiana and the Indiana State Museum.

"I enjoy philanthropic endeavors and a multitude of interests," says the electric Karen, a 1961 Indiana State University graduate, who surely never sleeps because how could there be time?

Vic, a 1960 Wabash College graduate, burns excess energy riding a bicycle more than 150 miles a week, volunteers with Karen at the White River Gardens, and lectures for the Indiana State Museum about Hoosier pioneer life to fourth graders at local elementary schools, along with other civic activities too exhausting and detailed to mention.

The three acres surrounding their home, barn, smokehouse, and summer kitchen include twenty-seven differing gardens abounding with hundreds of plant varieties. The 2001 spring issue of *Better Homes and Gardens Perennial Magazine* featured an article about their garden. Also that year, with the help of many volunteers, the Haslers conducted a "Friendship Garden Tour" with the proceeds going to Indiana University's Cancer Research Center.

"Living in something that's existed a long time gives you a sense of security," says Vic. "We are glad to have a share in preserving this historic property."

Keith and Geri Hathaway

Historic Name: HORATIO CHAPIN HOUSE

City: SOUTH BEND

County: ST. JOSEPH

Date of Construction: 1857

Architectural Style: GOTHIC REVIVAL

LISTED IN THE NATIONAL REGISTER OF HISTORIC PLACES, *Chapin Historic District*

It took workmen using tiny, delicate dental instruments more than eighteen months to painstakingly remove nearly 150 years' worth of dirt and bright orange stain, known as "pickling," from the crevices in the woodwork of the Horatio Chapin house near downtown South Bend. The new owners, Keith and Geri Hathaway, wanted the job done right. Geri is an interior designer. Keith is a commercial refrigeration engineer.

"We're perfectionists," says Geri. They bought the Chapin house in 1984, after living several years in a town-house on the St. Joseph River and deciding they wanted an interesting home. "We obviously didn't want to live in a suburb or gated community," says Geri.

Horatio Chapin, an early South Bend merchant and banker, built the Gothic Revival home in 1857 and owned it until his death in the late 1880s. In 1890, a local house builder and lumberman bought the house in a sheriff's sale and moved it about a mile, by placing logs beneath the structure. A team of mules then rolled it to its present location on Park Avenue, which must have been quite a sight in 1890.

It was a boardinghouse when Keith and Geri bought it.

"We didn't want it to look like 1890, with heavy drapes and patterned wallpaper, but we wanted the architecture, the details, and the woodwork to show," says Geri. It's now exquisitely furnished with classic modern furniture, much of it of Oriental design.

The 1905 house next door was a mess, however, a blight in the otherwise lovely neighborhood known as the Chapin Historic District. Keith and Geri bought the next-door blight in 1992, renovated it, and rented it to University of Notre Dame students. "We bought it because we wanted to protect ourselves," says Geri. The student renters proved to be noisy and tossed empty beer cans into the front yard during late-night parties.

"We now rent it to two nuns from the Sisters of the Holy Cross," says Geri, who grew up in Connecticut, graduated from the Moore College of Art in Philadelphia and the Harrington Art Institute in Chicago. She married Keith in 1966. Keith, a Limestone, Maine, native, graduated from the Illinois Institute of Technology in Chicago. They later moved to South Bend, where Keith worked for the refrigeration company that he eventually bought.

In 2000, he sold the business and retired. "I was afraid he'd sit at the computer and watch the stock market and I'd go bananas," recalls Geri. To avoid that state of affairs, they bought a fifty-five-foot-long oceangoing yacht in California. They'd never even paddled a canoe on the St. Joseph River, much less piloted a yacht on the Pacific Ocean, but they studied and took lessons and now spend six months a year piloting their boat along the Baja Peninsula around Puerto Vallarta, Mexico. They soon plan to cruise the length of the U.S. Pacific coast north to Vancouver, B.C., and eventually follow the Inside Passage to Alaska.

They named the boat *Escargot,* because it moves at a snail's pace and creates a slow, rolling wake, attracting schools of gentle dolphins.

At home in South Bend, Keith monitors the stock market on his computer and Geri still accepts an occasional interior design job. Her company, Hathaway 2, is in a 1935 house in downtown South Bend that she converted. Life is good for Keith and Geri. Half a year on the ocean, the other half in Horatio Chapin's house.

"We once worked all the time," says Geri. "Now we play all the time and have fun."

John Herbst

Historic Name: CHARLES AND SUSANNAH GAUSS HOUSE
City: INDIANAPOLIS
County: MARION
Date of Construction: 1890
Architectural Style: QUEEN ANNE

When John Herbst accepted the job as president and CEO of Conner Prairie Pioneer Settlement in Hamilton County in 1988, he was executive director of the Historical Society of Western Pennsylvania. He lived in downtown Pittsburgh in a nineteenth-century Victorian home, which was full of his family's old Victorian furniture and mementos, including an enormous photograph of his somber great-grandfather Lothar Herbst, a Brooklyn beer brewer.

Conner Prairie is a highly regarded fourteen-hundred-acre, reconstructed nineteenth-century Hoosier pioneer village and sixty-five-thousand-square-foot museum center. Herbst chose to live in downtown Indianapolis and commute thirty miles north to Hamilton County. He hired Joe Everhart, an Indianapolis real estate agent specializing in historic downtown homes, to find a Victorian home for his Victorian furniture and Lothar Herbst's picture.

"I needed to find a house that matched my Victorian furniture, which is not valuable to anybody but me," recalls John. The real estate agent showed him twenty homes. One night John had dinner at Joe's place, a Victorian home five blocks south of Monument Circle. Joe's house matched John's furniture. John bought his real estate agent's house right then and there, and it wasn't even for sale. He moved in a month later and hung Lothar Herbst on the wall.

The house was built in 1890 by German tinsmith Charles Gauss for his wife, Susannah, and their crowd of thirteen children. It remained in the Gauss family for 103 years, until Joe Everhart bought it in 1993. When Charles

Gauss built the house, the neighborhood was a thriving community of German Catholics and German Jews. Now there are few houses or Germans left in the neighborhood.

But John is happy. His house and furniture match and he lives in what's left of a German urban neighborhood. He grew up in a German neighborhood in Patterson, New Jersey. His father and grandfather were woodworkers. John graduated from Montclair State University in New Jersey in 1974, taught high school, and earned a master's degree

in history in 1984 from the Bank Street College of Education in New York City. He then ran a program for high school students with the New Jersey Historical Society, which led to a succession of museum administrative positions and finally the Conner Prairie job and the move to urban Indianapolis.

"I'm a city dweller," he says. He's got a unique view of the Soldier's Monument from his living room window. Because of a slight westward swerve in South Meridian Street,

121

his house is on a direct axis with the monument. It's the only house in Indianapolis in precise alignment with it: If you followed a straight line south from the monument you'd walk into the side of his house.

"I have the best of both worlds here in Indiana," he ex-plains. "I look out my office window at work and see cows and sheep grazing on the hills. I come home and see down-town Indianapolis and the Monument Circle straight out my living room window."

Betty Hohenstein

Historic Name: RACHEL NEAL HOUSE

City: CENTERVILLE

County: WAYNE

Date of Construction: CIRCA 1820

Architectural Style: FEDERAL

LISTED IN THE NATIONAL REGISTER OF HISTORIC PLACES, *Centerville Historic District*

After scraping and peeling wallpaper and paint one tedious inch at a time for two years, Keith and Betty Hohenstein uncovered a rare treasure and found themselves staring back in time. Beneath over 150 years of wallpaper and paint, they beheld a series of red and green stenciled-flower drawings on the plaster walls of their 1820s row house.

"We were so excited, you'd think we found gold," recalls Betty, a 1940 Indiana University graduate, who took several zoology classes from the famed sex researcher Dr. Alfred Kinsey. ("His hair stood straight up," she says of Kinsey.)

The Hohensteins bought the Centerville row house in 1969 but did nothing with it until 1979 when they retired. Betty owned a Centerville antique store and had long admired the cozy, one-bedroom Federal-style row house, one of Indiana's earliest examples of post-Colonial architecture. Until moving in, they lived in Richmond where Keith owned a tool rental business.

Betty never learned how to operate a car because she couldn't master parallel parking, so Keith drove her to her antique shop each day. She regularly reminded Keith they must one day buy the row house as a retirement restoration project and eventual home. "In order for us to be compatible, he had to go along with me," jokes Betty.

The two-story house was built as an inn on National Road around 1820 to serve travelers passing through Wayne County and east central Indiana. Rachel Neal is believed to be the original owner and innkeeper. It later became a wagon repair shop and a series of residences after Rachel succumbed to the lure of National Road, fleeing Centerville, never to return.

After discovering the delicate wall stencils, Keith and Betty learned that they had been created by Moses Eaton, a well-known, itinerant New Hampshire artist. He traveled throughout the east and eventually into Indiana, financing his journeys by stenciling the walls of inns in exchange for room and board. About a dozen of the original drawings were salvageable. Keith and Betty hired a Richmond artist to duplicate the stencils to replace the remaining damaged drawings.

The Hohensteins removed an entire kitchen that was added sometime in the early twentieth century and restored the original side porch. Keith scraped and refinished the poplar and ash floor by hand, methodically polishing each board like a piece of fine furniture. He also removed wall-boards and discovered the original fireplace where Rachel Neal cooked meals for her guests in the cramped kitchen.

While scraping purple paint from the stairway, he unearthed the original, light-blue featherbrush designs on the side panels. The Hohensteins moved into the house in 1984, filling it with simple, mid–nineteenth-century cherry furniture and oil paintings by early Hoosier landscape artists.

"This house looks almost exactly as it did when Rachel ran it as an inn," says Betty. Her house is across Old National Road from the historic Lantz House Inn, a bed-and-breakfast run by her daughter, Marcia Hoyt. Keith died in 1992 after fifty years of marriage.

"We both had this great love of beautiful wood," says Betty, sitting before Rachel Neal's cooking fireplace. "We always felt Rachel's presence in this house. Houses like this are so unique because they allow you to look back in time."

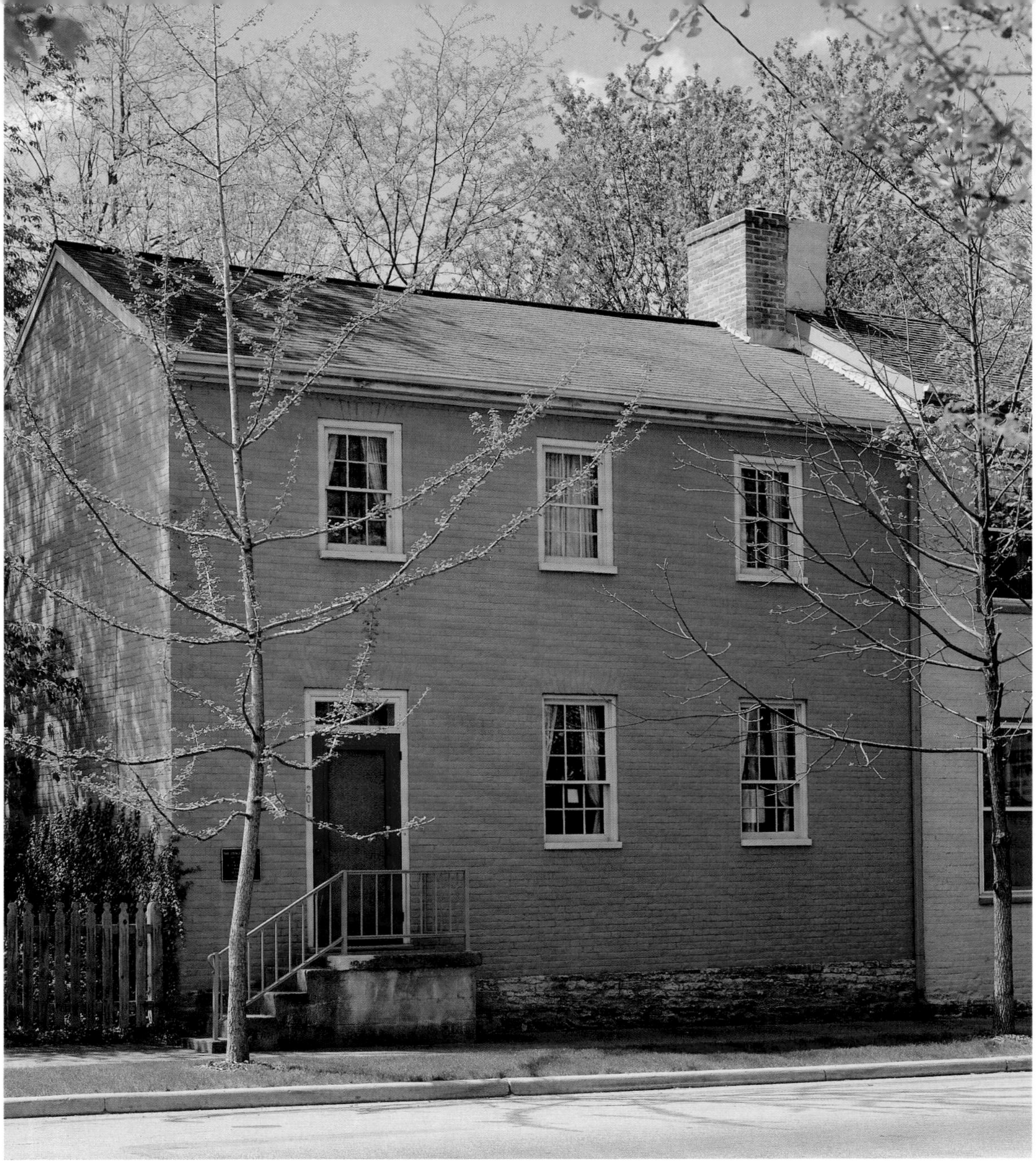

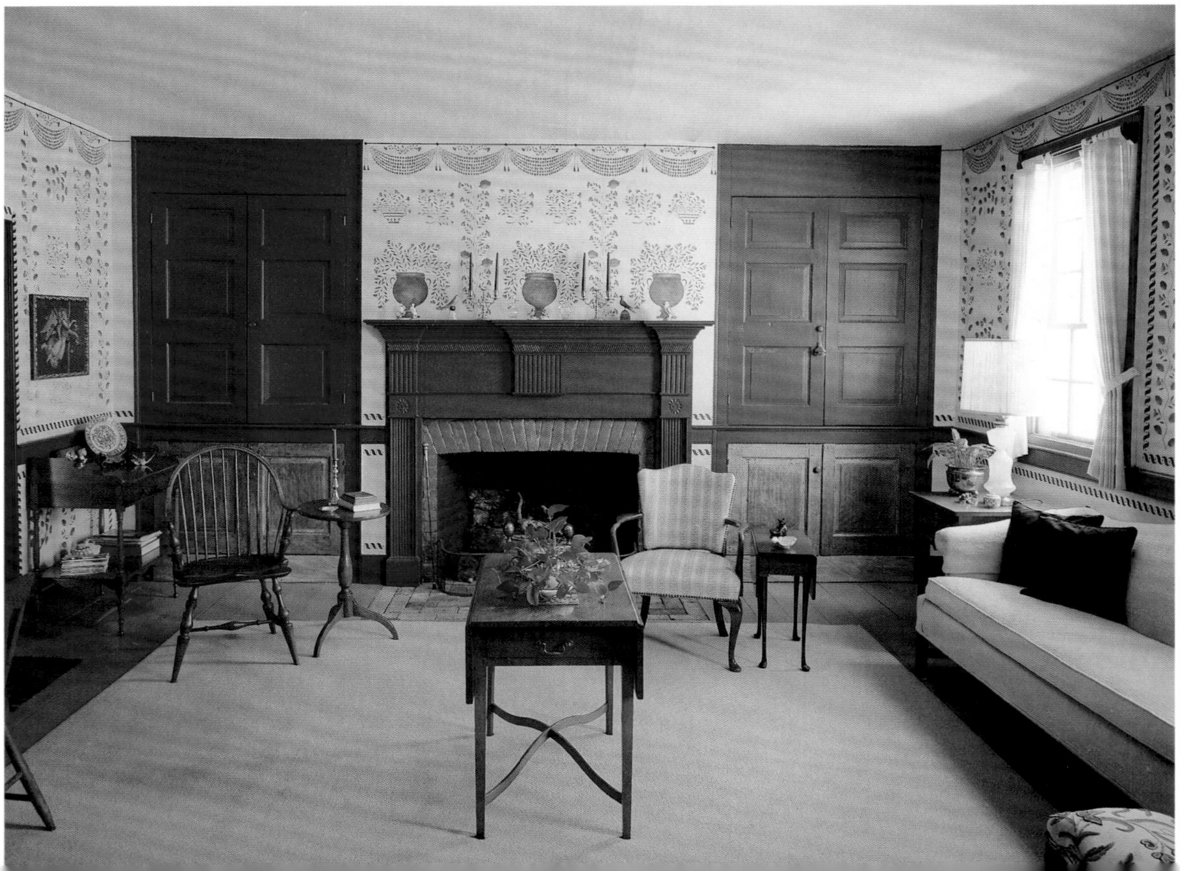

Dick and Marilyn Hornberger

City: MARTINSVILLE

County: MORGAN

Date of Construction: CIRCA 1830

Architectural Style: HALL AND PARLOR

In his younger years, truck driver Dick Hornberger worked the night shift, so he could visit secondhand shops and trash heaps during the day in search of inexpensive household furnishings.

"I couldn't afford new stuff," he recalls. Dick's first wife died young and he was raising four children alone, farming by day and driving a truck at night. In the 1950s, Amish and old hickory furniture was so cheap and unfashionable that Dick often found it broken and piled on sidewalks waiting for the trash man. He hauled the discarded tables and chairs home, repaired them, and slowly furnished his house with new treasures.

When he married Marilyn in 1967, they built a house on eleven acres near Paragon in Morgan County, but quickly decided it was too "modern." Marilyn, who grew up in

Martinsville, attended Central Elementary School at the southwest corner of Ohio and Jackson Streets. She often admired the old, neglected house across the street and dreamed of one day living in it.

"It always looked like home to me, even as a little girl," says Marilyn, who for years owned a wholesale restaurant-and-bar–supply business in Martinsville.

In 1975, they sold the modern Paragon home and bought the neglected, expanded hall-and-parlor–type house across from Marilyn's red brick elementary school. The six-room, 1830 post-and-beam structure is believed to be the oldest house in Martinsville, built eight years after the town was platted. It was moved a few blocks to its present location in 1880.

Unfortunately, the house was too small, because Dick

and Marilyn had three more children. He salvaged a collapsed, roofless 1820 church building near Wilbur in northern Morgan County and hauled the logs home. It took ten years, but Dick rebuilt the log church onto his house, adding one huge room.

"My wife and I never did have much money," he explains. "That's why it took ten years. We just learned to budget."

They've since filled the house with western art, images of Abraham Lincoln, American Indians, Civil War pistols, an 1813 flintlock rifle, moose antlers, an elk head, a stuffed black bear, the massive head of a twenty-five-hundred-pound bull buffalo, and the beautifully restored nineteenth-century hickory and Amish furniture he found in auctions and trash piles forty years ago.

"I don't hunt, but the bear and buffalo were already dead, so we bought them," says retired trucker Dick of the glassy-eyed animal heads. Over the years they've added mid–nineteenth-century furniture, which they are loathe to call antiques.

"We're not trying to make an antique collection," says Marilyn. "It's just things we like and use every day."

In the old pioneer house with its low ceilings, animal heads, Civil War weapons, Lincoln images, and cowhide rugs, you half expect a bearded trapper carrying a flintlock rifle to step in from the Morgan County wilderness, toss his pelts on the floor, and warm himself before the big stone fireplace.

And that's the idea.

"The house and the church logs are part of the pioneer history of the county and we want it to look like that," says Dick. "Shoot, my wife won't even allow a TV in here because it doesn't fit."

James and Sheila Hughes

City: INDIANAPOLIS

County: MARION

Date of Construction: 1958

Architect: EVANS WOOLLEN III

Architectural Style: INTERNATIONAL

It was the range of light and shadows that attracted Jim and Sheila Hughes to their classic modern home in a ravine on the northeast side of Indianapolis, beneath a canopy of towering white oaks and ancient beech trees.

The house was built in 1958 and designed by the great Hoosier architect Evans Woollen III, whose trademarks are clean lines and abundant light. Woollen has designed some of Indiana's most notable architectural landmarks: Clowes Hall on the Butler University campus in Indianapolis and the Musical Arts Center in Bloomington, among others.

"Clean design was always our goal," says Jim Hughes. "Why, I don't know. Why do some people like popsicles?"

The home's most dramatic feature is the ten-foot-tall glass outer walls providing an intimate view of the sur-

rounding acre of woods, a winding creek, and the slow movement of light and shadow. "It is the light that drew us to this house and has kept us here since 1967. It's the only house we've ever owned," explains Jim, an Indianapolis trial lawyer. "The hazard of this house is birds hit the glass in migrating season."

Best of all, "I don't own a lawn mower," he says. "There is no lawn, only thick ferns, wildflowers, and spring daffodils on the one-acre lot."

The house blends into the natural landscape over the creek and around the trees. The woods weren't destroyed nor the creek rerouted to accommodate the house. It accommodates the woods and the Barred Owls, hawks, and Pileated Woodpeckers that nest and hoot and screech and

peck in the big trees. The light, the seasons, the birds, and the angle of sun and shadows embrace the house both inside and out.

Jim is a Greencastle native and a 1966 graduate of Harvard Law School, with a deep interest in Indiana history and buildings that invite natural light. Sheila grew up in Chicago, graduated from St. Mary's College in South Bend, earned a master's degree from Northwestern University, and is the former director of development for the Indiana chapter of The Nature Conservancy. They raised three children in the four-bedroom, three-thousand-square-foot house of smooth lines and shifting shadows.

The furnishings are a mix of sleek contemporary pieces and nineteenth-century primitive antiques arranged on pre-1925 Oriental rugs. Historical biographies of Truman and Churchill, accounts of the Lewis and Clark Expedition, and environmental essays by Annie Dillard and Edward Abbey among dozens of others fill the bookshelves. An original Corita Kent serigraph hangs over the bedroom fireplace wall near a nineteenth-century postmaster's desk. Jim's grandmother's harvest table welcomes you at the entrance hall. His great-grandfather George Washington Hughes's framed commission as a second lieutenant in the Eleventh Indiana Cavalry hangs in the living room. A tight circular staircase winds to a lower level where the ground outside the big window is at eye level, a unique, contemplative perspective on the forest floor.

"This house has proven to be the best of all worlds because we're isolated and secluded in this little patch of woods but still within the city," says Sheila. "The outdoors is indoors in this house."

Jim Hughes passed away in July 2001.

Norman and Rosemary Hunt

Historic Name: WILLIAM E. EAGLESFIELD HOUSE

County: CLAY

Date of Construction: 1855

Architectural Style: GREEK REVIVAL

LISTED IN THE NATIONAL REGISTER OF HISTORIC PLACES

No hardship could persuade Norman Hunt to sell his splendid Clay County home along Old National Road (U.S. 40). Not a five-hundred-mile round-trip commute, which he undertook each weekend in the 1970s to his full-time teaching job at Ohio Northern University. Nor a hundred-mile-a-day (also round trip) drive in the 1980s to his staff psychologist job with the Indiana Department of Correction in Indianapolis.

"Everyone thought I was crazy, but I did what was necessary to live here, even if it killed me," recalls Norman, who married Rosemary in 1942. In 1949 they moved into the two-story house on seventeen acres with their two children and twelve hundred laying hens. Norman and Rosemary sold chickens, eggs, ham, bacon, and cold cider to travelers along Old National Road.

"Abraham Lincoln drank from this well," he proudly tells visitors, pointing to a pump on the side porch of the house built by railroad entrepreneur William E. Eaglesfield in 1855.

The striking house with its original wavy window glass, the dramatic rose and hosta gardens, the Concord grape vineyards, the sparkling white fences, and the magnificent three-story green barn was, and remains, an Old National Road landmark. The poplar barn was built in 1895. The three-bedroom house and barn were listed in the National Register of Historic Places in 1998.

In the early 1950s the Hunts moved a small house and converted it into a restaurant and a six-unit motel called Hunts' Pleasant Acres just west of the big house. Dinner cost $1.75 and included ice cream. A motel room cost $6.00 a night. Clay County native and Teamster's Union boss Jimmy Hoffa once paid for supper with a one-hundred-dollar bill.

The restaurant and motel thrived until October 31, 1969, when nearby Interstate 70 opened through Clay

County, thus draining traffic off Old National Road. A great silence descended on the house for the first time in decades. That's when Norman got his doctoral degree in psychology and began his exhausting commutes. No price was too high to remain in the house. No sacrifice too great.

"This house is our life. Most people take vacations and go somewhere," explains Rosemary. "We'd stay home to work on the house. Why leave? We love it."

The history of the country has passed before the wavy glass windows: Union soldiers marching off to war; the first automobiles bouncing down muddy National Road. The highway expanded to four lanes. The Hunts met travelers crossing the country during its post–World War II heyday, and then they watched the road grow quiet when I-70 opened three miles away. Now the traffic is mostly local. "We had a unique window on America from this house," says Rosemary. "The United States passed before us every day."

After more than half a century watching America from the side porch where Lincoln drew water, the Hunts remain as enthused and invigorated about the majestic house as the day they moved in with their two children and twelve hundred chickens.

"The house has been our friend for most of our lives," says Norman. "How could you ever leave such a friend?"

Phyllis Igleheart

Historic Name: EDGAR AND ALINE IGLEHEART HOUSE

City: EVANSVILLE

County: VANDERBURGH

Date of Construction: 1932

Architect: EDWARD J. THOLE

Architectural Style: FRENCH ECLECTIC

LISTED IN THE NATIONAL REGISTER OF HISTORIC PLACES

Shortly after their marriage in 1922, Edgar, president of the family-owned flour milling and cake mix company started in 1856 by his grandfather, and Aline Igleheart of Evansville visited Paris and were drawn to the French Château style of architecture. They took pictures of several French châteaux and upon their return bought twenty-three acres along a gravel road five miles east of Evansville. Two mid–nineteenth-century farmhouses on the property were moved from the hilltop and relocated in a little valley.

The Iglehearts hired architect Edward J. Thole to design and build a French château atop the hill, based on the photographs they brought back from Paris. The brick châ-

teau and a seven-stall horse barn were completed in 1932. The Iglehearts' cook, chauffeur, and horse groom lived in the two relocated farmhouses in the little valley.

The Igleheart place remains one of the most striking estates in the Evansville area, an enchanting masterpiece set amid rolling hills, big trees, and beautiful flower gardens. Unfortunately, air pollution in recent years has turned the coral pink concrete tennis court black. And the gravel road, long since paved, is the heavily congested Lincoln Avenue.

"The tennis court was pink for sixty years, now it's black," grumbles Edgar and Aline's daughter, Phyllis, who now lives in the family home. "When I was growing up I couldn't

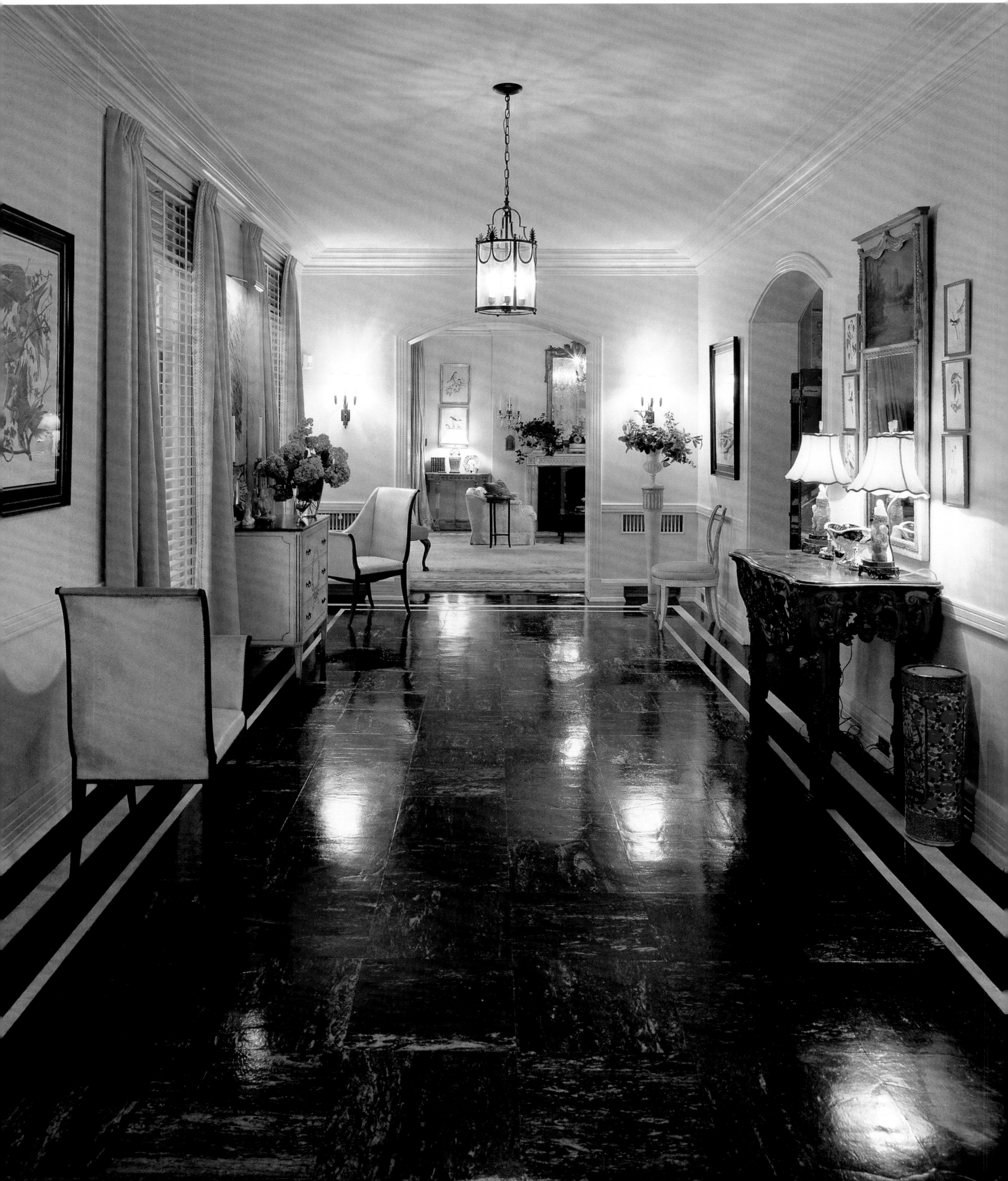

wait to get away from here, but now that I'm back I find it so very lovely," says Phyllis, who returned home in 1985 with her husband, Robert Kerdasha, a retired advertising executive.

Phyllis and Robert lived on the upper east side of New York City for twenty-six years, one block from the elegant Ritz Hotel. About the time Phyllis's mother died, Robert was stricken with Parkinson's disease. "A combination of events brought us back: Robert's illness, Mother's death, and a desire to see the home remain in the family," says Phyllis. Robert died in 1996.

Phyllis left home early to attend The Baldwin School in Philadelphia, an all-girls boarding high school. After graduation, she attended the University of Southern California for a couple of years, then lived in Florida and worked as an interior designer before moving to Paris and Rome and eventually New York City where she married Robert in 1961. Their daughter, Eve, is a Washington, D.C., artist.

"I always came back to spend a month with Mother in the summer. It was very comfortable," recalls Phyllis. "It's so delightful up here."

The house and the Depression-era furnishings remain virtually unchanged since 1932, except for the backyard pool where Phyllis swims her daily laps. "It's all the same stuff," says Phyllis, roaming through the towering buckeye and walnut trees behind the house. When she was six years

old, Phyllis remembers watching her mother plant sixty-five trees behind the house, a vivid memory she cherishes.

"Now when I walk among these big trees I'm reminded of Mother and my childhood," says Phyllis. "She was a lovely woman."

133

Paul and Elizabeth Jarvis
City: INDIANAPOLIS
County: MARION
Date of Construction: 1914
Architectural Style: CRAFTSMAN BUNGALOW

Having grown up in subdivision-saturated Orange County, California, Paul Jarvis was well versed in suburban life and wanted none of it when he arrived in Indianapolis in 1985.

"We wanted a common house," says the doctor who doesn't play golf. Paul, a 1981 graduate of the University of Southern California School of Medicine, came to Indianapolis as a public health doctor serving low-income residents in a Fountain Square neighborhood clinic.

Paul's wife, Elizabeth, who grew up in northern California, received a bachelor's degree in psychology from UCLA and a master's degree in biology from San Francisco State University. A midwestern city with big trees and seasons and common homes with a history beyond five years appealed to the lifelong Californians.

"The fun part about coming here from California is how green and lush everything is," Paul points out. "We felt a commitment to live in the city. Living in a suburb smacked of rich people running away from the city and those new houses are cheap and thin with no wood."

In 1988, they bought a modest, three-bedroom bungalow on tree-lined East 44th Street. The 1914 wooden house on the narrow street predates most of the larger homes on nearby historic North Meridian Street, which were mostly built in the 1920s. There were five kinds of linoleum nailed to the wood floors when Paul and Elizabeth bought the house. The bathroom had black wallpaper and the oak woodwork was covered in several layers of white paint, all of which they removed.

Dr. Paul examined the problem and bought books and *Old House Journal* and *Craftsman* magazines in search of answers. They knew nothing of Hoosier history, art, or 1914 homes. Between the books, the magazines, and the clues the house yielded, they found answers.

"The little, subtle things in the house nudged us in the right direction," says Elizabeth, who worked as a home inspector for the Marion County Board of Health before having two children, Daniel and Philip. Things like the oak rails near the ceiling. In his books Paul discovered they were picture rails. Picture rails require pictures. Paul looked into his books to research early twentieth-century Hoosier artists because he's a stickler for accuracy. He has since bought sixty period paintings, including seven by Richmond artist Charles Conner, and hung them from the picture rails throughout the two-story house.

"You've got to be devoted to something. The house is real and has a life of its own. You get connections with the past that aren't in a suburban house," Paul declares.

"With Paul, everything's got to be in keeping with the period," jokes Elizabeth. They are now in their second year of research to find the proper wallpaper pattern. "Part of the fun is the hunt and the planning," she adds.

They've since filled the house with American Arts-and-Crafts furniture, something they had never heard of when they first arrived from California.

"In California the roots of history are pretty shallow," says Paul, who left public health medicine when the government cut funds to the Fountain Square clinic and its low-income patients. He's now a pediatrician with St. Vincent Hospital.

"This is a very common house but the roots run deep and we like that."

Michael and Judy Kanne

Historic Name: KANNAL HOUSE

City: RENSSELAER

County: JASPER

Date of Construction: 1860

Architectural Style: GREEK REVIVAL

At the last moment, Indiana University graduates Michael and Judy Kanne canceled plans to attend the 1968 Rose Bowl to watch the IU Hoosiers play the University of Southern California. Instead, they put their $500 Rose Bowl money down on an old house in Michael's hometown of Rensselaer in northwest Indiana.

Not a bad decision, since USC, led by star running back O. J. Simpson, defeated the Hoosiers 14-3. The house, built by the Kannal family in 1860, is three blocks from the Jasper County Courthouse. Michael, an attorney, walked to work. In 1972 Governor Edgar Whitcomb named him to fill the unexpired term of the Circuit Court judge who died in office.

In 1982, President Ronald Reagan named Michael to the U.S. District Court in Hammond. No more walking to work. "It was very traumatic," says Judy, a professor and mother of two. "Houses are much more expensive in Hammond. The girls were young and involved in 4-H, Michael's parents were still alive, so Michael decided to commute so we could stay in our house in Rensselaer."

For five years Judge Kanne made the two-hour daily commute to Hammond. "When he was a judge here in Rensselaer, he would walk to work and be home by four or five in the afternoon. When he commuted to Hammond, he'd never be home before 8:00 P.M.," Judy recalls. "It was a hard time."

Then in 1987 President Reagan named him to the prestigious U.S. Seventh Circuit Court of Appeals in Chicago, a lifetime appointment. The Seventh Circuit Court of Appeals is one step below the U.S. Supreme Court. It handles all appeals of federal law from courts in Indiana, Illinois, and Wisconsin. Still, no thought of moving. "We both love Chicago but our house is very comfortable and it's the only house we ever owned," says Judy.

Judges at that high level are allowed to maintain two chambers, one in the Federal Building in downtown Chicago and the other wherever they choose. Judge Kanne chose the Federal Building in Lafayette, a shorter, 90-minute daily commute down I-65. Once a week he drives to downtown Chicago for hearings or conferences with his fellow judges.

"In the beginning all the commuting was difficult, now I'm used to it," shrugs the judge. "I guess we stayed for the girls." Daughter Anne Elizabeth, a Mercer University graduate, now lives in California and sells golf clothes. Katherine teaches anthropology at Purdue University and coaches the school's men's and women's polo teams.

They bought the brick house from former Rensselaer mayor Emmett Eger, a descendant of the original owners and longtime Kanne family friend. Michael's parents owned a restaurant on the courthouse square. Judy, who is now owner of a courthouse square antique shop, was born in Greencastle but grew up in the Irvington neighborhood of Indianapolis. She met Michael at IU and they married in 1963. In addition to being a shop owner, she is an assistant professor and director of student teaching at St. Joseph's College in Rensselaer and president of Historic Landmarks of Jasper County.

The Greek Revival house they bought instead of going to the Rose Bowl has proven over the years to be a stabilizing influence, a constant during difficult times. "Living here has kept Michael grounded," notes Judy. "We've just always been content in the house," she says. "It's very simple, very plain: four rooms up, four down. Very distinctive."

"I'm glad we didn't go to the Rose Bowl," Judy concludes.

Kenneth E. Keene Jr.

Historic Name: TUCKAWAY / GEORGE PHILIP AND NELLIE SIMMONS MEIER HOUSE

City: INDIANAPOLIS

County: MARION

Dates of Construction: 1906 / 1910

Architectural Style: ARTS AND CRAFTS

LISTED IN THE NATIONAL REGISTER OF HISTORIC PLACES

When Kenneth E. Keene Jr. went in search of a house in 1972, he was simply seeking a place to live. He wound up buying himself a new life, one of gramophones and ghosts, Persian rugs, dimly lit halls, and autographed photographs of Helen Hayes, James Whitcomb Riley, George Gershwin, and other early–twentieth-century luminaries who once visited the house called Tuckaway.

"I knew I was home when I saw it," recalls Keene. "My mystery house. I was mesmerized."

The house was christened Tuckaway in 1910 by its new owners, fashion designer George Philip Meier and his socialite wife, Nellie, a palm reader and arts patron. The cottage-style cedar clapboard house sits tucked away in a grove of ancient oak and ash trees a couple of miles north of downtown Indianapolis.

The one-story bungalow was built in 1906. The second story and a drawing room with a fifteen-foot arched ceiling was added in 1910 by the Meiers when they bought it to showcase their extensive art collection and accommodate elegant parties. The guests included distinguished writers, artists, actors, and musicians from around the United States and Europe.

The diminutive four-foot, seven-inch Nellie Meier was widely regarded for her "scientific palmistry," assessing a person's character by analyzing lines on the palms. Celebrities flocked to Tuckaway seeking scientific palmistry. The Russian pianist Sergei Rachmaninoff held a concert in the drawing room in 1941. Eleanor Roosevelt, Walt Disney, Helen Hayes, Raymond Novarro, Douglas Fairbanks Jr., and Joan Crawford, among other notables sought Nellie's palm-reading wisdom in Tuckaway. In 1942 Nellie reportedly warned actress Carol Lombard not to take her scheduled airplane flight from Indianapolis to Los Angeles. The actress failed to heed Nellie's advice, boarded a plane the next day in Indianapolis, and died when it crashed en route to California.

Ken Keene, an interior designer and wallpaper and paint consultant, knew nothing of the history of the place when he bought it from Nellie's elderly niece, Ruth Peaslee Cannon, a former Denis-Shawn dancer, who smoked imported Egyptian cigarettes in a twelve-inch-long cigarette holder. When Keene purchased the house he became the custodian of forty heavily beaded, hand-stitched, museum-quality evening gowns designed by George Philip Meier in the

1920s. Ruth Peaslee Cannon also gave him dozens of palm prints and autographed photographs given to Nellie by her famous visitors. There are also thousands of letters and notes she exchanged with visitors on palm-reading matters. The framed photographs line the dimly lit hallways beneath the massive, original chandeliers. "Best Wishes to Nellie Simmons Meier," wrote silent-screen star Mary Pickford.

Keene has devoted his life to studying Tuckaway's rich history and filling the house with 1920s furnishings to retain its original ambience. The house is listed in the National Register of Historic Places.

"This is my job, living here. I've learned to keep it the way it had been," he explains. "It pleases the house." Keene

fervently believes he is the spiritual caretaker of the Meiers' legacy and bears a sacred responsibility to the cottage in the trees.

"I'm here to keep the spirit of the house alive and please the ghosts who dwell in it," he says. "The house is haunted with the ghosts of Tuckaway. If you lived here, you'd believe that, too."

Charles and Shirley Kerkove

Historic Name: ANDREW ZIEGLER HOUSE

City: ATTICA

County: FOUNTAIN

Date of Construction: CIRCA 1840

Architectural Style: GREEK REVIVAL

LISTED IN THE NATIONAL REGISTER OF HISTORIC PLACES, *Attica Main Street Historic District*

When Shirley Kerkove's parents died within two months of each other in 1975 she inherited the responsibility of raising her younger brother in addition to her own four children. In addition to parenting, Shirley operated a beauty salon in the kitchen of her Attica ranch home.

"We needed a bigger house to hold a bunch of kids and my beauty shop," says Shirley, a 1960 graduate of the now-defunct Approved University of Beauty Culture in Indianapolis. Shirley and Charlie bought the Andrew Ziegler house on Main Street in downtown Attica, which was built in either 1832 or 1847, depending on which Fountain County history you believe. Shirley didn't care when it was built.

The history and architecture of the four-bedroom house with the inset front entrance and Ionic columns was secondary to more pressing matters.

"We never thought of the history of it. We just needed space. The location was good for business, there was a grocery next door, and I needed to keep an eye on five kids while I was cutting hair," recalls Shirley. "That's what we needed. Something handy, that worked for us. I needed to be home with the kids while I worked."

It was a good fit. Shirley set up her beauty shop in the original basement kitchen and stores her supplies in the butler's pantry. In 1990 the Kerkoves installed new plumb-

ing, heating, and air conditioning and replaced all the windows. The house requires fifty gallons of paint every seven or eight years.

"I now have an appreciation for historic homes. It would have been cheaper to put up vinyl siding, but it would sure look stupid," says Shirley. "We don't have antiques, I tell you that, I wish we did. We have traditional furniture, nothing out of the ordinary. I don't know anything about decorating. I wanted to put the right things in here but I didn't know."

Straight-talking Shirley grew up in Benton County where her parents owned and operated Senesac's Restaurant in Fowler. While attending beauty school she met Charlie and married him in 1961. They moved to Attica in 1962 and Charlie sold fuel oil before being hired by Eli Lilly and Company to work at its Lafayette drug development plant.

Shirley became interested in the stories of the house when her elderly customers talked about its history and how the corner cupboards in the dining room are supposedly identical to the cupboards in George Washington's headquarters at Valley Forge, Pennsylvania. Who knows if they are, but

the story is part of the oral history of the house and Shirley finds it interesting. When another ancient customer told her that the black iron fireplace coverings are identical to the fireplaces in Abraham Lincoln's home in Springfield, Illinois, Shirley took a drive.

"One day we went to Springfield to look," says Shirley. "Lincoln's house and fireplace sure looked the same, but I don't know." Someone else told her Lincoln visited the Attica house, which is highly questionable. However, Lincoln did appoint his Attica friend Dr. John Evans territorial governor of Colorado in 1862, so who knows? It doesn't matter, because the stories are woven into the real or imagined lore of the house and the history of the town, which sits on the bluffs of the Wabash River in western Indiana along the route of the old Wabash and Erie Canal.

More importantly, the house served its purpose. Shirley still cuts hair in the basement. "We're just high school graduates," Shirley notes, "but all our kids graduated from Purdue University and now the grandkids run all over the house."

Jim and Jill King

Historic Name: CONKLIN-MONTGOMERY HOUSE

City: CAMBRIDGE CITY

County: WAYNE

Date of Construction: 1838

Architectural Style: GREEK REVIVAL

LISTED IN THE NATIONAL REGISTER OF HISTORIC PLACES

It is hard to imagine a family more devoted to a historic home in small-town Indiana than Jim and Jill King. Jim is a senior vice-president and CIO (Chief Information Officer) with McGraw-Hill Company in New York City. He commutes to a fiftieth-floor office near Times Square, about five hundred miles from his home along Old National Road in Cambridge City. "I leave home about 4:30 A.M. Monday, drive to the airport in Indianapolis or Dayton and I'm in my office in New York by 9:00 A.M.," says Jim. He then flies home Friday afternoon to spend the weekend with Jill and their two children and to work on the house. His previous position was director of strategy and planning with computer giant Microsoft in Seattle, a mere thirty-five-hundred-mile weekly commute. His easiest commute was in the 1980s and early 1990s when he only drove 122 miles a day to his job with the National Cash Register Company in Dayton, Ohio. He says he doesn't get tired.

"I made a commitment to Jill that we would never move," says Jim. "This is our home and we're never gonna leave it."

Jim's father managed gypsum plants around the country and the family moved every two years. Jill grew up in Pulaski County and never moved anywhere until she went to Ball State University, where she met Jim. After getting graduate degrees in computer science, they moved to Valley Forge,

Pennsylvania, in 1984 to work at General Electric Company. They didn't much like Valley Forge, a historic Revolutionary War town now awash in malls and subdivisions.

"It was Yuppieville," says Jill. "I missed Indiana."

The Kings acquired their home through collecting. "Collecting is a disease in our family," says Jill, who collects coverlets, just as her father, John Simmermaker, does. One of his best friends was Cambridge City Latin teacher and Hoosier coverlet queen Pauline Montgomery, author of *Indiana Coverlet Weavers and Their Coverlets* (coverlets are bedspreads that were hand-woven in the early 1800s).

Pauline and a clutter of cats lived in a house built in 1838 by Benjamin Conklin, a Wayne County merchant. Pauline, a widow with no children, died in 1982 and left the house to Jill's father, her coverlet-collecting pal. He already had a house in northern Indiana and didn't need another one, which smelled like cats. In 1986, Jim and Jill returned to Indiana, bought the house, fumigated the cat smell, removed moldy wallpaper, and began a long and ultimately magnificent restoration project.

"I'm a Hoosier and I wanted to come home," says Jill. Thus Jim began his grueling commutes. Jill got breast cancer in 1987. She beat it. Two years later while pregnant with her daughter, she had a recurrence. She beat that, too.

"Life is a roller coaster," says Jill, who now laughs all the

time because why not? She has since been elected to the town board twice and works to preserve Cambridge City's historic architecture of which their house is a prime example.

"The house kept us focused," says Jim, who serves on the board of the Golay Community Center in town. "The house is our fun. It's what we do together."

They also attend antique auctions throughout the Midwest and have accumulated an impressive collection of 1830s American Empire and Sheraton-style furniture, Overbeck pottery, nineteenth-century wax portraits, and an unusual hair wreath made in 1865 by Boston, Indiana, elementary school students to honor Abraham Lincoln.

"We could live anywhere," explains Jim. "But this is our home. We like the idea of improving our town and rehabilitating a historic house. We're proud of what we've done here. I never had roots as a kid and now I do."

Pat and Nancy Kirgan

Historic Name: SCHEMMEL-KECK HOUSE

City: UNION CITY

County: RANDOLPH

Date of Construction: 1927

Architectural Style: TUDOR REVIVAL

There was only one way that Pat and Nancy Kirgan could afford to buy the sixty-seven-hundred-square-foot Schemmel-Keck mansion in Union City, five blocks from the Ohio border in Randolph County. It had to pay for itself. Produce income.

"We didn't need a seven-bedroom, four-bathroom monster house," says Pat, "but we wanted it because we like living in old places." At the time, Pat ran a family grain farm in nearby Darke County, Ohio, and Nancy owned a crafts shop in Union City, specializing in dried flowers. She grew and dried flowers on the Ohio farm and sold them in the Indiana shop.

In addition, shortly after getting married in 1997, they began designing and manufacturing crafts items including wooden pilgrims, bunnies, Santas, and painted apple crates,

which are sold in Cracker Barrel Old Country Stores around the country. They make their products in a hog barn on the Ohio farm. The Kirgans are highly skilled at turning their hobbies and passions into lucrative business. They applied those money-making skills to The Mansion.

They bought the Schemmel-Keck house in 1988 and converted a portion of it into a bed-and-breakfast, although neither Pat nor Nancy knew anything about the hospitality business. They did know there were only two, small motels in Randolph County and no bed-and-breakfasts.

They furnished the house with Chippendale reproductions and antiques from scratch-and-dent shops in wealthy Ohio neighborhoods. The Kirgans use one bedroom. Their teenage son, Matt, and Nancy's sister, Jennifer Buckingham, sleep in two third-floor bedrooms. The four

remaining bedrooms are rented out for $65–$75 per night, which includes breakfast.

Because there are no motels in Union City, the occupancy rate was nearly 100 percent almost immediately. Business travelers book it through the week. Local people fill it on the weekends for weddings, parties, and high school reunions because The Mansion is perhaps the premier residence in tiny Union City and has been a local curiosity for more than seventy-five years.

The massive English Tudor Revival with marble floors, winding brass stair railings, and a walnut-paneled elevator was built in 1927 by R. C. Schemmel as a wedding gift for his daughter, Estelle, and her new husband, Paul Keck. Schemmel's wife died while giving birth to Estelle, their only child.

R. C. Schemmel manufactured bus and automobile interior upholstery in Union City and by 1927 was worth about $60 million. R.C. lived in the house with Paul and Estelle until his death in 1953. The Kecks raised three daughters in the house, one of whom, Marilyn, lived in it until 1994.

Because Pat and Nancy believe in deriving income from a variety of sources, all the chairs, tables, lamps, light fixtures, paintings, wall hangings, sheets, bedspreads, pillows, pillow cases, towels, and blankets in The Mansion are for sale. "It's kinda like a furniture store. You want to buy something, we'll sell it," says Nancy. "People sleep on our mattresses, they like 'em and buy 'em. It's funny. By doing

all this, the house supports itself and we've saved a piece of Union City history."

The Mansion has done so well supporting itself that the Kirgans recently bought the 1905 three-bedroom Victorian house next door and are renovating it into an extended-stay bed-and-breakfast for their corporate visitors.

"We're making it pay," says Pat.

Mike and Deb Klink

Historic Name: CHARLES ECKHART HOUSE

City: AUBURN

County: DEKALB

Date of Construction: 1903

Architectural Style: ARTS AND CRAFTS

When Mike Klink was a senior at DeKalb County High School, he drove his girlfriend to the Eckhart mansion on Main Street in Auburn, parked the car, produced a diamond ring, and proposed. "If you marry me, one day we'll live in this house," Mike promised her. In 1972 Mike and Deb married and in 1997 they moved into the Eckhart mansion,

an Auburn landmark for nearly a century. It took a while, but Mike kept his promise. "I kept saying, soon as it's for sale, I'll buy it," says Mike.

The cavernous brick home was built in 1903 by Charles Eckhart, founder of Eckhart Buggy Works, which later became Auburn Automobile Company, the manufacturer of

147

the famed Auburn and Cord roadsters. The house attracts a lot of attention.

"People knock on the door asking if they can use our house for their group's parties," says Mike. "I say, 'Are you kidding? No, it's my house. I live here.'"

After Mike graduated from Tri-State University in Angola in 1974 with an engineering degree, they moved to San Bernardino, California. Mike worked for the Bechtel Corporation, the world's largest engineering and construction firm. A year later they moved to Washington, D.C., where Mike worked on the new underground transit system. When he quit Bechtel, they lived briefly in Indianapolis, then returned to Auburn.

"We wanted to come home," says Deb. Mike worked as a civil engineer. In 1981, while Deb remained in Auburn with their four children, Mike rejoined Bechtel and spent two difficult years in Saudi Arabia building a town on the Persian Gulf called Jubail. "I saw two men beheaded and a woman stoned to death for having premarital sex," recalls Mike. "I went there for the good money."

With that good money he bought a small concrete company in 1986, built a new plant, and expanded Klink Concrete Company to twenty-five trucks, with offices in Auburn, Angola, and Kendallville. When he kept his high school promise and bought the Eckhart mansion, Mike promptly launched a major renovation and expansion project.

"Some moron had painted the cherry woodwork with car enamel and glued linoleum to the floors," says Mike.

He set up a woodworking shop in the basement and made new floors, paneling, side molding, and baseboards to duplicate the enameled woodwork and ruined floors. He added a big four-car garage, big kitchen, seven big heating units, big family room with big-screen TVs, and filled the house with big things. Mike, a burly former high school linebacker, likes big.

"It would have been easier to build a new house," he shrugs. "Hell, I just looked on it as a great challenge to see if I could do it. Sure was expensive."

Even though they don't entertain, he ordered a handmade, fourteen-foot-long walnut table and fourteen chairs for the big dining room. When his daughter pleaded for the house to please be finished in time for her 1998 high school graduation party, Mike said sure and hired thirty more people to help him.

"After making concrete all day I stayed up until 2:00 A.M. making molding for the guys to hang the next day," he says. "I promised my daughter."

Two of the Klink children attend Valparaiso University Law School, son Simon goes to Purdue University, and their third daughter studies at St. Mary's College in South Bend. "I write a lot of tuition checks," laughs big Mike. "Hell, we love our kids."

While in the midst of making the big brick house even bigger, he figured why not build an elevator from the basement to the third floor.

"In case I get crippled," he says. "Because I'm not moving. I'm gonna die here."

Fred and Sandy Koss

Historic Name: BICKNELL COLE HOUSE
City: NOBLESVILLE
County: HAMILTON
Date of Construction: 1840
Architectural Style: FEDERAL

One of the first things Fred Koss did when he bought the Bicknell Cole house near downtown Noblesville was rent a jackhammer and remove the concrete Colonial-style porch that had been added in the 1950s.

"The neighbors asked why we were removing the beautiful porch and I said, 'Because it doesn't belong on this 1840 house,'" says Fred, a stickler for historic accuracy. Naturally, he's not pleased with what's going on around him now. "The development is so fast and so destructive that historic homes, barns, and farms are getting bulldozed

every day," continues the devoted and emotional advocate for old neighborhoods and the irreplaceable history they represent.

Fred and Sandy bought the Bicknell Cole home ten blocks north of the courthouse in 1978 and spent years restoring it. Now they are locked in a battle with Noblesville officials who hope to knock down several old homes one block from the historic courthouse to build a massive, suburban-style $39-million city hall complex.

"People are working hard to restore neighborhoods in

Noblesville and they want to put that thing in the heart of town. They keep encroaching and encroaching. Zoning is a mess and every day is a new battle," attests Fred, past president and charter member of the Noblesville Preservation Alliance and fierce defender of historic neighborhoods.

"We love it here, though," says Sandy, a medical technologist and 1964 graduate of St. Mary's College. She married Fred, a Notre Dame graduate and social worker, in 1965. They met in high school in Indianapolis. Sandy's grandfather Walter Brant started the Indiana Oxygen Company in downtown Indianapolis in the 1920s. Sandy spent sum-

mers at her grandfather's farm on Highway 32, just west of Noblesville. The farm remains in the family but is now surrounded by Sandpiper Lakes, Pebble Brook, Pine Ridge, Emerald Village, and The Arbor subdivisions, although there are no visible signs of sandpipers, pebbles, pines, emeralds, or arbors. "It used to be beautiful country," she remembers.

Financial wheeler-dealer Bicknell Cole built his narrow, two-story brick home in 1840. He was a broker for Indianapolis financier Calvin Fletcher, owned dry-goods stores in Strawtown and Noblesville, and served in the state senate. It took twenty years for the Kosses to add a kitchen and

fully restore Bicknell Cole's house because they were working, raising two sons, and didn't have an abundance of time or money.

Because of a narrow stairway, they hoisted their massive walnut four-poster bed up a rope from the side yard through a second-story window and into the bedroom. They bought the antique bed while attending the National Flatpick Championships in Winfield, Kansas. Fred is an accomplished guitar and dulcimer picker and a collector of antique tools. "I never ended up making anything with the tools," he says. "I like how they look."

One of Fred's most prized possessions is a framed 1930 black-and-white photograph of Nobel Peace Prize winner social activist Jane Addams, founder of the American social work movement and a continuing inspiration to Fred in his endless battles with city hall.

Fred is pleased to have an elementary school across the street. Noisy children running through the yard don't bother him.

"Music to my ears," he says. "CVS can't buy a school and knock it down to build a pharmacy. At least this corner is safe."

Monica Lorimer and Matt Troy

Historic Name: RED OAK

Town: LONG BEACH

County: LAPORTE

Date of Construction: 1925

Architect: JOHN LLOYD WRIGHT

Architectural Style: PRAIRIE

After graduating from medical school and marrying in 1995, surgeons Monica Lorimer and Matt Troy lived in Mankato, Minnesota, which they didn't like for a variety of reasons. They both grew up in the Chicago area. Monica graduated from the University of Illinois medical school and Matt from Loyola University in Chicago.

After a couple of years in Mankato, they contacted a medical recruiter who told them that St. Anthony Memorial Hospital in Michigan City, Indiana, was in need of staff surgeons. "We wanted to come home. We didn't want to live or practice medicine in Chicago, because it's crazy there, but we wanted to be close," explains Monica, who is now the director of the hospital's Center for Breast Health. "We either wanted to live in the country or near Lake Michigan."

A real estate agent suggested a house three blocks from the big lake in the small town of Long Beach, a quick commute to the hospital in Michigan City. The sprawling, white stucco house known as Red Oak, which was built in 1925, was one of seventeen homes in Long Beach designed by architect John Lloyd Wright between 1923 and 1946. John Lloyd Wright is the son of fabled eccentric architect Frank Lloyd Wright. John Lloyd Wright, who lived in Long Beach at the time, also designed the elementary school and the town's administration building. In addition to designing buildings, he created the wildly successful Lincoln Logs building kits for children.

"It looked like Grandma's house but the architecture was incredible," Monica says of her initial impression of the hilltop house surrounded by towering red oaks. It was dark, worn-out, and depressing, despite a soaring twenty-one-foot cathedral ceiling in the large living room. The original carpeting with horsehair padding was still on the floor. Paint had peeled and heavy draperies covered the windows.

"Luckily, I struck gold with Matt. Not only is he cute but he knew how to renovate a house," notes Monica. In Mankato, they had renovated and lived in a 1912 house along the Minnesota River.

In 1998, they moved into the seventeen-room, six-bathroom Red Oak and lived in two rooms with three young children while methodical Matt renovated and painted the place, one big room at a time. "He's happy with chores," says Monica. "The only thing we hired out was a painter to do the living room. It required scaffolding because of the high ceilings."

Coincidentally, Matt's family goes back a long way in Long Beach, which was developed in the early 1920s as a summer resort for wealthy Chicagoans. Over the years, it has evolved into a permanent community of about two thousand residents and eight hundred homes, most of which are tucked deep in the trees and sand dunes of northeast LaPorte County. Matt's grandfather Chicago Alderman Matthew Bieszczat, bought a house in Long Beach in 1963. In the 1970s, his parents bought a beachfront home not far from Grandfather.

Life in Long Beach has mellowed Monica, a self-described hard-charging overachiever. "All my life I was a type-A competitive person. Living here, I've learned there's more to life," says Monica.

"Long Beach has big old homes and small ranch houses, so there's a good mix of people here. When people ask where we're going on vacation we say, 'Right here.' This is a vacation place," she adds, nodding out a second-story window at the forest of red oaks surrounding the house. "We live in the trees."

Harold F. Mailand

Historic Name: SNEPP HOUSE

County: SHELBY

Date of Construction: CIRCA 1850

Architectural Style: GREEK REVIVAL

The first thing Harold F. Mailand did in 1994 when he bought the old Snepp farmhouse in Shelby County was drive to Florida and buy two cows named Little Butch and Bovina. They are an endangered breed of small Longhorn known as Florida Crackers and were first brought to North America by the Spanish centuries ago. "This was the breed of cattle that also fed the Confederate army," notes Harold. "I needed something to clear this place of brush and weeds. Cattle are a good way of trimming and civilizing a property." He liked providing a home for endangered animals while working to civilize and restore an endangered home. The Snepp house had been abandoned for twenty-five years, had no roof, thirty-five broken windows, no water, heat, or pipes and was once used to stable horses. It was an overgrown, two-story brick shell on a beautiful hill above the rolling green grass valley of the Big Blue River.

Harold grew up on a northern Indiana farm, received

art education degrees at Ball State and Indiana Universities, taught a while, and spent twelve years as a textile conservator at the Indianapolis Museum of Art. In 1986 he founded his own company, Textile Conservation Services, which rehabilitates and restores historic flags, tapestries, and other old fabric for private collectors and museums around the country.

He lived in and ran his textile business from an early–twentieth-century row house in the St. Joseph Historic District in downtown Indianapolis, thirteen feet from Alabama Street.

"I was getting tired of downtown, all the noise and congestion, and wanted more ground under my feet," Harold recalls. He began driving around on weekends searching for an old home within a forty-five-minute radius of the Indianapolis airport. Harold is a frequent business flier. A friend told him about the Snepp house, which was referred

to locally as the haunted house, the kind of place that scares children.

"Something about it pulled me in," says Harold. "The house had a pure architectural form and was built in the period of great optimism before the Civil War. That appealed to me." Harold is an optimist.

For the next three years, he commuted thirty-five miles to work in Indianapolis and lived in a tiny two-wheel trailer behind the house, working to make it livable. While Harold worked on the house, Little Butch and Bovina civilized the brush and tall grass.

The next project is stabilizing the enormous barn that is already half-collapsed but salvageable. On August 18, 1881, D. J. Hoskins carved his name into one of the logs while building an addition to the barn. Harold would like to save the barn for D. J. Hoskins, although things have taken a depressing turn in the valley of the Big Blue River.

In 1994, when Harold bought the place, he looked out north-facing windows toward land largely unchanged since the Snepp family built the house. Harold fled the noise and density of downtown Indianapolis in search of a quiet, contemplative place that evoked memories of his boyhood farm. The farmstead he civilized is now rapidly being surrounded on three sides by an aggressively encroaching suburban development, a generic subdivision marketed as "A New Place to Live." The contrast between Harold's home and the new arrivals jars the senses, providing affirmation of the need to contain sprawl and preserve something of the rural and historic landscape.

While the beauty of the landscape that surrounded the Snepp family farmstead is irretrievably lost, for now Harold and Little Butch and Bovina will remain, along with the old brick house and the sagging barn, to maintain a vestige of civilization in the valley of the Big Blue River.

Ray and Lou Marr

Historic Name: JAMES MARR HOUSE

County: BARTHOLOMEW

Date of Construction: 1871

Architectural Style: GREEK REVIVAL

LISTED IN THE NATIONAL REGISTER OF HISTORIC PLACES

On November 2, 1901, Ray Marr, who was ten years old, stood barefoot in wet cement that his father had poured for a ramp leading to the barn on their Bartholomew County farm. Ray then scratched the date in the cement beneath his little footprints.

"Isn't that amazing, Pop's feet," marvels Ray's son, Ray, more than a hundred years later, as he studies the footprints beside the barn he now owns. It is the most poignant and striking reminder of the Marr family's long history in Bartholomew County. The original Marrs left Harrison County, Kentucky, in 1819 and settled along the Hawpatch plateau, a flat, sandy plain north of Columbus, named for the abundant Hawthorne trees.

Shortly after the Civil War, the current Ray's great-grandfather James built a fine house on Three Notch Road in the Hawpatch made of bricks fired on the nearby sand hills. Ray, his wife, Lou, and their five children are the fourth and fifth generation of Marrs to live in the house and farm the rich, sandy soil. Three Notch Road was renamed Marr

Road in the 1930s, a gesture of respect for one of the county's original pioneer families. Across Marr Road is the Columbus Airport, a portion of which was once part of the Marr farm. Ray, Lou, and their children moved into the family home in 1972 when Ray's mother, Jean, died.

Copies of Great-Grandpa James's original ledger books reveal a thrifty man who diligently recorded every penny he ever spent. "Look at this," says a laughing Ray, opening the ledger copy. On March 27, 1875, James bought two brooms and a half-ball of twine for sixty cents. A week later he bought a dish of oysters for forty cents, a five-cent beer and a thirty-five-cent pint of whiskey. He paid two dollars for a pair of boots and bought three balls of twine for twenty-five cents.

Ray grew up visiting Grandpa's farm. Grandpa stubbornly farmed with mules, believing them superior to the obnoxious internal combustion engine. Ray remembers riding the mule wagon into town with Grandpa to sell corn. Ray learned to read upside down while watching Grandma

sell eggs. As the egg buyer wrote down prices, suspicious Grandma mentally computed the math upside down across the desk so she wasn't cheated.

During World War II Ray, a graduate of the U.S. Merchant Marine Academy, sailed cargo ships. Lou, a Shelbyville native, graduated from DePauw University in 1950 and married Ray a year later. Ray managed the old family-owned Hotel St. Denis in downtown Columbus where Ed Sullivan slept one night. A Republican, Ray served two terms in the state legislature and one term as county commissioner, following in the footsteps of his father and grandfather.

When they moved into Great-Grandpa's house, the circle was complete for yet another generation of Marrs. "I just kind of felt it would always be my house because I always wanted to farm like my Dad," says Ray. The hall wallpaper that Grandma Maggie put up in 1917 is still there. James's oil lamp remains on the shelf. Ray still uses Dad's 1945 black dial telephone. Bricks in the smokehouse are black from decades of smoking hams. The goldfish in the outdoor brick pond are descendants of the original fish Ray dropped in the water in 1975. The brick shed where Grandpa stored wood and Dad parked his car is now Lou and Ray's festive party house.

"You learn to live with old things," says Lou, who refuses to install a dishwasher because it would wreck the old family china plates.

But, more importantly, the concrete footprints are still visible on the barn ramp.

"Pop's footprints still make me emotional," says Ray.

Michael and Ellen Mauer

Historic Name: T. G. WILKINSON HOUSE
City: MUNCIE
County: DELAWARE
Date of Construction: 1936
Architect: LESLIE AYRES
Architectural Style: ART MODERNE

If Michael and Ellen Mauer's gleaming white house were in the wild and crazy Deco District of South Beach in Miami, Florida, it wouldn't attract much attention. However, it attracts considerable attention in Muncie, which has no sandy ocean beaches (but *was* once home to the world's oldest canning jar manufacturer in the world).

Delaware County financier T. G. Wilkinson built the streamlined Art Moderne–style house with portal front windows in 1936 near the Ball State University campus. He obviously wanted to make a dramatic, eye-catching statement about something. Himself, probably.

The chromed-brass doorknobs are square, the interior wall paneling and shelves are teak. There are two dark blue porcelain sinks in the main upstairs bathroom. The large sink is for washing and the small one for brushing teeth. T.G. apparently didn't believe in brushing his teeth in the same sink in which he washed his hands. The front porch features an enormous red neon light.

"I had to screen in the red neon porch light because it lit up the whole neighborhood," says Michael. "It seems obvious Mr. Wilkinson liked being noticed."

Michael is from Liberty, Missouri, and met Ellen at the

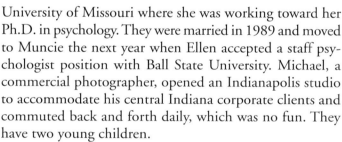

University of Missouri where she was working toward her Ph.D. in psychology. They were married in 1989 and moved to Muncie the next year when Ellen accepted a staff psychologist position with Ball State University. Michael, a commercial photographer, opened an Indianapolis studio to accommodate his central Indiana corporate clients and commuted back and forth daily, which was no fun. They have two young children.

In 1995, they began searching for a new house in the country south of Muncie to reduce Michael's dreaded I-69 commute to Indianapolis.

"The only way I would stay in Muncie was if we could buy this house," he says. He'd often drive out of his way to admire the unusual, curved house with the sleek lines and Art Deco look. As luck would have it, a real estate agent told them it was about to be listed for sale. They bought it and discovered that the bricks were crumbling.

"We were in tears and a state of panic," he recalls. Michael went into manic home repair overdrive and taught himself how to mix mortar and replace bricks.

"I replaced thousands of bricks by myself," says Michael. "I'm a perfectionist. It's a character flaw that's bad for me, but good for the house. I won't be happy until I get every floorboard in perfect alignment. I could work on this house twenty-four hours a day."

He ponders, researches, and agonizes over every household repair. For example, he cleans the original 1936 toilet mechanisms with a toothbrush and is currently obsessing about the source of a small roof leak he can't locate. "It's emotionally expensive to be insane like this," he says, only

half-joking. You can imagine his reaction when teenagers egged the front of the house one Halloween night. Or how nervous he gets when golfers across the street in Guthrie Park drive golf balls in his direction.

"I try to stay calm," he laughs. "Ellen thinks I'm nuts. She'd be happy if we left the white carpet on the floor, but there's wood parquet underneath and that's my next project." He still commutes to his Indianapolis photography studio a couple of times a week but the drive is less grueling because he uses the time to analyze his next home repair project.

"I drive everyone nuts with my obsession," he says. "A friend told me I'm the right owner for this house because I care about it so much and want everything perfect.

"I'm calm today."

Hank McLain and Barbara Douglas

Historic Name: DUDLEY PEAK CRAIG HOUSE

Town: VEVAY

County: SWITZERLAND

Date of Construction: 1895

Architectural Style: FREE CLASSIC

In 1994, despite already having one home in Anderson, Hank McLain and his wife, Barbara Douglas, bought two more right next to each other in the picturesque town of Vevay in Switzerland County. Hank, who retired in 1989 after teaching high school social studies for thirty-three long years, needed something to do. "I'm an old house guy," he asserts.

Both houses overlook the Ohio River on Market Street. Enormous old trees form a canopy over the quiet street that handles more walkers, dogs, and cats than cars. In its nearly two-hundred-year existence, Vevay's population has never exceeded two thousand and 63 percent of the 492 homes in the downtown historic district were built before 1883. It is the Switzerland County Seat and it has one stoplight and no noise.

"We irrationally fell in love with the houses because Vevay is so unique and tranquil. We just happened to drive by," says Barbara of the spontaneous decision to buy two houses 2¹/₂ hours from their Anderson home. Barbara is a music professor and lyric soprano at Anderson University. Hank moved to one of the Vevay houses and Barbara commutes on weekends during the school year. They renovated one house and rented it. When the renters wrecked it, they sold it in 1997 and concentrated on the other house, which continues to be a slow work in progress.

"We're just teachers, not rich people," says Barbara. "It takes a lot of time and patience but it's the most fun we've ever had. We've done most of the work ourselves." The house, which hadn't been painted in thirty-five years, was built in 1895 by Dudley Peak Craig, who previously lived

across the river in Ghent, Kentucky. After his second wife died, Dudley tried changing his bad luck by moving to Vevay and marrying his first cousin, Mattie. Luckily for the Craig family gene pool, cousins Mattie and Dudley had no children. Mattie was twenty-seven years younger than Dudley, who was a member of one of northern Kentucky's most prosperous slave-owning families during the Civil War.

Dudley and Mattie's grim wedding portrait hangs in Hank and Barbara's front parlor. Dudley and Mattie appear ready to face a firing squad. Hank and Barbara stumbled across the wedding portraits at an antique auction and paid too much for them, but felt honor-bound to return them to the house.

"This is a special place. Their pictures belong in this house," says Hank. Dudley spared no expense for his cousin-bride. Solid-brass doorknobs and chandeliers throughout the house, an elaborate oak stairway, and a most unusual extravagance for a nineteenth-century home: clothes closets.

"Everything was intact in this house. No matter where we looked we saw something beautiful," says Hank, a board member of Historic Southern Indiana and Historic Vevay.

Dudley died in 1923 and his funeral was held in the front parlor. Mattie died in 1945; her funeral was held someplace else. At one point, the house was bought by former Louisville mayor and Kentucky congressman Charlie Farnsley, who kept it until the late 1980s. It remained empty until Hank and Barbara had their irrational moment that they've never regretted, despite the vandalizing renters and long commute to Anderson.

"We have friends down for the weekend all the time and they always say how well they sleep here," says Hank, rocking on the front porch, waving and shouting howdy at passing neighbors. Happy guy Hank knows everyone in the 300-block of West Market, which he oversees from his front porch rocking chair.

"It's the best porch in Vevay," says Hank, now waving with both hands.

Mac and Sarah McNaught

Historic Name: JOHN WOOD HOUSE

County: RUSH

Date of Construction: CIRCA 1830

Architectural Style: FEDERAL

LISTED IN THE NATIONAL REGISTER OF HISTORIC PLACES

One spring day in 1996, Mac McNaught was wandering around Rush County near Flatrock River when he topped a slight hill and knew a long journey had ended. For twenty-two years, Mac, an Indianapolis attorney, had searched for an old farmhouse and a good piece of land in a relatively unspoiled setting, an increasingly difficult challenge in Indiana.

Every time he checked a prospective home, it would be too close to a noisy interstate or power lines, or in the path of advancing subdivisions, malls, or people who drive

SUVs and talk on cell phones, a sure sign the area is in imminent decline. Then he spotted the simple white house on Mulberry Hill, the three old barns, the corncrib, and the nearby stand of old trees, and knew that his twenty-two-year search was over.

The house was built around 1830 by British immigrant John Wood, who constructed the first grist- and sawmill on Flatrock River near the tiny town of Moscow. Over the long years, the simple farmhouse had the usual succession of owners, the last being a woman who lived there for thirty-five years while the house experienced a lingering case of benign neglect.

Mac and long-suffering wife, Sarah, bought the Mulberry Hill house and 250 surrounding acres of pasture and woods and began a costly restoration project.

"At first Sarah was shocked. We have two busy teenage kids, how could we do this? I said, 'One step at a time.' I think she humored me throughout my wanderings, now that part was over," he says of his saintly wife who patiently endured his decades-long obsession with finding the ideal farmhouse.

"I'd always thought since I was a kid it would be a good thing to be part of restoring an Indiana farmstead and

keeping it going," says Mac, who grew up in Logansport and graduated from Wabash College in Crawfordsville and from Duke University Law School in 1979. His parents divorced when he was young and he spent his childhood riding a 26-inch Schwinn bicycle up and down country roads in Cass County. He'd hike and fish Eel River and Pipes Creek, wander the woods, and let his imagination roam free. He worked on a farm in high school, which deepened his interest in old barns and houses and open spaces and quiet places.

Then, of course, the usual dream-killers intruded: high-pressure corporate law in downtown Indianapolis, growing children, financial demands. Yet in Mac's case, he never forgot about open spaces and quiet places, a tribute to his character and a reminder that childhood dreams don't have to die.

The family spends weekends on Mulberry Hill working to restore the house and outbuildings to their original 1830 condition. Mac is a stickler for historical accuracy. One day he hopes to live there full-time and walk the woods and fields every day. Until then, several times a week, he escapes his job in the late afternoon, drives the forty miles by himself and hikes the good land, collects wildflower and prairie grass seeds, and watches the coyotes and fox dart across the rolling fields. He hopes to use the collected seeds some day to restore the land, refilling it with native wildflowers and blue-stem grass.

His childhood enthusiasm for simply wandering, watching, and becoming part of something greater than himself in a quiet place remains undiminished.

"I'm in a whole different state of mind when I'm walking down a ravine or through the woods. It sure beats a health club," he says. "I found my dream."

On Mulberry Hill.

Harriet McNeal

Historic Name: HENRY MILLER PARROT HOUSE

City: TERRE HAUTE

County: VIGO

Date of Construction: 1894

Architectural Style: QUEEN ANNE

LISTED IN THE NATIONAL REGISTER OF HISTORIC PLACES, *Farrington's Grove Historic District*

Harriet McNeal was newly divorced with three children when she arrived in Terre Haute in 1967 to teach renaissance art history at Indiana State University. She was eager to buy a house and called a real estate agent and guess what?

"The realtors showed me houses in every stupid subdivision in town," recalls Harriet, who still rides a bicycle twenty to thirty miles a day, although she is now retired after thirty-seven years of teaching. She finally demanded to be shown real houses in real neighborhoods because she had no interest in living in a generic, treeless subdivision.

When she walked into the cavernous Queen Anne–style house a few blocks south of the Vigo County Courthouse,

she spotted a medieval tapestry hanging on the living room wall and sun streaming through stained-glass windows.

"This house is mine," Harriet told the confused agent. The house was built in 1894 by Henry Miller Parrot, who owned a bakery known for its crispy crackers. In the 1930s it was bought by beer baron Oscar Bower and his flamboyant wife, Lillian, a former Ziegfeld Follies dancer, known for her long legs.

Then along came Harriet, three children, twenty thousand color art slides, a concert grand piano, and a moving van full of books, art, and old furniture she hauled from her previous life in Englewood, New Jersey. "I never bought

a new piece of furniture and never will," says Harriet during a tour of the four-thousand-square-foot house with bedroom bay windows that extend into the tree branches.

"It's like sleeping in a tree house," she explains. The only thing missing from the Queen Anne house is Queen Anne herself. Harriet's interest in European art and history is reflected in her extensive collection of seventeenth- and eighteenth-century furniture and paintings. "I'm not a person for style, just what I like."

Harriet grew up in an old house full of antiques in Highland Park, Illinois. Her mother was a pianist, her father a pediatrician. She attended the University of Colorado and received a Ph.D. in art history in 1970 from Columbia University in New York City. She reads German, French, and Italian. In 1977 she wrote a book exploring the life of Florentine architect and sculptor Michelozzo, who died a few years ago—in 1472.

Harriet was instrumental in having Farrington's Grove, her neighborhood of big trees, declared a National Register historic district. When old buildings in Terre Haute are demolished to make way for more strip malls, chain drugstores, subdivisions, and other twenty-first-century forms of "progress," Harriet gathers stone samples from the sad wreckage.

"I've collected stone from every building torn down in Terre Haute in the last twenty-five years," she explains, noting the backyard stone mountain. "If I can't save the buildings, I'll save part of them."

In her seventy-second year, she took three months to

bicycle through Thailand, Cuba, Vietnam, Mexico, and Spain, simply to learn about new cultures and art. When she wanted to meet Georgia O'Keeffe, she flew to New Mexico, drove into the Ghost Ranch Mountains, and knocked on the great artist's door. Harriet explained to the maid that she'd studied and taught O'Keeffe's modernist paintings for thirty years and wanted to shake her hand.

"Hell, if someone likes my work and teaches me, I want to meet her," said Georgia O'Keeffe, who invited Harriet in for a twenty-minute visit.

"I love traveling but I always love returning to Terre Haute and the charm and graciousness of the old homes in this neighborhood," says the charming Harriet McNeal.

J. Irwin and Xenia Miller

City: COLUMBUS

County: BARTHOLOMEW

Date of Construction: 1956

Architect: EERO SAARINEN   *Landscape Architect:* DAN KILEY

Architectural Style: INTERNATIONAL

NATIONAL HISTORIC LANDMARK

He was born in 1909 when ox-drawn wagons slogged through the muddy streets of downtown Columbus. He attended Yale University, majored in Greek and Latin classics, received a master's degree in political science at Oxford University in England, and returned home to run the family business, about which he knew nothing. When he took over Cummins Engine Company in 1934, it employed sixty people and was near collapse. Eventually, he built Cummins into a Fortune 500 empire, employing twenty-five thousand workers in a hundred countries.

In 1942, Mr. Miller commissioned architect Eliel Saarinen and his son, Eero, to design the First Christian Church in Columbus. It was the first of more than fifty architectural commissions by the Miller family for designs by some of the world's great architects, transforming Columbus into an international architectural gem.

In the early 1950s, Mr. Miller and his wife Xenia lived in a house several blocks from where he was born. They had five children and space was limited, so the Millers bought a thirteen-acre corn and tobacco patch on Flatrock River one mile from the Bartholomew County Courthouse and in 1952 commissioned Eero Saarinen to design a family home.

"We wanted a house in town so the kids could walk to school because I wasn't about to chauffeur them around," says Mrs. Miller, who predates the soccer-mom era. "The house had to accommodate kids but we didn't want to feel like we were rattling around in it after they were gone."

"I'd take Eero out to get a hamburger and we'd talk and became good friends. We thought alike," recalls Mr. Miller. In 1948 Eero Saarinen designed the soaring, 630-foot Gateway Arch at the Jefferson National Expansion Memorial in St. Louis.

Largely completed in 1957, the low-slung, seven-bedroom home showcases Mrs. Miller's extensive contemporary and Impressionist art collection, Saarinen-designed furni-

ture, and floor-to-ceiling living room bookcases, containing hundreds of volumes on history, art, and architecture. Mr. Miller reads Greek and Latin and plays Bach on a Stradivarius.

Mrs. Miller has renovated and preserved dozens of historic Columbus buildings. "She just insisted we not tear down the good, old stuff," says Mr. Miller. "We never wanted to live in an old house but we wanted to save them."

His downtown office was built in 1881 by his great-grandfather, a friend of Abraham Lincoln's. Mr. Miller's wisdom has been sought by seven U.S. presidents. He is chairman of the Irwin-Sweeney-Miller Foundation, which donates millions of family dollars to build schools, hospitals, museums, and churches throughout the world. During more than fifty years on the Cummins payroll, he donated 30 percent of his pre-tax salary to charity.

"It's harder to give away money than it is to make it," he says. "My parents always said, 'You didn't make this money all by yourself. Other generations laid the foundation and you have an obligation that is not self-centered but in the interest of other people who have gone before you.' The highest priority should be the legitimate claims of those left behind in society." Clearly, he's not the stereotypical greed-driven American businessman.

The Millers obviously could live in splendor anywhere in the world. They chose instead to anchor their entire lives within a few blocks of Mr. Miller's birthplace in a house built to accommodate kids, within walking distance of public school.

"We weren't concerned about style, only that it be useful and serve our family's purpose," says Mr. Miller. "It has."

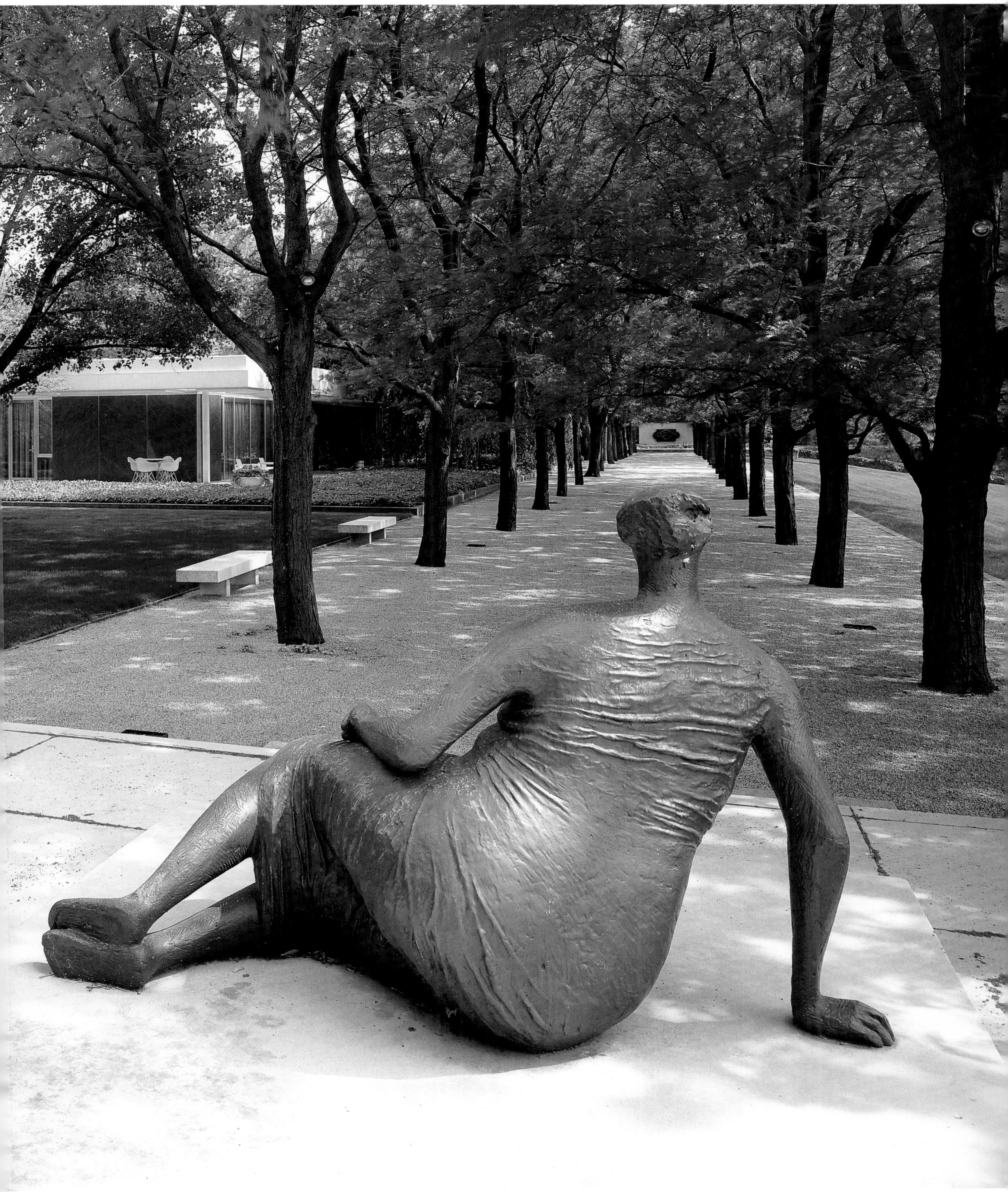

Elizabeth Brand Monroe

City: ZIONSVILLE

County: BOONE

Date of Construction: CIRCA 1895

Architectural Style: QUEEN ANNE COTTAGE

In 1989 when Elizabeth B. Monroe received her Ph.D. in American history at the University of Florida in Gainesville, she moved to Indianapolis to teach at Indiana-Purdue University. She rented an apartment because she didn't plan to stay long. She didn't like big cities.

"I decided I could stand Indiana about two years," Liz recalls. A year later, Dr. Monroe was named director of the Indianapolis-based National Council on Public History and later director of the university's Public History Program. She decided Indiana wasn't so bad, especially if she could find the right house.

In 1993 she found it, a small T-shaped Queen Anne cottage built around 1895, in the pleasant tree-lined village of Zionsville in Boone County, twenty-five miles northwest of downtown Indianapolis and the IUPUI campus.

"I wanted to make an old house suit my needs," she says. She wanted something instantly livable but old so it could be restored and would accommodate her books and scholarly pursuits in an atmosphere dominated by clean lines, ample sunshine, and a sense of history and place.

Zionsville's narrow, brick streets and closely built nineteenth-century houses remind her of small towns in northern Virginia where she grew up, the only child of bankers. On weekends they often attended garden tours of the stately nineteenth-century homes in northern Virginia. This led to a lifelong interest in legal and public history and the preservation and restoration of old buildings.

From 1978 to 1983 Liz was the Florida State Historic Preservationist and architectural historian for the $11 million restoration of the 1845 state capitol building in Tallahassee. The restored building is now the Florida Museum of Political History.

Since buying the twelve-hundred-square-foot, two-bedroom Zionsville house on Poplar Street, she has added a bathroom and a closet, and lined the walls with bookcases. She's currently writing a biography of Virginian William Wirt at her dining room desk. He was America's longest-serving attorney general, holding the post from 1817 to 1829.

Dr. Monroe wrote *The Wheeling Bridge Case,* a book that examines an 1852 legal dispute between railroads and steamboats over the use of the thousand-foot-long West Virginia suspension bridge over the Ohio River. She co-authored *The Main Stem: The History and Architecture of North Meridian Street* for Historic Landmarks Foundation of Indiana.

Dr. Monroe's home is tailored for scholarship, combining

all elements of her life in a fairly small space on floors of bare wood beneath sloping ceilings. "I like interesting and carefully thought-out, clean designs, something I could walk into and say, 'This is different,'" she explains. The wall surrounding the brick fireplace is lined with framed etchings, drawings, paintings, and photographs reflecting her interest in British and American history, ranging from a nineteenth-century print of British thinker and furniture de-

signer Charles L. Eastlake to a steel engraving of the famed South Carolina Swamp Fox and Revolutionary War hero Francis Marion.

There is also a Civil War–era oil painting of a man and a woman, which was found in her late mother's belongings. Her mother labeled it, "No One We Knew."

"In addition to teaching and writing, this house is my job," she says. "Getting it right."

Jim Morrow

Historic Name: IMRE AND MARIA HORNER HOUSE

Town: BEVERLY SHORES

County: PORTER

Date of Construction: 1949

Architect: OTTO KOLB

Architectural Style: INTERNATIONAL

LISTED IN THE NATIONAL REGISTER OF HISTORIC PLACES

In 1991, Jim Morrow, a retired real estate broker, bought a curiosity called a Lustron Home in Chesterton in Porter County. It is an all-steel, porcelain-enameled, prefabricated, futuristic-looking house built in 1950. The Lustron Corporation of Columbus, Ohio, only sold twenty-five hundred before going out of business due to inadequate funds.

"I like 'em," says Jim, a restless, curious soul. He converted the house into a museum, which was open to the public and dedicated to the story of the Lustron Home. After five years, he declared his mission accomplished, sold the house, and redirected his quirky passion north to the unique town of Beverly Shores on Lake Michigan. "I've

been tramping around northwest Indiana for years and this looked like a good place to be," explains Jim, who prefers not to waste words.

Beverly Shores was created in the late 1920s by developer Fred Bartlett, who built Mediterranean Revival–style homes and marketed the new resort town to affluent Chicago residents seeking relief from city heat and smog. He transported prospective buyers forty miles from Chicago to Beverly Shores on the South Shore railroad line and wowed them with the spectacular beauty of the lake and the windswept sand dunes.

In 1935, several buildings from the 1933–1934 Chicago

World's Fair were barged across the lake to Beverly Shores and soon a fully functioning town was in place, populated mostly by Chicago residents in search of summer fun.

Beverly Shores is now surrounded and protected from encroachment and development by the Indiana Dunes National Lakeshore, a federal park. There are about five hundred homes in the tiny town, about half of them occupied only in the summer. Jim Morrow, however, is a dedicated full-time resident, living in a spectacular home with floor-to-ceiling windows that was built and designed in 1949 by Swiss architect Otto Kolb for Chicago doctor Imre Horner and his wife, Maria.

Kolb, born in 1921, came to the United States in 1948 to join the industrial design faculty of the Illinois Institute of Technology in Chicago. His clean, modernist designs reveal the influence of such twentieth-century architectural giants as Mies van der Rohe, Walter Gropius, and Marcel Breuer. Kolb's work has been measured favorably against that of the Bauhaus greats, and the International-style home he designed in Beverly Shores is no exception.

The house sits on the isolated tip of a sand dune overlooking the big lake on one side and a heavily wooded ravine on the other. With the same intensity he devoted to the Lustron Home, Jim, a passionate preservationist, has immersed himself in the history of Beverly Shores. He recently authored a fine book entitled *Beverly Shores: A Suburban Dunes Resort.* He's also on the committee of the Beverly Shores Museum and Art Gallery where he works one day a week and serves as a self-appointed curator. The museum and gallery are located in the 1929 South Shore Line Depot, which is on the National Register and still serves railroad commuters traveling between South Bend and Chicago.

"I got hooked on Beverly Shores and this house the same way I got interested in the damn Lustron. I like the area and there was an interesting house on the market and I bought it," grumbles Jim, who grew up in Gary, fought in Europe during World War II, and graduated from Mexico City College in Mexico in 1949. "I went there because it was cheap and I only had the GI Bill," he explains. He returned to Gary, worked in his family's lumber business, and later started his own real estate business, which shifted around northwest Indiana, depending on his mood.

In keeping with his continued devotion to modernist designs of the 1930s and '40s, Jim furnished the small house with 1930s steel and leather furniture. It's a small house, two rooms up and two down. He lives alone, and it suits his modest needs.

"You don't live in your bedroom," he grumbles. "So why the hell would you need a big one."

Paul Myers

City: EAST CHICAGO

County: LAKE

Date of Construction: 1917

Architect: HOWARD VAN DOREN SHAW

Architectural Style: ARTS AND CRAFTS

LISTED IN THE NATIONAL REGISTER OF HISTORIC PLACES, *Marktown Historic District*

Growing up in the Marktown section of East Chicago, Paul Myers thought snow was supposed to be pink. Marktown snow was tinted pink by iron oxide spewing from the towering smokestacks of the massive steel mills that surround the tiny community like canyon walls.

When Lake Michigan froze solid from one end to the other, the U.S. Shipping Canal, which borders Marktown, never froze. Pollution control devices have since stopped the pink snow, but the canal still steams and never freezes and the mighty blast furnaces roar twenty-four hours a day.

"I love it. I know everyone in every house," says Paul of this unique forty-acre enclave built in 1917 to resemble an English Tudor garden village. Nearly a hundred buildings—small single-family homes and duplexes—were designed by noted architect Howard Van Doren Shaw, who was hired by industrialist Clayton Mark to build housing for his Lake County steel-plant workers. It's the old company town concept, but with an emphasis on tasteful housing in a humane environment.

The narrow streets require that the cars park on the sidewalks and the people walk in the streets. There is nothing else like it in Indiana, or possibly even the country: a tiny

residential island dwarfed and isolated by one of the densest industrial complexes in the world.

"I couldn't live anywhere else," says Paul, whose great-great-grandfather, a steelworker, lived in one of the first homes built in Marktown. Each succeeding generation of his family has also lived in Marktown and worked in the steel mills. Paul worked in the mill after graduating from Purdue University Calumet in 1976 and is now a business manager for a Chicago industrial design company.

In 1976 he bought his one-thousand-square-foot Marktown duplex, which he has decorated with Japanese calligraphy, antique swords, and a bust of architect Howard Van Doren Shaw. Paul is director of the Howard Van Doren Shaw Society, an organization dedicated to preserving his architecture, which includes a few Indianapolis homes and the famed Quadrangle Club at the University of Chicago.

Paul is a delightful character, an endearing eccentric who works tirelessly to preserve, protect, and promote his beloved Marktown. He knows every resident by name, their family histories, their dogs and cats, their troubles and triumphs.

"I could live in a nicer place and never help anyone but myself," says Paul, who patrols the streets, notes broken street lamps, potholes, junk cars, uncollected garbage, and other problems and notifies the East Chicago authorities.

It is a blue-collar, low-income community where the

small homes and duplexes sell in the $12,000 to $15,000 range. The location tends to depress prices. There are about a hundred homes and no businesses within the sixteen-square-block island known as the Marktown Historic District.

"It takes a certain kind of person to live in here," says the irrepressible Paul. "My family's always been here," he notes proudly. "I still see the potential."

175

Frank and Judy O'Bannon

INDIANA GOVERNOR'S RESIDENCE

Historic Name: SCOTT WADLEY HOUSE

City: INDIANAPOLIS

County: MARION

Date of Construction: 1928

Architects: RUBUSH AND HUNTER

Architectural Style: TUDOR REVIVAL

LISTED IN THE NATIONAL REGISTER OF HISTORIC PLACES, *North Meridian Street Historic District*

Each year, about ten thousand visitors tour the imposing English Tudor home at 4750 North Meridian Street in Indianapolis, the official governor's residence for the state of Indiana. Since Governor Frank O'Bannon and his wife, Judy, moved into the residence in 1996, it has become, among other public interests, a showcase for contemporary Indiana artists, young pianists, adult literacy programs, and a neighborhood gardening center.

"I call it the state's living room," declares Judy O'Bannon. The First Lady's Art Series exhibits the work of Hoosier artists on the first floor of the Governor's Residence, arguably the most prestigious address in Indiana. Exhibits are rotated every three months. The governor and first lady host a reception for each new exhibit in honor of the artists and participating galleries and schools, although the relatively small first floor can only accommodate 125 visitors.

"We have a great many practicing artists in Indiana and the Governor's Residence should be a showcase for the best Indiana has to offer," Judy explains. "We see this as a place set apart for people to do important things."

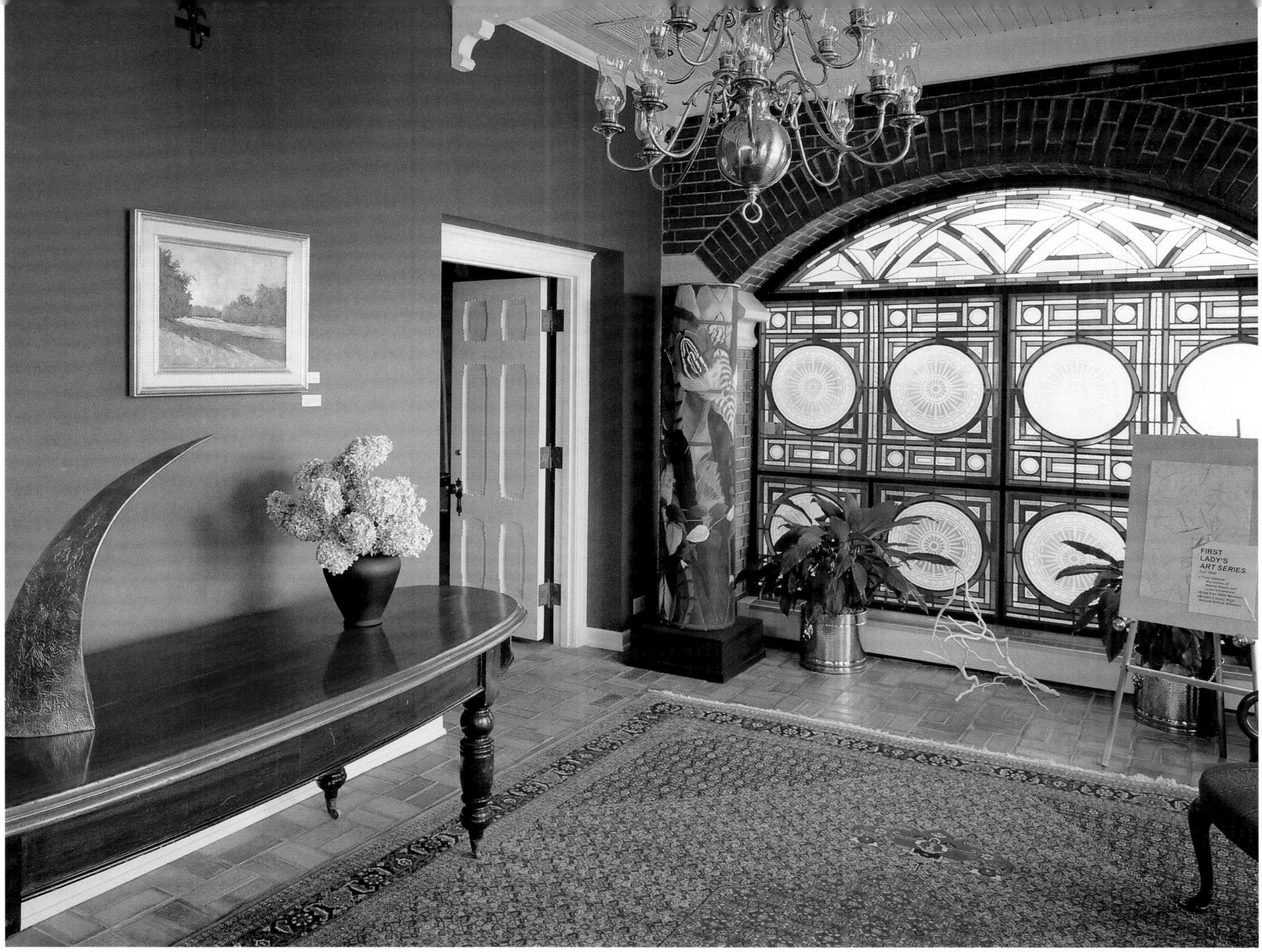
FIRST
LADY'S
ART SERIES

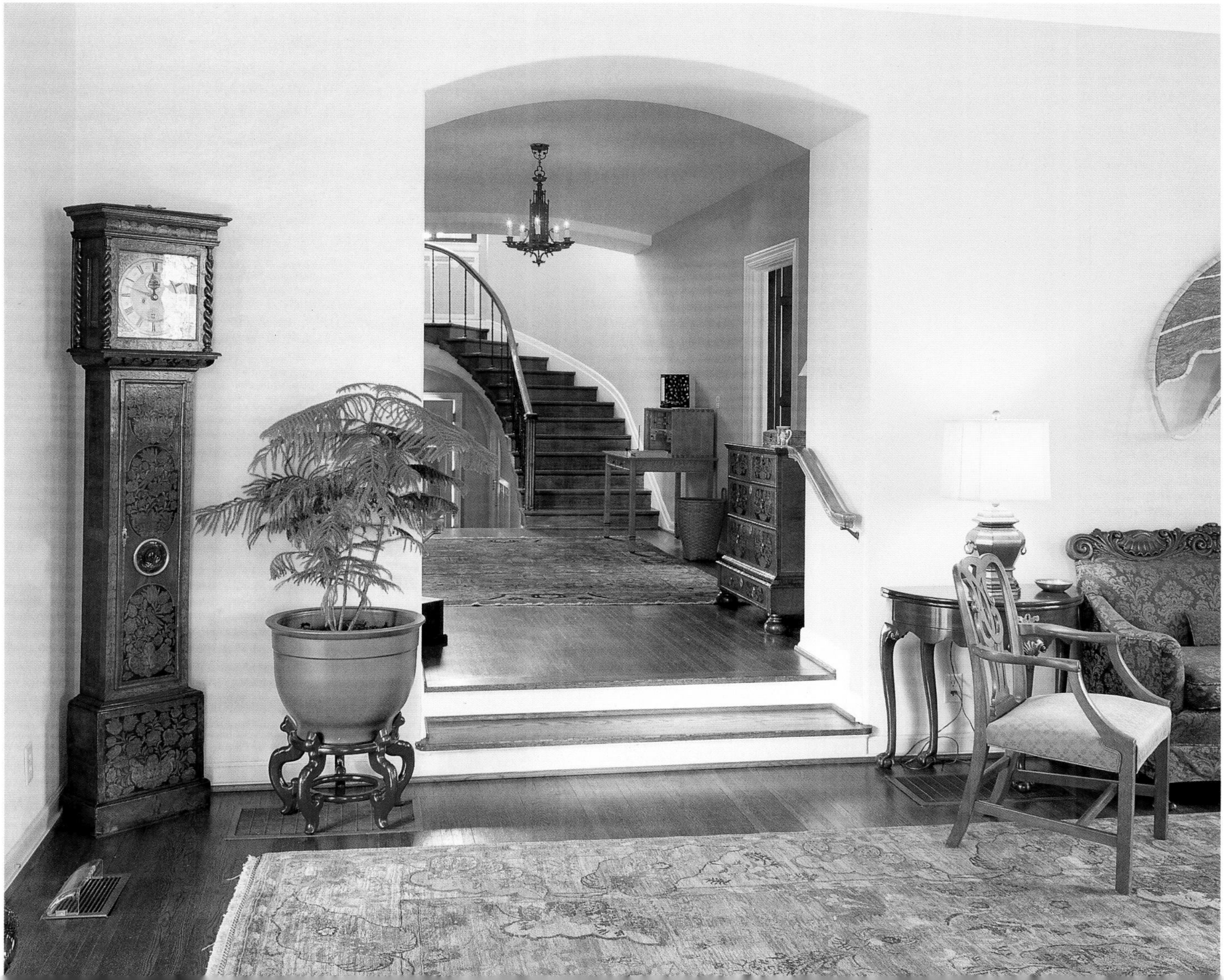

The 2½-story brick home was built in 1928, but did not become the Governor's Residence until 1973 when the state purchased it from Indianapolis attorney C. Severin Buschman for $242,000. The previous Governor's Residence at 4343 North Meridian Street was home to seven governors dating back to 1945. The seven bathrooms in the current residence are not accessible to wheelchairs, which could result in a massive remodeling project or in moving the governor's home to yet another location, which would be the seventh since Indiana became a state in 1816.

The Governor's Residence is a unique facility serving a dual purpose as a public building and a private home. Governor and Mrs. O'Bannon's living quarters are on the private second floor, which is off limits to visitors.

"We live over the store," Judy notes. Most of the furniture in the house is owned by the state of Indiana and is a diverse collection ranging from Colonial reproductions to Asian chairs and Chinese artwork, reflecting the tastes of the previous three first ladies.

Judy O'Bannon, a devoted collector of Hoosier antiques, brought thirteen pieces of personal furniture with her, most of which are in the second-floor living quarters. "There are traces of all the people who have lived here. We looked for historically interesting things," she explains. Mrs. O'Bannon eliminated the heavy drapes from the leaded-glass casement windows and removed much of the carpeting in favor of the original hardwood floors and oriental rugs. She also removed the white paint from the wrought-iron staircase railings. "This house is part of the fabric of the historic neighborhood," she notes.

While she has primarily used the residence to promote the arts, a large neighborhood garden is planted and harvested each summer on the north side of the six-acre estate by volunteers, public-school children, and visiting inmates from the Indiana Girls School. The O'Bannons also host several large, outdoor summer festivals on subjects ranging from the environment and urban forestry to the arts and community development projects.

"We've tried to treat it as the people's house," says Mrs. O'Bannon. "This is not our house. We're just temporary squatters."

Charles and Cheryl Owens

Historic Name: WILLIAM AND HELEN KOERTING HOUSE
City: ELKHART
County: ELKHART
Date of Construction: 1936
Architect: ALDEN DOW
Architectural Style: PRAIRIE

In the winter of 1968 there were only four houses for sale in Elkhart that would comfortably accommodate Charlie and Cheryl Owens and their five children, all of whom were younger than seven years old. They chose a house on the St. Joseph River because it had basement maids quarters, a good place to bunk the two boys.

Charlie, a University of Notre Dame graduate, was an executive with Miles Laboratories, an Elkhart-based pharmaceutical manufacturer. They lived across the state line in Edwardsburg, Michigan, but Cheryl didn't like the school system. She preferred the school system in Elkhart, where she grew up, so they moved back.

It was only after they settled into the distinctive, Japanese-style home that Cheryl became curious about its history. It was built in 1936 for William and Helen Koerting and designed by architect Alden Dow, a student of Frank Lloyd Wright. Cheryl had never heard of Dow but soon launched into a study of his architecture.

"I see, I read, I love beautiful things and I get interested in the history of everything," she explains. She arranged to meet Dow in his Midland, Michigan, office to seek his advice on replacing the home's aging roof and adding a kitchen with big windows so that she could admire the river and her long, sloping backyard and colorful perennial gardens.

"I didn't want to mess up the original design but I had to see the river from my kitchen," says Cheryl. "My husband couldn't care less. Between my husband and the kids there are eleven college degrees in this house and only two of us have any common sense, me and my son." Cheryl didn't go to college. "My degree is in common sense."

At Cheryl's request, Dow dispatched the home's original construction supervisor to Elkhart to insure that the kitchen addition and new roof installation were done properly, in keeping with the original design. The original flat roof withstood forty-six years of rough northern Indiana winters before it had to be replaced. The kitchen windows added a glorious new dimension to the house.

"What I must have missed all those years with no kitchen windows," laments Cheryl. In the solarium outside the kitchen windows are her bonsai trees. Bonsai is the Japanese art of dwarfing or miniaturizing trees by growing them in pots, pruning branches, cutting roots, and carefully balancing the amount of water and soil so they remain small. She's been dwarfing trees for forty years.

"It's a delicate process," she explains, "a combination of art and gardening."

She often accompanied Charlie on his job-related trips around the world and they've accumulated an extensive collection of African and Oriental art, including dozens of Lladró porcelain figurines. Cheryl, ever curious, also developed an interest in Native American art and miniature totem poles from tribes in the Northwest and Alaska. That collection now includes Navajo rugs, sand paintings, beadwork, and arrows.

179

"The only disaster we ever had was when a kid lassoed a big clay Japanese vase and broke it," recalls Cheryl. "After that, they rowdied outside. I had a heavy hand."

Charlie retired in 1983 and their leisure travel increased. With the children grown and gone, they must hire a bonsai tree–sitter when they travel. The delicate trees require daily care and constant vigilance. The graceful bonsai trees, says Cheryl, are a perfect outdoor complement to the Dow style of Oriental architecture.

"This house must always stay this way," she says. "You can't ever change it because it's an Alden Dow house. It's a piece of art, not just a house. Even Charlie now realizes it's important."

Frank and Patte Owings

Historic Name: JOSEPH E. COLE JR. HOUSE

City: INDIANAPOLIS

County: MARION

Date of Construction: 1932

Architect: FREDERICK WALLICK

Architectural Style: FRENCH ECLECTIC

LISTED IN THE NATIONAL REGISTER OF HISTORIC PLACES, *North Meridian Street Historic District*

Amid the towering pine trees in the quiet side yard of this North Meridian Street house is a ten-ton concrete block bearing the name "Cole Motor Car Co." It was once embedded over the door of the old automobile manufac-turing plant in downtown Indianapolis.

In 1967, the Cole building was bought by a hardware wholesale supplier, Service Supply Company of Indiana. Frank Owings, grandson of Service Supply founder Edger Seitz Sr., worked in the family business selling nuts, bolts, and screws. He was intrigued by the history of the building that held the Cole Motor Car Company, which produced 40,717 handcrafted luxury automobiles between 1909 and 1925.

Frank and his wife, Patte, an artist and fine arts photographer, were living in an 1870 Victorian home in the historic eastside Irvington neighborhood. They heard that the Cole house on Meridian Street was for sale. Joseph Cole Jr., son of the car company founder, built the twelve-room French Normandy farmhouse–style home for $15,000 in 1932 and lived there until his death in 1955.

The family crest and its Latin motto *Cole bonus est,* "Cole is good," is carved in limestone above a bay window.

"Had I not worked in the Cole building, it would have been just another house," says Frank, who is now a writer, musician, and historical researcher. They bought the Cole house in 1989, covered the swimming pool, moved the concrete façade from its downtown location to the side yard, and bought one of the few Cole automobiles left in the world, a 1925 V-8 Brouette in mint condition. Then Frank and Patte decorated the basement with rare Cole Motor Car Company memorabilia, including framed original stock certificates, promotional items, advertising posters, and owners' manuals—a tribute to the home, the Cole family, and their quality automobile. In 1996, the Cole house was listed in the National Register of Historic Places.

"We're custodians of this house and its history. Some of us believe in leaving things in better condition than we found them," says Patte, who met Frank in 1976 while working at Service Supply. The company closed its doors in 1998. The 1914 Cole building is now part of the Marion County Jail, but the carved limestone nameplate survives in the Owings's side yard beneath the big pines.

In another contribution to Hoosier history and preservation, the Owings are also restoring a 1952 Frank Lloyd Wright–designed home they bought in Fort Wayne, one of only eight Wright homes in Indiana.

"It's a person's moral responsibility to care for things,"

says Frank, a Wright scholar and lecturer. "When you study the history of a place it becomes so much more important."

The Cole house, with its distinctive round limestone tower, is in the North Meridian Street Historic District which runs from 40th Street north to Westfield Boulevard. Most of the 175 buildings in the district date from the 1920s and '30s.

The twelve-room house contains an elegant mix of Arts and Crafts and Wright-designed furniture, modern art, and Thomas Hart Benton lithographs, reflecting the Owings's interest in classic American art forms. They've also framed the home's original design drawings by architect Frederick Wallick. The original clay tile roof shingles and copper gutters still remain and have never leaked, a testimony to the architect's lasting belief in permanence.

"As Mr. Wright said, 'The evidence of a culture is the architecture that remains,'" notes Frank. "I believe that applies to this house."

Walt and June Prosser

Historic Name: MELVILLE FITZALLEN McHAFFIE HOUSE / RISING HALL

County: PUTNAM

Date of Construction: 1870

Architectural Style: ITALIANATE

LISTED IN THE NATIONAL REGISTER OF HISTORIC PLACES

When Walt and June Prosser first looked at the dilapidated Melville Fitzallen McHaffie house along Old National Road (U.S. 40) in Putnam County, they briefly questioned the wisdom of buying such a mess. It had been abandoned for years. Rodents scurried through the dirt and cobwebs, and farm animals, unaccustomed to toilet habits, roamed freely through the rooms and halls. The house had no plumbing or electricity. The walnut and ash staircase had been painted pink. The slate roof leaked. Of the five chimneys, three were crumbling and two were missing entirely.

"It looked like the Addams Family house, a black hole in which to throw money," recalls the energetic, irrepres-

sible, obsessive Walt, a retired Indianapolis businessman who can't sit still. "But I was looking for a rewarding challenge to keep me busy the rest of my life."

It's kept him busy since 1982 and elevated his obsessive tendencies to maniacal levels. "It's taken me over heart and soul," he says in his rapid-fire manner of speech. "It's consumed me and stirred my soul."

McHaffie, a Greencastle banker, horse and mule breeder, and friend of Abraham Lincoln, built the two-story brick Italianate house and twenty-five-hundred-square-foot barn in 1870. The brick barn has fourteen porthole windows. It is believed that the great Dan Patch, the early-twentieth-

century trotting horse who held the world record in the mile for thirty-three years, performed stud services in the barn on several occasions.

A grand and striking landmark on the eastern line of Putnam County, it remains the most prominent home on Indiana's western stretch of the venerable Old National Road, the first federally funded road across America. President Thomas Jefferson, who ordered the road built into the interior of America in 1806, called it "The Long Road."

"The history of this country passed along that road," says Walt, nodding toward the long road out beyond his vast tulip and rose gardens. "As a lawyer, Abraham Lincoln traveled the road many times on horseback."

Walt and June have meticulously restored the house, which they rechristened Rising Hall for its spectacular, multi-flight central-stair hall. They have filled it with period furnishings and have immersed themselves in its history and connection to Jefferson's Long Road and the spirit of Dan Patch, Abraham Lincoln, and the countless travelers who've passed by out front.

Walt is a founding member of the Indiana National Road Association and a major force in having the 156-mile Hoosier stretch of highway declared a National Scenic Byway to honor its historic and cultural value to the country.

The McHaffie house, which was a rodent hotel when June and Walt bought it for $40,000, is now listed in the National Register of Historic Places and has been featured on the Home and Garden TV channel. They held an open house in 1992 to satisfy curious onlookers and thirty-two hundred people showed up, jamming traffic on Old

National Road for miles. The Prossers recently conveyed a legal easement to Historic Landmarks Foundation of Indiana, which guarantees the exterior of the house and barn can never be changed.

"I've become obsessed with it never changing. Ever. Ever. Ever," says Walt, shouting out the words "never" and "ever." "It belongs to the ages so generations forever can see, touch, feel, and smell this place and get some sense what it was like in the 1870s."

Ted and Kim Reese

Historic Name: CASA DEL LAGO / DR. WILLIAM SCHOLL HOUSE

Town: LONG BEACH

County: LAPORTE

Date of Construction: 1928

Architectural Style: SPANISH ECLECTIC

After a long day at the office, Ted and Kim Reese usually sip wine in their living room overlooking Lake Michigan, admiring the Chicago skyline thirty-four miles to the north-west. Their front yard is a 280-foot–long stretch of white sandy beach, framed by the vast waters of the lake.

They don't have to stop at the liquor store on their way home, either. There are four thousand bottles of vintage wine in their climate-controlled, fifty-eight-degree wine cellar. Not a bad way to end the day.

"We enjoy it," says Ted, a chemical engineer and founder and president of the Michigan City–based Cadence Environmental Energy, which converts waste into energy to help power and reduce the emissions of forty-four cement kilns around the world. Kim is the company's business development director.

The four-story, eight-thousand-square-foot home was built in 1928 for Dr. William Scholl, who grew up on a LaPorte County farm and later made a vast fortune developing and marketing foot-care products. He called his summer estate *Casa del Lago*—"House by the Lake." Dr. Scholl, who never married, spent summers at Casa del Lago and the remaining seasons in residence at the Chicago Athletic Club.

After Dr. Scholl died in 1967, the house fell apart through years of neglect. In 1990 Ted bought it at a bankruptcy auction. His first thought was to demolish the top two floors and begin anew. Luckily, he realized the potential of the house and hired a Chicago architect to restore the estate, which is located in the unincorporated town of Long Beach in LaPorte County.

"It was the last chance to buy a significant piece of property on Lake Michigan," he says. "I also liked the idea of owning Dr. Scholl's house because of the similarities between us: He was a pioneer in his business and so am I in mine."

In July 1999, Ted and Kim invited more than eighty members of Dr. Scholl's family to the house for a celebration of the completed renovation. Grateful family members presented their hosts with a plaque and a photo of the world-famed foot doctor.

Ted grew up in Schenectady, New York. He graduated from Syracuse University in 1964, worked for Shell Chemical Company in New York City, and later developed more than twenty waste-to-energy recycling patents.

When he decided to start his company in 1975, he looked around the country for a good harbor for his fifty-three-foot racing sailboat, *The Cadence.* "Michigan City is one of the greatest harbors in the country," he says. After starting his company, he bought a house in Long Beach with his first wife and two children, a few blocks from the deteriorating Casa del Lago.

Kim is from Lancaster County, Pennsylvania, and graduated from Millersville University. She worked as an air traffic controller at Andrews Air Force Base outside Washington, D.C., frequently guiding the U.S. president's plane, Air Force One, to safe landings. After receiving her M.B.A. at Central Michigan University, she went to work for a cement company in Virginia. In 1991, by then divorced, Ted Reese hired her. Ted and Kim married in 2000.

"He was starting to be a confirmed bachelor like Dr. Scholl," Kim laughs.

Ted recently retired from competitive sailboat racing and now he and Kim cruise the Gulf of Mexico and the Great Lakes in one of their thirty-seven- and fifty-three-foot offshore power boats.

"I've been fascinated by boats since my Dad, a locomotive tester, took me fishing when I was two years old," says Ted. "I like the water, the sky. It's always changing and makes me keenly aware of everything. For us, this is the best home: on the water, a great comfortable house, and only seventy minutes from the third-largest city in the country, a city which I can see from the many windows facing the lake."

Vernay and Dotti Reindollar

Historic Name: MAYWOOD / SHADRACK WILBUR HOUSE

City: MADISON

County: JEFFERSON

Dates of Construction: CIRCA 1835 / CIRCA 1920

Architectural Style: GREEK REVIVAL

LISTED IN THE NATIONAL REGISTER OF HISTORIC PLACES, *Madison Historic District*

As a child, Dotti Inglis dreamed of one day living in the big house on Wilbur Point, high above the enchanted city of Madison with a commanding view of the beautiful Ohio River and the Kentucky hills to the south. It was one of Jefferson County's premier homes, a grand mansion built in the 1830s by riverboat and railroad tycoon Shadrack Wilbur and owned over the years by some of the town's leading citizens.

In the 1920s Drusilla Cravens—granddaughter of J. F. D. Lanier, a prominent Civil War–era banker—enlarged and remodeled the house. She added a Greek Revival roof, portico, and massive columns to the imposing home. That was the house Dotti Inglis admired, the shining mansion on the hill.

Dotti left Madison after graduating from the University of Cincinnati and moved to New York City to work at an advertising agency. In 1957 her father, John, suffered a stroke and she returned home to run the family drugstore on Main Street. It had been started by her grandfather in 1884 in Milton, Kentucky, and relocated across the river to Madison in 1910.

Dotti met Vernay (Vern) Reindollar at a dog obedience class and soon they were engaged. Dotti's friends George and Mildred May now owned the house on Wilbur Point and held an engagement party for Dotti and Vern. The Reindollars were married in 1960 and moved onto the grounds of the Madison State Hospital, a psychiatric institution, where Vern worked. Hardly the mansion on the

hill, but soon fate intervened: George May died and the house on Wilbur Point was for sale.

In 1966, the Reindollars bought the house, a nearby cottage, and thirty-three adjoining acres. They filled their home with family antiques, artwork, musical instruments, books, and a grand piano at each end of the double parlor. They raised four children in this house of music, books, and art. Much like previous occupants of the Wilbur Point house, Dotti became one of Madison's premier civic leaders, active in all manner of good causes, and a tireless crusader on behalf of historic preservation in Jefferson County. Among other things, she served five years on the city council and was a charter member of Historic Madison, a citizens organization formed in the 1960s to protect the town's architectural heritage. In the 1990s she was instrumental in protecting Eleutherian College, a National Historic Landmark building and Underground Railroad site in

nearby Lancaster. She was a tireless promoter of her community's rich heritage.

"I would do anything for Madison," she often said of her beloved river town.

In a stunningly cruel twist of fate, an electrical fire roared through Dotti and Vern's house on a cold night in January 2000. Dotti, known as the matriarch of Madison, a woman of incomparable grace and goodwill, suffered a heart attack while fleeing the inferno. She died at 3:00 A.M. on the frozen ground beside the burning mansion on the hill. She was seventy-one years old. Vern leaped from a second-floor window, fracturing his heel, but he survived.

"Everything was lost," says Vern a year later. The walnut and cherry family furniture, artwork, musical instruments, clothes, wedding pictures, books, Stephie the dog—thirty-five years of accumulated personal belongings, all gone. The mansion on the hill, the object of Dotti's childhood

dreams, the shining symbol of Madison's magnificence, was suddenly reduced to soggy, blackened ashes.

Vern moved to a rented home on another hill overlooking Madison and the great river of dreams. "My kids have a very strong attachment to that place," he says. "I don't know whether to rebuild or not."

The loss of Dotti was painful for the community. Though nothing but memories remain of Maywood, Dotti's efforts on behalf of her city will continue through the work of her countless friends. And her dedication to historic preservation and to her community will be remembered and honored each year by Historic Madison with the presentation of the Dorothy Inglis Reindollar Preservation Award.

Lamar and Jean Richcreek and Mary Sinnock

Historic Name: LAWRENCE GEORGE HOUSE

City: INDIANAPOLIS

County: MARION

Date of Construction: 1909

Architectural Style: ARTS AND CRAFTS

LISTED IN THE NATIONAL REGISTER OF HISTORIC PLACES, *Meridian Park Historic District*

Locating one of the first residents of the old home you just bought would certainly be a stroke of good fortune. When Lamar and Jean Richcreek met the elderly Mrs. Gardner, daughter of the man who built their home in 1909, she gave them a remarkable collection of photographs of its first years.

The three-story, seventeen-room Arts and Crafts–style home just north of Fall Creek and not far from downtown Indianapolis was designed and built by Lawrence George on the site of the nineteenth-century Osgood family farm. The George family and their African American maid, Addie, lived in the brick and stucco house for several years.

Addie accessed her bedroom via a back staircase from the kitchen. Her bedroom floor was rough pine. The floors in the rest of the house are oak. Addie's bedroom door had no lock or knob on the inside. The lock and knob were on the outside, controlled by Master George. On Addie's side

of the swinging kitchen door, the push plate was cheap metal. Mr. George's white hands pushed an elegant brass plate when entering the pine floor kitchen.

"Mr. George made a strong statement about class distinctions. Pretty obnoxious," notes Lamar, pointing out the original push plates, floors, and locks designed to remind Addie and Clarence, the chauffeur, of their subservient status.

Newlyweds Lamar and Jean and their longtime friend Mary Sinnock were in their early twenties in 1978 when they bought the expansive six-bedroom home with its Arts and Crafts interior of oak beam ceilings, brass light fixtures, and stained- and leaded-glass windows. The once-elegant neighborhood was in steep decline, the $30,000 price was right, and the extra bedrooms could be rented for extra income.

"We didn't want anything modern but we wanted a large home with a fireplace," says Lamar, a leader in the successful

effort to revitalize the stately neighborhood, now designated the Meridian Park Historic District.

Lamar, formerly a banker, is now a much happier professor of fine art photography at the Herron School of Art. Jean is a utility company executive and Mary, a social worker. "Our model was an alternative family," explains Jean. "We knew none of us wanted kids but we wanted a sense of family. It's worked out for almost twenty-five years."

Mrs. Gardner's classic photographs allowed them to nearly duplicate the 1909 interior. They bought similar Mission-style furniture and positioned it as shown in the pictures. They placed china plates on the wooden wall rail and a round table and a china cabinet in the dining room, all similar in shape and style to the Lawrences' original furnishings. Turn-of-the-century landscape paintings by Hoosier artists hang on the walls.

"We wanted to learn about the culture and style of the era and re-create what it looked like in 1909," says Lamar. "Those photographs were our guide, getting us interested in the era and Arts and Crafts furnishings and learning to respect the history and integrity of the house."

The photographs also show neighbors in turn-of-the-century clothing strolling down the sidewalks, proudly posing before their early–twentieth-century automobiles, and relaxing on the long front porches, fanning themselves in the summer heat, as Addie and Clarence stand at attention.

"We use the front porch to know our neighbors. We wave and talk at people walking down the street," says Lamar. "You move into an old house and you become interested in the history and it changes you."

Frank Ricketts and Gregory Bales

Historic Name: OLIVER KEELY HOUSE

City: INDIANAPOLIS

County: MARION

Date of Construction: CIRCA 1865 / 1991

Architectural Style: GABLE-FRONT

LISTED IN THE NATIONAL REGISTER OF HISTORIC PLACES, *Lockerbie Square Historic District*

The Lockerbie Square Historic District reveals what an American neighborhood can look like when it resists the tendency to adopt suburban qualities of homogeneity and commercial franchise encroachment.

Which is why Greg Bales and Frank Ricketts live in Lockerbie, roughly a six-square-block protected neighborhood just east of downtown Indianapolis, where "modern" buildings, fast food franchises, and billboards aren't allowed. It is a tranquil neighborhood dominated by shade trees, narrow streets, picket fences, brick sidewalks, and a variety of mid–nineteenth-century architectural styles–right on the edge of downtown.

"We wanted to live in something distinct and alive in a real downtown urban area," explains Greg, a retired hotel manager. Greg collects Limoges china eggs, painted vases, and little boxes, which he displays throughout the house with other delicate family artifacts, such as his grandmother Katherine Shipley's peacock feather opera fan. In 1991 Greg and Frank bought a tiny one-and-a-half-story, cottage-style home built circa 1865 by contractor and fireplace dealer Oliver Keely. They doubled the size of the house, adding a second bedroom, bathroom, two-car garage, office, and arbor. They followed strict guidelines set forth by the Indianapolis Historic Preservation Commission, which must approve every construction detail, right down to the color of paint and species of plants, shrubs, and trees.

"Lockerbie is a little-changed world within a changing world," says Frank, a men's fragrance salesman, volunteer director of the Miss North Central Indiana beauty pageant,

and the bass soloist for the Broadway United Methodist Church.

"My life consists of three things," says Frank, the son of an Indianapolis minister and 1981 Butler University graduate. "Miss America, Aramis [the men's fragrance], and my church." Frank collects antique Miss America dolls and has been to nine Miss America pageants.

"My goal is to coach Indiana's first Miss America," he says. "Greg is Mr. Green Thumb." Greg, a 1970 graduate of Ohio University, is a devoted gardener, filling the small yard with plants, flowers, and shrubs that bloom from April to October.

The neighborhood, first platted in 1821 by Janet and Thomas McQuat, blossomed during the Civil War as German immigrants poured into the city and built homes. It thrived through the turn of the century and served as home to many of Indianapolis's early luminaries, including the famed Hoosier poet James Whitcomb Riley, who lived at 528 Lockerbie Street. Following World War I, the neighborhood entered a long period of steep decline.

Faced with losing the whole neighborhood to slumlords, decay, and demolition, the city of Indianapolis formed the Indianapolis Historic Preservation Commission to assist in protecting the unique charm of this and other historic neighborhoods and to enforce design guidelines. Lockerbie residents chose strict guidelines, and now it's one of the most desirable and costly neighborhoods within Center Township and home to about twelve hundred residents, including Frank and Gregory.

"We're proud to say we live in Lockerbie," says Frank.

Joe and Judy Rohleder

Historic Name: THE GREEN TREE HOTEL / JOHN AND MARGARETHA OPEL HOUSE

City: JASPER

County: DUBOIS

Date of Construction: CIRCA 1858

Architectural Style: FEDERAL

LISTED IN THE NATIONAL REGISTER OF HISTORIC PLACES

Judy Rohleder's mother was not pleased with her daughter's new home. "My God, Judy, don't buy this house," she gasped. Then she sat on the back porch and cried a while. Judy and Joe Rohleder bought it anyway. They'd been haggling with the owners for seven years to buy the crumbling house known as The Green Tree Hotel.

"We bought four brick walls," says Judy. The house has an enormous second-floor ballroom and a barrel-shaped, stone wine cellar. It was built around 1858 by John and Margaretha Opel southeast of Jasper in Dubois County.

The hotel served travelers and farmers hauling grain and driving cattle to the port town of Troy on the Ohio River. The German-born Opels and their six children lived on one side of the house, while renting sleeping space and serving food, beer, and wine in the other half. Many fine parties were held in the spacious ballroom, including the annual Fourth of July dance and an 1864 banquet honoring Civil War veterans from the local regiment.

The Rohleders bought it in 1977 and spent the next seven years renovating the grand old building and getting

it listed in the National Register of Historic Places. "We quit everything we were involved in—golf, tennis, everything—and focused on nothing but this house. Good thing we had our slaves back then to help us," Judy says, referring to her three children. "We worked the kids hard," adds Joe. "We lived in the big parlor and ate off a hot plate the first year we lived here. The kids couldn't wait to leave home for college."

At the time, Joe taught biology and coached football and wrestling at Jasper High School. Judy was a surgical nurse but later quit to raise the children and buy and renovate three historic structures in nearby Huntingburg, including The Ideal Hotel building. "We can't stand to see things torn down, so we buy 'em and fix and rent 'em out," says Judy, who runs Green Tree Antiques in one of her renovated Huntingburg buildings.

The Green Tree home is a Dubois County cultural treasure because of the unusual ballroom with its rare and intricate floor-to-ceiling stencils as well as the curved stone cellar that remains a constant fifty-eight degrees even in the steamy summer heat. In keeping with the German wine-making tradition of southern Indiana, Joe now brews and bottles his own brand of wine in the cellar. "It's very strong and not very good," he says.

Joe retired in 1999 after thirty-one years of teaching and coaching at the high school. He now sells textbooks part-time and recently re-sided a long chicken coop on the Green Tree property with old barn wood. He made a path between the house and the converted chicken coop using old stone grinding wheels. "I appreciate them every time I walk on them," he says. "If they were just stacked somewhere, you couldn't appreciate them as well."

In 1982, Joe heard that the owner of an 1830 two-story log barn near Beaver City was about to tear it down. He bought it for $125, took it apart, numbered the logs, and reassembled it near the Green Tree house. "I won't tell you how much that $125 barn has cost us," he says. The Green Tree property, which once covered hundreds of acres of farmland, had dwindled to five by the time the Rohleders bought it. A subdivision borders their property on the north side, a furniture factory on the south, and a combination pizza/fried chicken–mini-mart–convenience store is down the hill and across the road. The new America is taking over, even in Dubois County along the old Troy Road, where weary travelers once spent the night in The Green Tree Hotel.

"The good news is they'll never touch this place," says Judy. "And Mother finally quit crying."

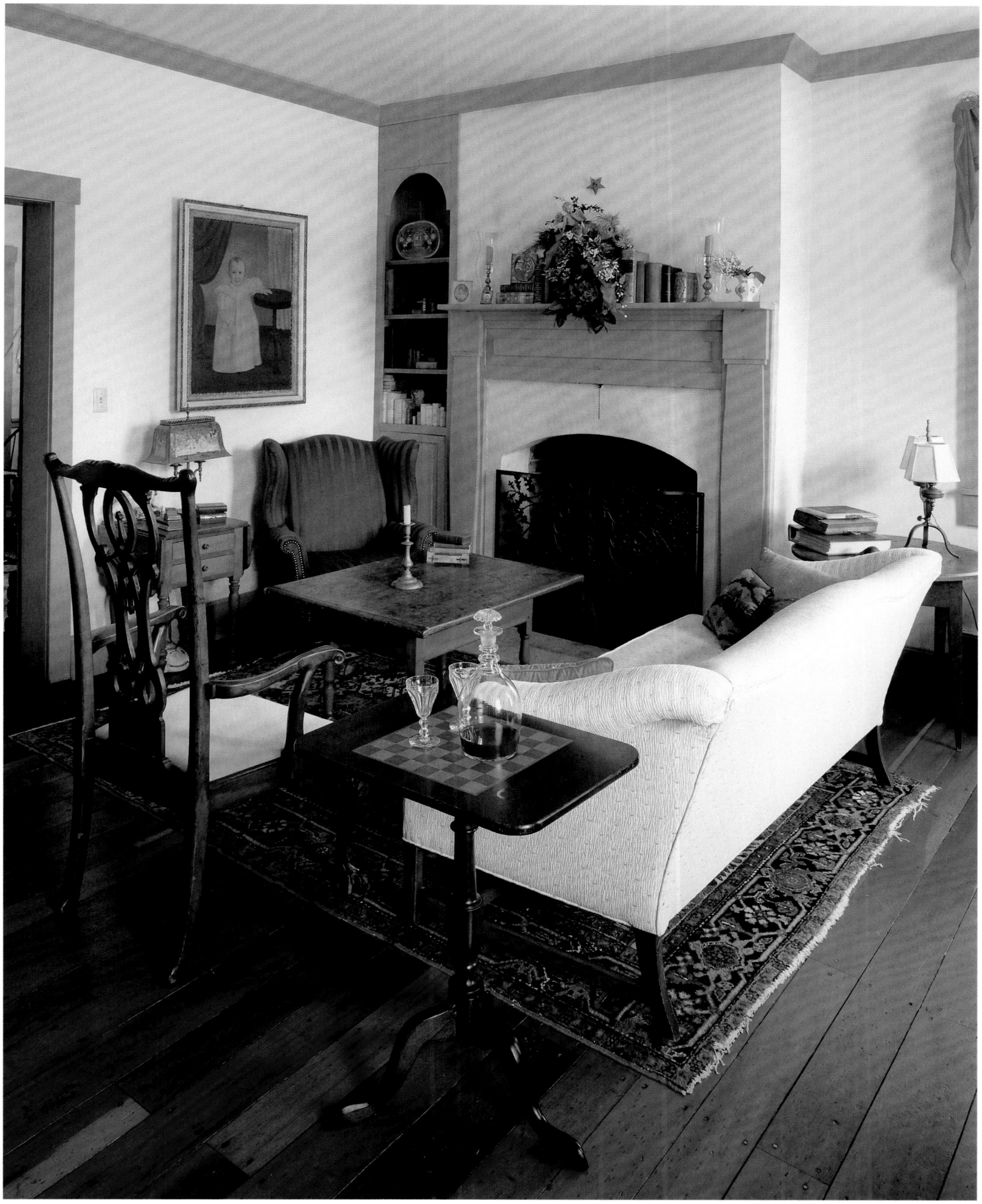

Kenneth and Barbara Russell

Historic Name: JAMES ALVERSON HOUSE

Town: CARP

County: OWEN

Date of Construction: 1838

Architectural Style: GREEK REVIVAL

Southern California natives Kenny and Barbara Russell had never lived in Indiana and had certainly never heard of Carp, a tiny Owen County settlement along U.S. 231, ten miles north of Spencer. So naturally they decided to move there. To Carp, where the post office closed in 1904 for lack of residents.

Kenny's father, Earl, was born in Franklin and migrated to California in the 1920s to work in the oil fields. Kenny and Barbara met in 1942 in high school in Fullerton, California, and married on October 29, 1948. Kenny worked in the post office after serving as a cook in the navy during World War II. Barbara was a spot welder. They have four children.

In 1978, they decided their jobs were boring and southern California had become a nerve-wracking, overdeveloped mess of malls, subdivisions, and crazy people. "We were fifty and decided it was time to retire and have fun," says

Barbara. Kenny still had cousins in Johnson County and asked them to look for an old farmhouse anywhere between U.S. 40 and the Ohio River. The Russells spent a month in southern Indiana, scouting the cousins' recommendations, which led them to Owen County, one of the least-populated counties in the state with a mere sixteen thousand people spread over 386 square miles. Just what Kenny wanted. Then he saw the house in Carp.

"As soon as we drove up the driveway Kenny said, 'This is it,'" recalls Barbara of their first glimpse of the 1838 Greek Revival farmhouse overlooking a big pond and cornfields rolling to the horizon. "I loved the fireplace in the kitchen and Kenny loved the whole thing. Period."

When Kenny was a kid, his grandmother gave him an old cup and saucer, which triggered a lifelong interest in antiques. The Russells spent their honeymoon in Mexico visiting antique shops. After moving into the house in Carp, Kenny began buying antiques for fun. He furnished the house but kept buying and soon the garage was filled with antiques. Pretty soon he decided to open an antique shop in the garage. He stuck a sign in the front yard proclaiming Russell's Plantation House Antiques was open for business.

Kenny had never been happier, buying and selling high-quality antiques, swapping stories with his customers, laughing, joking, and proudly showing off the big brick house. Between customers, he sat at his easel in the backyard and painted birds, wildlife, and the sweeping rural landscape. It sure beat southern California and the monotonous old post office job, Kenny told visitors.

"The first years here we just played. We did everything together and had fun. Kenny had his antique shop and I'd fish in the pond," recalls Barbara. "Our first year here in 1978 we had that big blizzard and we laughed and played in the snow and pulled each other around in a sled."

Kenny's primitive and Victorian antiques were soon drawing buyers from Ohio, Kentucky, and Tennessee. He built a sixteen-hundred-square-foot addition on the back of the house to handle the booming business. Even so, the antique shop never made much money.

"Kenny, he just loved this big old house and talking to people about antiques," says Barbara. "Fun was always the point with Kenny. Never money."

When they fled California their children thought them crazy. Mom and Dad at age fifty, moving to a godforsaken place called Carp to live in a 140-year-old house because it sounded like fun. Come on! Well, it worked just as they planned, until Kenny had a heart attack. He died on August 7, 2000.

"He was running the shop and having fun right up until he died," says Barbara. "It was an ideal life. Quiet, peaceful, and fun, just like we wanted."

Greg and Judy Rust

City: GREENSBURG

County: DECATUR

Date of Construction: 1917

Architectural Style: CRAFTSMAN BUNGALOW

"My first thought when I moved in was, 'Let's sell the house,'" recalls Judy Rust. "It was a single guy's house. Very depressing and I couldn't see any redeeming features."

On that positive note, Judy and Greg began their marriage in 1989 on busy Michigan Avenue in Greensburg, not far from the Decatur County Courthouse, which has a tree growing in the tower. Greg, a stockbroker and financial planner, had four children from a previous marriage and Judy had a little girl, all of them younger than twelve years old. Within a year they had yet another child together. The 1917 stucco bungalow had only one bathtub and two toilets, creating daily bathroom traffic jams for the two adults and six kids.

Greg bought the house in 1976 because he needed something to live in. It qualified. It had a roof, floors, walls, and wasn't falling down or leaking. With Judy's 1989 arrival,

they struggled and debated for a couple of years, unsure what to do. In 1992, the elderly couple who lived next door died and the Rusts bought their dilapidated house, which was in such disrepair that mushrooms grew from the living room floor, watered by the leaking roof. They salvaged the marble fireplace and stained-glass windows and tore the rest down, giving them space to expand their house by adding bathrooms and a solarium, and enlarging the kitchen.

"Then we started obsessing; we're both very compulsive people," says Judy. "We wanted the addition to look seamless on the outside, so then we thought why not on the inside, too? One thing led to another, then another, and another."

They obsessively and compulsively restored the house inside and out, spending weekends scouring salvage yards in Indianapolis, Louisville, Cincinnati, and Chicago for

the appropriate brass light fixtures, bathroom faucets, furniture, artwork, and marble countertops that replaced the avocado- and orange-colored plastic junk in the kitchen.

"We wanted stuff that looked like the house," says Greg.

They bought a 1923 six-burner Clark-Jewell gas stove for the huge kitchen, which became the hub of social activity for the herd of kids and their friends.

"We wanted a child-friendly house. Now there's room for all the kids when they come home," says Judy.

"The intensity peaked and stayed at a high level," says Greg, a 1966 University of Notre Dame graduate, whose father, Oskar D. Rust, was the longtime and well-known owner of a variety store on the courthouse square that was called The Fair Store. Judy, an Indiana University graduate and volunteer science teacher, filled the new solarium with her collection of sea shells, animal bones, rocks, nests, and stuffed birds.

They refuse to air-condition the restored house because the required vents would mar the character and integrity of the interior and that, of course, would never do. On hot summer evenings, they eat on the big back porch overlooking Judy's extensive flower gardens. They don't even own a television. They did, but a couple of years ago it blew up.

"Like good Americans we dutifully ran out to buy one, couldn't find what we wanted right away, and noticed the kids had started reading at night," says Greg. "We decided we didn't need one."

Judy, who in 1989 found her new home depressing and without any redeeming qualities, is now president of the Decatur County Alliance for Preservation.

"The house changed us," she says.

Mike Sanders and Shari Rodriguez

Historic Name: WILLIAM BARNETT HOUSE

City: DELPHI

County: CARROLL

Date of Construction: 1857

Architectural Style: GREEK REVIVAL / ITALIANATE

LISTED IN THE NATIONAL REGISTER OF HISTORIC PLACES

One of the most interesting stories of how people got their house has to be that of Mike Sanders and his wife, Shari Rodriguez, of Delphi in Carroll County. Mike and Shari work at Purdue University in Lafayette, twenty miles southwest of Delphi. Mike is the director of undergraduate programs at the Krannert School of Management and Shari is development director in the mechanical engineering department.

In 1993, after nine years living in Lafayette and battling its seemingly endless street reconstruction and daily traffic snarls, they began looking for an old house in Delphi. Mike had previously lived and taught school in Delphi and had admired the William Barnett house, which was listed in the National Register of Historic Places.

When it was listed for sale, Mike and Shari got into a bidding war with Earl and Vera Johnson, retirees from Valparaiso. The Johnsons won.

"We were devastated when the deal fell through," recalls Mike. "I never wanted anything so bad." He phoned the Johnsons before they moved in to ask if they had changed their minds. No, they hadn't. Well, said Mike, please call us first if you ever want to sell. "We'll buy it in a second. I have very strong feelings about one day living in the house," Mike told Earl, who seemed unusually receptive.

A few days later, a grief-stricken Vera called to tell Mike that Earl woke up that morning and died. Did they still want to buy the house? They did.

"I'm not very spiritual but the spirits were working that day," says Mike. Shortly after Earl's funeral, Mike and Shari bought the house, one of downtown Delphi's premier historic residences. While on a whistle-stop train trip across the country, Franklin Roosevelt stopped by for tea when the house was owned by powerful state Democrat and Delphi newspaper publisher Henry B. Wilson.

The table where Roosevelt sipped tea has stayed with the house. "The rule was, you buy the house, you buy the table, which was fine," says Mike, although how could you ever prove Roosevelt used it? Who cares, it's a good story, part of the folklore and history of the house.

William Barnett, the man who built the house, was a prosperous merchant who shipped goods up and down the old Wabash and Erie Canal during its brief heyday. Barnett was later elected mayor of Delphi.

Since the house has historically served as a focal point of civic activity, Mike chose to carry on the tradition and served one term on the Delphi City Council. "I like public service but I don't like politics so I didn't run again," he says.

They have opened their home to civic historic-preservation groups and for Purdue alumni receptions, again in keeping with its long tradition. "We always felt like it had been a prominent public house and we want to keep that tradition alive," Mike explains. They even host meetings of the Oracle Club, a Delphi literary society that began in the nineteenth century. Mike, Shari, and neighbors organized the Delphi Preservation Society in the Barnett house living room. They often bring Purdue students over and attempt, usually without much success, to interest them in the home's history.

"I explain the wonder of it all, how it was built without power tools, before time zones, before the Civil War, that Franklin Roosevelt ate here, and all that. Most of them can't grasp it, they just look at you," says Mike, who still marvels at the sad and unusual circumstance that brought them into the house. Fate and spirits, he supposes.

"We were meant to be in this house and I sensed it that day I spoke with Mr. Johnson," he says. "Some things are beyond understanding."

Donald and Pamela Schmidt

Historic Name: JAMES KEENAN HOUSE
City: FORT WAYNE
County: ALLEN
Date of Construction: CIRCA 1917
Architectural Style: COLONIAL REVIVAL

When Fort Wayne hotel owner and poker player James Keenan built his spacious brick home in the Forest Park neighborhood around 1917, his wife insisted on a purple sink, toilet, and bathtub in her upstairs bathroom. She also demanded heavy red velvet drapes on the parlor windows and doorways and an extra tall closet to accommodate her ball gowns.

Helen Keenan ordered the purple bathroom fixtures because she liked purple. She insisted on the heavy velvet drapes to block the sounds of her husband's late-night poker parties.

"We got rid of the red velvet," says the home's current owner Pam Schmidt. "We kept the purple bathroom because it is so distinctive and original to the house. Don keeps his referee uniforms in the ball-gown closet. Refereeing is the single most passionate thing in his life."

Don is a longtime high school football referee and professor of mechanical engineering at Indiana University–Purdue University at Fort Wayne. He's also president of the Fort Wayne City Council. He was first elected to the council in 1971, five years after marrying Pam, an elementary school teacher.

They bought the Keenan house in 1977 because they had two young boys and were enchanted with the peaceful Forest Park neighborhood, its magnificent trees and wide boulevard. "The kids could play baseball in the boulevard and we didn't have to worry about them," says Pam.

The neighborhood was developed in 1913 by Louis Curdes on the site of the former Fort Wayne Trotting Association track, just north of downtown. The original fifty-six large lots soon became home to many of the city's prominent families, including James Keenan, who owned the

Keenan Hotel and annoyed Helen with his poker parties. The Keenan Hotel has long since been demolished.

The Keenan home, however, now houses Don's collection of Hoosier sheet music. He's a trumpet player and former member of the Purdue University marching band. Pam collects black iron cooking utensils, baskets, and heat register grates that she salvages from abandoned and demolished buildings. In the front and back yards they've placed old Fort Wayne street lamps, one of which illuminates the grave of Rommel, their eighteen-year-old dachshund who died in 1994.

In another corner of the yard is the gravestone of America Boyer who was two years and three months old when she died on February 21, 1854, near Logansport. Pam found the headstone in a ditch after the pioneer cemetery was destroyed by the State Highway Department in the 1970s. "At least America Boyer gets some respect here," says Pam.

Pam, born in Detroit, was raised in Murray, Kentucky, a couple of months after her father, Billy Atkins, died in the 1944 Allied invasion of Normandy Beach during World War II. He was nineteen years old and his wife, Ruby, was sixteen. Pam has two framed pictures of her father, one taken when he was an infant, the other in his army uniform, snapped weeks before his death. "It's very sad," she comments. "He's my father but he died before I was born."

Pam is chairman of the Fort Wayne Historic Preservation Review Board, appointed by the mayor. The Schmidts chose not to air-condition their house because it would require reconfiguring the exterior window frames.

"We've done a lot of interior remodeling because you have to live in a home and adapt it to fit your family, but we feel the exterior should never be altered or compromised," says Pam.

Tim and Meg Shelly

Historic Name: CONN MANSION

City: ELKHART

County: ELKHART

Dates of Construction: 1874 / CIRCA 1910

Architectural Style: NEO-CLASSICAL

Colonel Charles G. Conn claimed he was punched in the mouth in a fight with fellow soldiers during the Civil War. The punch mangled his lips, which made it difficult to blow his small brass trumpet, called a cornet. Charles played the cornet when his unit marched into battle. To ease his sore lips, he devised a more comfortable, rubberized mouthpiece. Following the Civil War, he began manufacturing brass horns with rubberized mouthpieces in Elkhart. School bands throughout the country were soon buying millions of Conn brass instruments with rubberized mouthpieces.

That, at least, was the story Charles told when explaining the origin of the wildly successful Conn Instrument Company, which later became the largest band instrument manufacturer in the world. Charles was a notorious showman and self-promoter, so who knows if the busted-lip story is true, but there is no doubt that his success spawned dozens of other musical instrument–related businesses in Elkhart. By the middle of the twentieth century Elkhart proclaimed itself the "band instrument capital of the world."

Around 1910, Charles bought what was then the largest home in Elkhart. It was built in 1874 by banker Samuel Strong who even named the street after himself. Charles

Pringles, the uniformly shaped potato chip in a tube. Tim grew up in Bloomington, met Meg at DePauw, graduated from the College of William and Mary Law School in Virginia in 1985, and was thrilled to be invited to join an Elkhart law firm.

"My grandfather was from Elkhart and I wanted to come home," says Tim, an appointed member of the Elkhart Historic and Cultural Preservation Commission.

The expansive thirty-nine-hundred-square-foot house with wraparound first- and second-floor porches remains an Elkhart curiosity. "We get a lot of people stopping by to take pictures or ask if we have rooms for rent," says Tim, who, despite the nearly non-stop, year-round maintenance the grand old riverboat-looking house requires, still finds it awe-inspiring. A couple of years ago an enormous tree snapped in a windstorm and crashed into the sturdy roof, yet did almost no damage. Such a tree would have reduced a new home to splinters, he marveled.

In 1884, Colonel Conn commissioned a portrait of himself in his Civil War uniform. Somehow it wound up in the Masonic Hall. When the Masons vacated the building after a fire, they offered the portrait to the Shellys who display it in the parlor.

"He belongs here," says Meg.

promptly remodeled the Strong house on Strong Street, adding sixteen two-story-tall wood-and-plaster pillars topped by three-foot, six-hundred-pound capitals. The enormous house where Charles reportedly entertained John Philip Sousa soon looked like a landlocked Mississippi riverboat. His ego and flair for the dramatic was boundless.

After Charles's death, the house passed through a series of owners and by 1992 was occupied by an antique dealer and his mother-in-law who wanted to sell it. Several interested parties hoped to turn it into a boardinghouse. Attorney Tim Shelly and his wife, Meg, a high school teacher, often admired the house on their walks through the neighborhood. If it became a boardinghouse, it would slowly slide toward ruin, Tim and Meg concluded. So on New Year's Eve, 1992, they bought it.

They had also needed a bigger house and yard for their two little boys.

"We needed more space and boy we got it," says Meg, a DePauw University graduate who grew up in Cincinnati. Her father, a chemical engineer at Procter & Gamble, invented

Randall T. Shepard and Amy MacDonell

Historic Name: HENDRICKSON-LANDERS HOUSE

City: INDIANAPOLIS

County: MARION

Date of Construction: 1925

Architect: FREDERICK WALLICK

Architectural Style: COLONIAL REVIVAL

LISTED IN THE NATIONAL REGISTER OF HISTORIC PLACES, *Golden Hill Historic District*

In the first years of the twentieth century an ad appeared in the Indianapolis newspapers promoting a new neighborhood on the scenic bluffs overlooking White River. A neighborhood of curving streets, enormous trees, and elegant homes just two miles northwest of soot-choked downtown Indianapolis.

"Living In Golden Hill Will Be Like Living In A Park," proclaimed the promotional material. And it was true, despite being written by a real estate developer. And it remains true today, which is why Randall Shepard and his wife, Amy MacDonell, left the far busier North Meridian Street for the peacefulness and limited traffic of secluded Golden Hill.

"We got tired of the sound of suburban commuter traffic on Meridian Street," says Amy, the former director of Indiana's Main Street program.

"Living in Golden Hill is like living in heaven," she adds. "I'm at work in ten minutes," says Shepard, chief justice of the Indiana Supreme Court, an Evansville native, and a passionate student of Indiana history.

Buggy-maker David Parry bought the Golden Hill land around 1900 and built a fifty-six-acre estate for himself. When he died in 1915, his family hired landscape architect George MacDougall to subdivide the land and design a neighborhood for fifty-four homes. The Shepards bought the neighborhood's eleventh house. The three-story, five-

bedroom Colonial Revival house was built in 1925 by the Hendrickson family, who sold it in 1930 to insurance agent Fisk Landers and his wife, Mary Louise, an ardent gardener. The Shepards bought the house with shutters that really work in 1996 from the Landers estate.

The neighborhood is so well hidden that few people in Indianapolis know it exists, tucked in the trees south of 38th Street and west of Michigan Road (U.S. 421). Residents hold an annual dinner, a Christmas party, and a Fourth of July gathering on the site of a legendary thirty-foot-tall Alaskan Indian totem pole which isn't there anymore. David Parry secured the totem from the 1905 World's Fair and installed it near his estate. It blew down during a storm in the 1940s and disappeared. Now a historical marker on Totem Lane marks the spot where the fabled totem once stood, and a re-creation of the Golden Hill totem pole stands in the Eiteljorg Museum of American Indian and Western Art in Indianapolis.

"We can probably call forty of the fifty-four homeowners here by their first name," says Shepard, who graduated from Princeton University and Yale University Law School and was appointed to the Indiana Supreme Court in 1985.

"It works like an old-fashioned neighborhood, people take walks at night and visit," says the chief justice, merrily strolling past the period revival–style homes down the winding, tree-lined streets, where their daughter, Margaret, happily plays on her scooter.

In keeping with the history of the house, they restored Mrs. Landers's beloved gardens, rebuilding the flowerbeds with the original bricks and planting two hundred pots of perennials in the first summer. The house is furnished with Shepard and MacDonell family heirlooms, although the stately dining room ensemble consists largely of the Landers's furniture, which was purchased from the estate. The room

does not have an overhead chandelier because Mrs. Landers believed in formal, candlelight dining beside the fireplace, a respectable tradition that is continued by the Shepards.

"I can't imagine living in a new house," says Amy, a banker's daughter who grew up in another 1920s Colonial Revival house, in Lima, Ohio. "Old houses have good, strong bones."

John and Janet Simmermaker

Historic Name: DR. GEORGE W. THOMPSON HOUSE

City: WINAMAC

County: PULASKI

Date of Construction: 1897

Architectural Style: QUEEN ANNE

LISTED IN THE NATIONAL REGISTER OF HISTORIC PLACES

In 1970 Florence Simmermaker of Star City in Pulaski County began burning her possessions—furniture, family photographs, and personal belongings. Florence was tough, stubborn, and ninety-eight years old. She told her family she didn't want her stuff sold or tossed into the dump after her death. Why she thought that would happen, no one knows.

The family finally halted Grandma's burning binge. One item saved from the fires was Grandma's coverlet, which she kept draped over a fainting couch in the parlor. She gave it to her grandson John. A coverlet is an early–nineteenth-century term for bedspread. They were hand-woven of wool or cotton on jacquard looms between 1830 and

1860, usually by European immigrants. Mechanization rendered the jacquard loom and the weavers obsolete.

John Simmermaker has since accumulated more than four hundred coverlets, the largest collection in Indiana. His daughter, Jill King, lives in a Cambridge City house that John inherited from Pauline Montgomery, who wrote a book in 1974 called *Indiana Coverlet Weavers and Their Coverlets.* If you ask John about coverlets, be prepared for a highly informed, detailed answer.

The prized coverlets are stored in John and Janet's Winamac home, which was built in 1897 by Dr. George W. Thompson. The local newspaper called Dr. Thompson's new house "the most modern and complete dwelling house in the County." It had flush toilets and running water at a time when everyone else used buckets and outhouses.

John and Janet were living in Star City in 1975 when the schools closed and were consolidated into a countywide system. Their five children were transferred seven miles north to the Winamac schools, so the family moved. "I'd always had my eye on this house, never dreaming we'd own it," says Janet, a chronic collector of punched-paper needlework samplers, old grocery store signs, antique children's toys, black wrought-iron fences, early–twentieth-century Wils Berry Hoosier landscape paintings, and other items too numerous to mention.

"She gave me a big hug when we bought the house, so that made it worth it," says John. "I love the house because Janet loves the house."

John was a production manager at a rubber-bushing factory before retiring in 1993. John and Janet lived next door to each other in Star City and got married in 1955. Their children's names, like theirs, all begin with J and they aren't sure why. "Easier, I guess," supposes John.

Being self-described compulsive collectors, they quickly filled up the house. Then the two-story brick carriage house filled to the ceiling. It contains old tables, chairs, five hundred feet of black wrought-iron fencing, and a 1923 Studebaker, among other things ranging from basketball hoops to bridles, harnesses, and anything with the name Parker on it. Janet's maiden name was Parker. She also collects Parker pens.

"We never sell anything," says John. "That's our problem." In 1999, an 1874 house two blocks away was for sale. The black wrought-iron fence around the large corner

lot caught Janet's eye. The Simmermakers bought the property. Their daughter, Jolie, now lives in the enormous house. She collects turn-of-the-twentieth-century silver souvenir spoons.

"We're all nuts," laughs Jolie, an Indiana University graduate.

"We were afraid someone would tear it down or put vinyl siding on it," says Janet. "I also like the wrought-iron fence and it gave us another place to store our stuff." They also own two Pulaski County farms and their old house in Star City.

"We haven't led a boring life. Put it that way," laughs John. "Boy, do we have fun. I guess we need to sell some of this stuff."

Suzanne Skaggs and Peter Lessaris

City: MADISON

County: JEFFERSON

Date of Construction: 1838

Architectural Style: FEDERAL

LISTED IN THE NATIONAL REGISTER OF HISTORIC PLACES, *Madison Historic District*

What a wonderful retirement idea, thought Suzanne Skaggs and Peter Lessaris. Move to beautiful Madison on the Ohio River, buy two adjoining row houses, operate a small bed-and-breakfast, and entertain travelers who shared their enthusiasm for Madison's stunning architecture and rich riverfront history.

Suzanne and Peter pursued that idea in 1992 when they retired to Madison from Champaign, Illinois, and bought two of the three units in an 1838 row house on East Main Street. Suzanne was an interior designer and had worked at the University of Illinois Performing Arts Center. Peter and his two brothers had operated a family-owned chain of twelve Top Boy drive-in restaurants in central Illinois since 1958.

"I had an itchy feeling to leave the flat farmland and live in rolling country," says Suzanne. Years earlier, Suzanne's mother had visited Madison and spoken highly of its hills and bluffs, the beauty of the great river, and the restored historic homes that lined its streets. Suzanne's interior design skills and Peter's years in the restaurant business were well suited to operating a bed-and-breakfast. They called it the Federal Inn and, boy, what a mistake.

"We were worried we'd be retired with nothing to do," explains Suzanne. "A bed-and-breakfast sounded good. We romanticized about people staying with us who'd come to Madison to explore the architecture and history. We couldn't have been more wrong." Most of the guests were only interested in "antiquing," complaining about the lack of fast food franchises, and wondering where the nearest Wal-Mart could be found.

"We looked at each other and said, 'What are we doing?'" recalls Suzanne. They closed the Federal Inn in 1999,

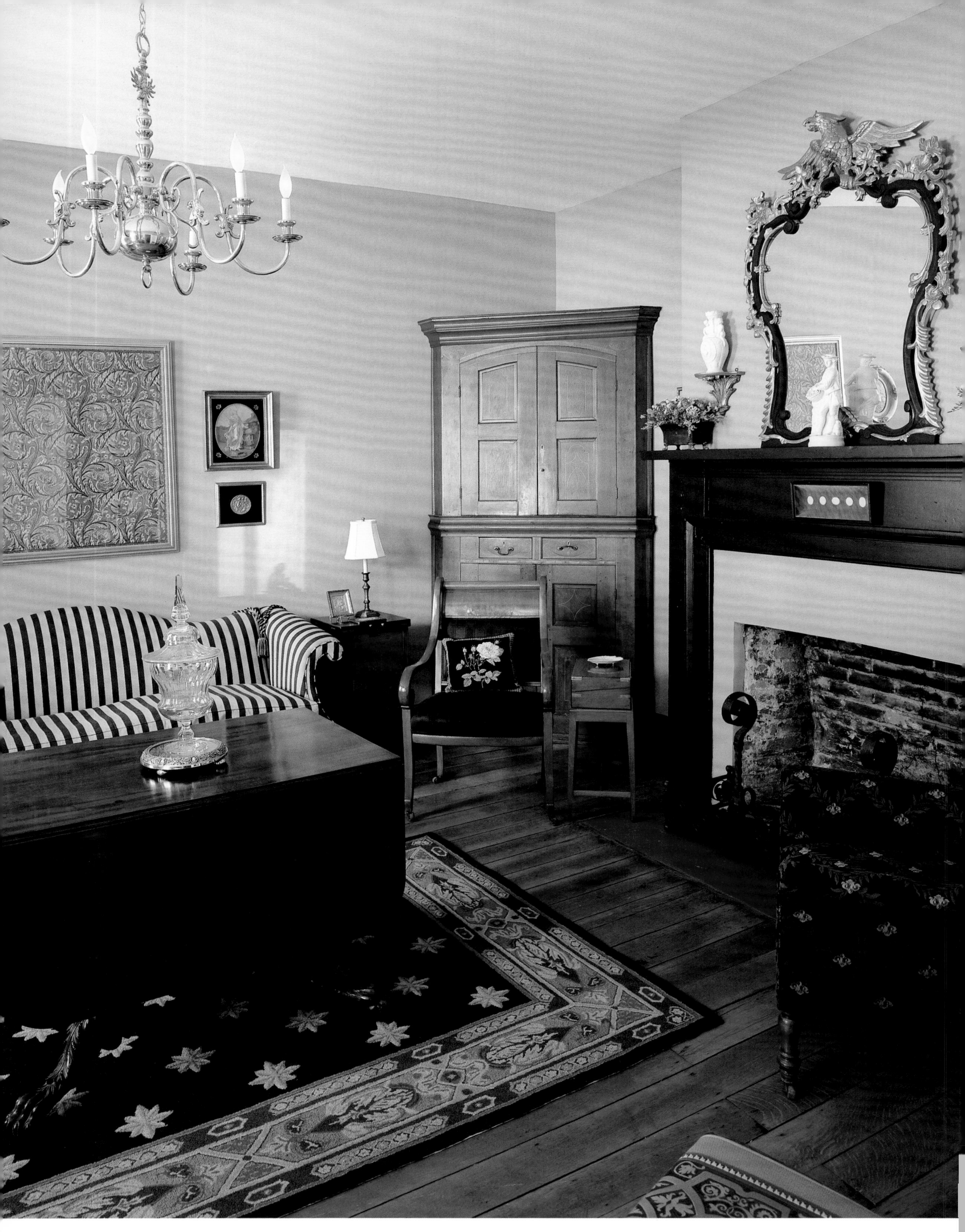

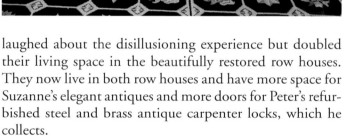

laughed about the disillusioning experience but doubled their living space in the beautifully restored row houses. They now live in both row houses and have more space for Suzanne's elegant antiques and more doors for Peter's refurbished steel and brass antique carpenter locks, which he collects.

"I've learned a lot about locks," says Peter. "Some of the leaf springs are 150 years old."

To keep busy, they diligently monitor the actions of the Madison City Council and the Historic Board of Review, which are supposed to enforce the local preservation ordinance throughout the 131-block historic district.

Outspoken Suzanne and fellow members of the Cornerstone Society, a local preservation organization, point out that officials too often ignore preservation guidelines and, among other things, allow vinyl siding to be nailed to historically significant homes.

"You whittle away at the architecture of this town and pretty soon, the very thing that makes Madison attractive will be gone," warns Suzanne. "The bankers and realtors have wormed their way onto the historic boards and you know what that means?" It means the money-changers are vinyl-siding the temple.

While Suzanne fumes about the temple invasion, Peter marvels at the mysteries and wonders of little, easily overlooked things, like lock leaf springs that still work after 150 years and a turnip carved into the basement stone foundation on October 4, 1838, by a construction worker.

"It's fascinating to think that 130 years ago some guy might have stood on this very floor and yelled to his wife that Lincoln had been shot," says Peter. "I'm pleased I followed Suzanne over here."

Don Smith

Historic Name: ISAAC P. SMITH HOUSE

City: NEW ALBANY

County: FLOYD

Date of Construction: CIRCA 1848

Architectural Style: GREEK REVIVAL

LISTED IN THE NATIONAL REGISTER OF HISTORIC PLACES, *Mansion Row Historic District*

In the 1850s New Albany was Indiana's largest city, a bustling port on the Ohio River known as the steamboat-building capital of the country. Between 1817 and 1867, the golden years of riverboat traffic, New Albany shipyards built over 350 steamboats.

Great fortunes were made in the years preceding the Civil War and general contractor Isaac P. Smith built dozens of homes, churches, and civic buildings for the prosperous community. Around 1848, he also built a fine home for himself overlooking the river in what is now known as the Mansion Row Historic District.

Shipbuilding in New Albany ended with the coming of the railroads during the Civil War and the city underwent assorted economic convulsions during the next fifty years as its population dwindled. In 1937 a monstrous flood nearly floated New Albany off the map. Following the flood an enormous levee was built through downtown, visually cutting off the city from the river. Now, without a map, you'd never know New Albany is on the Ohio River.

"You can't see the very river that made this town," says

Don Smith, who now lives in Isaac P. Smith's house on Main Street, which once had a splendid view of the river. Now it faces the great earthen levee. Don grew up north of town on a farm that is now an industrial park. As a kid interested in history, he'd always admired the magnificent mansions along Main Street that were built when you could see the river.

After graduating in 1976 from the University of Cincinnati with a degree in interior design, Don worked across the river in Louisville while living with his parents and looking for an old house in town.

"The other house I wanted was torn down when I was away at college," he says. In the 1970s New Albany went on a demolition binge. The Culbertson Mansion, which is now a State Historic Site and one of the grandest homes in Floyd County, was nearly torn down in the late 1960s to make way for a gas station. The old home next door to Don's was torn down, became a floodlit used car joint, and is now a VFW parking lot.

Despite all that, Don bought the Isaac P. Smith house

in 1979 and transformed it into a showplace for nineteenth-century Regency Empire–style furniture, Viennese pianos, and other exquisite European artwork, including a harp with no strings. Hand-painted wallpaper in the dining room depicts Paris and the River Seine in 1825. Don's roommate, Sid Spear, a laboratory inspector for the state government of Kentucky, has filled his bedroom with Catholic religious artifacts, including a painting of the martyred Saint Sebastian tied to a tree with arrows in his heart and not looking very good.

The elegantly restored home looks like a museum befitting New Albany's glory days, despite being next door to the VFW, which features Karaoke on the first and third Wednesday of the month. "Beats a used car lot," shrugs Don, who now operates his own interior design business. "I put easements on this property so it can never be torn down." A few years ago, the electric utility that serves New Albany cut down all the big trees, except one, along Don's stretch of Main Street, and replanted suburban stick trees.

The chain saws spared Don's Catalpa Tree, which Isaac P. Smith probably planted when he built the house.

"Over my dead body you'll cut it," Don told them. "I meant it, too. The madness has to stop somewhere. It's bad enough we can't see the river."

John Martin and Barbara Clark Smith

Historic Name: WILLIAM AND MARY CORNELL HOUSE

County: DEKALB

Date of Construction: CIRCA 1860

Architectural Style: ITALIANATE

LISTED IN THE NATIONAL REGISTER OF HISTORIC PLACES

When John Martin Smith graduated near the top of his 1965 Indiana University Law School class, he received lucrative job offers from big law firms in New York and Chicago, none of which interested him. He grew up on a hog farm in DeKalb County.

"Hogs put me through law school, my family's been in the county since 1840, and I love it here, so I rented an office, put out a cardboard shingle and said, 'By golly, I'm a lawyer,'" laughs John Martin, tugging on his country lawyer red suspenders.

Luckily for DeKalb County he came home. In 1972 he helped start the Auburn Cord Duesenberg Museum in Auburn, the county seat. It draws eighty thousand visitors annually to the small northeastern Indiana town. He's also president of the National Automotive and Truck Museum of the United States, which he founded in 1989 in Auburn.

"I like old buildings and I like old cars," he says. "By starting these museums, I've saved two old buildings and hundreds of old cars." The Auburn Cord Duesenberg Museum is in the original 1930 Auburn factory showroom. In the first thirty years of the twentieth century, Auburn was a major automobile manufacturing center. The cars were known worldwide for their style, power, and advanced engineering.

In his spare time, John Martin, the DeKalb County Historian, wrote a massive two-volume county history. He's just completed four more books of reproductions of his collection of four thousand postcards printed between 1905 and 1915 depicting various locations in Steuben, Noble, Allen, and DeKalb Counties.

"That was the golden era of postcards," he notes. "Now I'm researching nineteenth-century horse-thief detective associations and writing a book about the pacifist Shakers of Knox County, Indiana." In 1969, John Martin and his

wife, Barbara, a schoolteacher, bought the brick shell of a farmhouse built circa 1860 by Maryland abolitionist and farmer William Cornell. The Indiana Cornell house was a stop on the Underground Railroad. William and his wife, Mary, hid slaves who were fleeing north to Michigan in a compartment above the basement cistern.

In 1974, after a lengthy restoration, John Martin obtained National Register status for the house to provide some protection if the state highway department tries to build an interchange off I-69, which is a mere eighth of a mile to the east. An interstate interchange onto John Martin's quiet road would trigger a development free-for-all and, of course, ruin everything.

National Register status sparked a new activity for John Martin. "I assumed when you got on the National Register the government sent you a nice plaque," he says. The government doesn't do that, so John Martin and Barbara started a company to manufacture and sell cast-bronze historic plaques. Many of the historic plaques seen on National Register homes were made by their company, which they sold in 1991.

The inexhaustible John Martin, who practices law in Auburn with his son, Thompson, wakes up at 4:00 A.M. to squeeze a couple more hours into the day. He heads to the basement and the former slave hiding place, which contains thousands of books on Indiana history, his postcard collections, Civil War artifacts, and toy wooden boats.

Scattered across his rolling fifty-four acres is an assortment of old automobiles in various states of restoration,

including a 1926 Auburn touring car. "I want to drive it in parades," he says, rocking on the front porch where William and Mary Cornell once sat.

"I need to live another hundred years to complete all my projects," he sighs.

Patrick and Laura Smith
Historic Name: WILLIAM H. COULTER HOUSE
City: FRANKFORT
County: CLINTON
Date of Construction: CIRCA 1885
Architectural Style: QUEEN ANNE

When developers representing CVS pharmacy slunk into Frankfort and optioned fifteen old homes four blocks east of the Clinton County Courthouse, the Reverend Patrick Smith and his wife, Laura, were not pleased. CVS optioned the homes to tear them down and build a square block, twenty-four-hour pharmacy/food mart with ample, well-lit parking and a drive-through window. This, of course, would have destroyed the character and ambience of tree-lined Clinton Street. The Smiths live one block from the proposed project in one of Frankfort's premier historic homes, a magnificent Queen Anne.

The mild-mannered Reverend Mr. Smith was in no mood to love his new, well-lit, corporate neighbor, never mind what the Bible says. He organized hundreds of furious residents and held strategy meetings in his living room to combat the pharmacy giant that is wrecking neighborhoods throughout Indiana.

"I started all the trouble," he says. The reverend-led band of protesters packed zoning board meetings, lobbied city council members, and demanded CVS's rezoning petition be denied. Amazingly, it worked. CVS went away. The good guys won and downtown Frankfort was saved . . . until the next corporate "development" assault.

"I met with those developers," recalls the Reverend Mr. Smith, pastor of the First Presbyterian Church. "They were just like those guys in the movies. Expensive suits, big grins, and you couldn't believe a word they said."

Strong words from a man of God, but the reverend believed he was defending his neighborhood and the legacy of William H. Coulter, the hotel, clothing, and furniture store magnate who built the house in the 1880s when the area was called Christian Ridge.

"God brought us to this house," explains Laura, a Kansas City native, gifted pianist, and 1976 graduate of Wheaton College in Illinois. She met Pat in his hometown of Murfreesboro, Tennessee, shortly after he graduated from Middle Tennessee State University with a degree in historic preservation. They married in 1977 when he was mulling over his future.

"I then thought I would study architecture in graduate school or become a Marine Corps officer like my father," explains Pat, whose roots in Rutherford County, Tennes-

see, stretch back to 1790. "But for some reason I felt a gentle but strong pull to become a minister."

He graduated from Trinity Evangelical Divinity School in Deerfield, Illinois, and served as a church pastor in Knoxville, Tennessee. In 1990 he was transferred to Frankfort where God guided the family to the red brick Coulter house and a future rendezvous with CVS. The Smiths raised two sons in the house.

"This house is a piece of Frankfort history," says Pat, proudly leading the tour and noting significant details, like the green Art Deco–tile bathroom floor and what he believes is Frankfort's first built-in bathtub, installed in 1910. Much of the furniture came from the old Smith plantation in

Tennessee, which the family lost in the 1929 stock market crash. Then there's the kitchen, where in 1933 William Coulter's widowed daughter, Edith Harding, murdered her two little girls and killed herself by opening the gas valve on the stove. She was distraught over the death of her husband, said stunned friends.

"People still remember those two, little white caskets sitting in this living room," says Laura, a special-events coordinator for a Frankfort nursing home.

"I was born thinking about history because it mattered in my family," says Pat. "That's why CVS got me so worked up."

Amen.

Lynn Thomsen and Mike Jones

Historic Name: THE HALF-WAY HOUSE / NATHANIEL WILSON HOUSE
County: CARROLL
Date of Construction: 1848
Architectural Style: GREEK REVIVAL

On Sunday afternoon excursions, Cliff Thomsen often drove his family along the quiet, unmarked roads that wind along the Wabash River in rural Carroll County. As a little girl in the back seat of Dad's car, Lynn Thomsen cast a young artist's eye at an old farmhouse nestled at the base of a slight hill overlooking the wide river.

"I thought it was the most beautiful house in the most beautiful place I'd ever seen," recalls Lynn, who later moved to Indianapolis, graduated from the Herron School of Art in 1980, and became an accomplished landscape painter and art teacher. Over the years, on trips home to her parents, she'd drive by the farmhouse or stop along the river to paint or sketch.

The post-and-beam house she admired for decades was built by Nathaniel Wilson in 1848 and is one of the oldest structures still standing in Carroll County. In the mid–nineteenth century it was known as The Half-Way House, serving travelers along the old Wabash Highway, which followed the river south from Fort Wayne to Terre Haute. It had been owned since 1948 by one-legged dairy farmer Charles Munson and his wife, Waneita. Charles's leg was chewed off in a corn auger. As they grew older and weaker, unable to care for the old Half-Way House, it slowly deteriorated. The Munsons had incubated chickens with a kerosene heater in one upstairs bedroom and stored grain in another. The paint had worn off the exterior, exposing

bare wood, there was no heat or water upstairs, and the toilet flushed directly into the river.

In 1996, Lynn married Indianapolis computer programmer Mike Jones. She heard that the Munsons had recently died and the house was for sale and in danger of being torn down by two prospective buyers. "It needed to be saved and looked to us like the perfect place to spend summer weekends," says Lynn.

In May 1998 they bought the house and fourteen acres, including one-third mile of riverfront from the Munson children. That first summer, they hauled away forty cubic yards of trash from inside the house, put sixty gallons of paint on the exterior, installed a septic tank, tore up shag carpet and linoleum, and removed a concrete front porch. In the barn, lashed to the rafters, they found the original wooden front porch columns and re-installed them.

Lynn, a schoolteacher, spent summer vacations working on the house and hunting arrowheads. Mike commuted on weekends. After removing 150 years of paint and wall-

paper from an enclosed back porch, they uncovered names of visitors penciled on the original plaster. Ben "Bean" Burrows scribbled his name on the wall on 1-20-1906.

"The fun of this place is discovering its history," says Mike, who grew up in Muncie and graduated from Ball State University in 1976.

Their Indianapolis home is an 1899 three-story telephone company building they renovated into a loft apartment upstairs and an artist studio on the first floor. "I'm a rural and city dweller and I like living in both worlds," says Lynn.

Centuries ago the Indians called the river the Wah-Bah-Shik-Ki, which meant "pure white," something it isn't anymore. However, Lynn and Mike's remote stretch of river valley and the revitalized Half-Way House is one of the most picturesque places in Indiana, a tranquil scene from a T. C. Steele landscape.

"It was a lifelong dream of mine to own this house," says Lynn. "And I did it."

Ted Toler

Historic Name: CLEM AND FANNIE GAAR HOUSE

City: RICHMOND

County: WAYNE

Date of Construction: 1886

Architectural Style: QUEEN ANNE

LISTED IN THE NATIONAL REGISTER OF HISTORIC PLACES, *Starr Historic District*

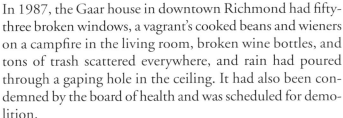

In 1987, the Gaar house in downtown Richmond had fifty-three broken windows, a vagrant's cooked beans and wieners on a campfire in the living room, broken wine bottles, and tons of trash scattered everywhere, and rain had poured through a gaping hole in the ceiling. It had also been condemned by the board of health and was scheduled for demolition.

"My wife, Nancy, loved it," recalls Ted Toler, a maintenance supervisor at an automotive parts factory. "I had a dumb-ass attack so we bought it four months before it was scheduled to be torn down."

They rented a nearby house to live in while tackling the extensive restoration project. Three months later, they were forced from the rental house when the owner sold it. They moved into the Gaar house, although it had no heat and snow blew in through the hole in the ceiling and cracks in the walls. They huddled near a wood stove, feeling like vagrants.

"My son wouldn't bring kids home because he thought it looked like the Addams Family house," says Ted. "Tom

Hanks in the movie *Money Pit* had nothing on me. I'd work ten to twelve hours middle shift at the factory and come home and work on the house. I didn't sleep much. Then my daughter and her newborn baby moved in."

He completed the restoration in seven long years, during which he was divorced and had a mild heart attack. He did everything but the plumbing and the drywall. Most of the magnificent walnut, chestnut, beechnut, and mahogany woodwork and floors had been destroyed over the years. Using his Shop Smith saw in the basement servants quarters, he duplicated the damaged woodwork, floorboards, bookshelves, cabinets, and door panels. "I tongue-and-grooved everything," he says. He cut seven thousand diamond-shaped parquet floor pieces with a handsaw and miter box.

"The house had the fundamentals, I just put it back together," he explains.

Then he painted the Victorian house pink, put an enormous above-ground swimming pool in the small backyard, helped form the Starr Historic District Neighborhood Association, and took a class to learn how to make ceramic

cherubs for the living room fireplace. He filled the house with Victorian furniture and hundreds of paintings, drawings, and statues of cherubs and angels. Nancy painted winged angels and cherubs on most of the ceilings.

"I felt the house needed guardian angels, although I'm not religious," he shrugs. The house is a popular stop on the neighborhood Christmas tour. Ted decorates the pink house of angels and cherubs inside and out with hundreds of twinkling lights and Santa Clauses. He likes the holidays so much that he leaves the decorated living room Christmas tree up all year.

The house was built in 1886 by Clem Gaar, whose family manufactured stoves and threshers. Ted grew up in Muncie, graduated from high school in 1964, worked in factories,

bought a small farm, and tried following the *Mother Earth News* suggestions for self-sufficiency and living off the land. That didn't work. He got divorced, a new job in Wayne County, and a new wife, and was planning to restore an old round barn to live in when he had his dumb-ass attack and bought the condemned house.

"I wasn't into saving homes but I got hooked," says Ted. "The house drives you."

His new projects are to get married again and convert the attic ballroom into a giant, year-around Christmas game room with pool tables, more angels and cherubs, Santas, and fully decorated Christmas trees.

"Wait till you see it then," says Ted.

John Watson

Historic Name: AUGUST BUSCHMANN BUILDING
City: INDIANAPOLIS
County: MARION
Date of Construction: CIRCA 1894

managing historic apartment buildings throughout the Midwest, largely in Indianapolis and Madison, Wisconsin.

John's mother, Betty, taught him how to fix things. "I never saw my dad with a tool but my mom taught me how to use a power saw," he says. "She would tackle any project and ask questions and not be afraid to do anything."

John's spacious loft apartment and company headquarters is in the thirty-three-thousand-square-foot August Buschmann Building. It was built around 1894 by August Buschmann to house his plumbing supply company. Buschmann sold the building in 1933 and over the subsequent years it housed a grocery, hardware store, hat shop, dance academy, barbershop, tavern, restaurant, and pool hall before being diced into apartments. In the late 1970s it was abandoned and taken over by drifters and vandals who built fires in barrels to keep warm.

John and Carl bought the building in 1989 and moved their company offices into the first floor in 1991 while still renovating the upper two stories into additional office space and the enormous loft apartment. John moved into the loft in 1998 and began his one-step, one-second commute to his office.

John Watson's commute to work is brief: about one second. One step through the second-story door of his six-thousand-square-foot loft apartment in downtown Indianapolis into the adjacent offices of Van Rooy Properties, which he co-owns with Carl Van Rooy, and he's there.

John started his building rehabilitation career in 1986 when he bought an abandoned thirty-eight-unit HUD apartment building in downtown Indianapolis for $76,000 and spent another $525,000 rehabilitating it. Soon afterwards he partnered with Carl Van Rooy. They have since built a successful business buying, rehabilitating, and

"Lofts are my hobby," says John, a Munster native, who graduated from Indiana University in 1980 with a degree in finance and a strong drive to become wealthy. After working briefly in the finance department at GTE in Connecticut, he moved to Indianapolis and began selling real estate. "I discovered real estate was the way to get rich," he says. After joining forces with Carl Van Rooy, he worked seventy brutal hours a week in pursuit of wealth; when he was thirty-five years old his father died.

"I was a workaholic but when my dad died I refocused my life," he says. "Now I only work about thirty-five hours a week and only do deals that are fun." Fun is the predominant theme of his loft, which was once used as a meeting place for the local veterans of the Spanish-American War. Among other toys, it contains foosball, air hockey, and pool tables. A golf net, sixty-inch television, lavish bar, a gargoyle, statues of Neptune and King Tut, his grandmother's piano, and a series of 1920s black-and-white photographs of the Marott Hotel, which John now owns and manages as apartments. Parties are held in the spacious ballroom, which overlooks the downtown Indianapolis skyline.

"This is the ultimate bachelor pad," he says. "I have two sons and when they visit the three of us kids play here."

Van Rooy Properties employs four hundred people and manages nine thousand apartment units from its headquarters on the other side of the door from John's playhouse. John works in blue jeans and no tie and his office contains an old red leather barber chair and a vintage F-14 Tom Cat pinball machine.

"We chose to stay small. We don't have partners and we don't have to answer to anyone," he says. "Basically, we just have fun, messing around with old buildings."

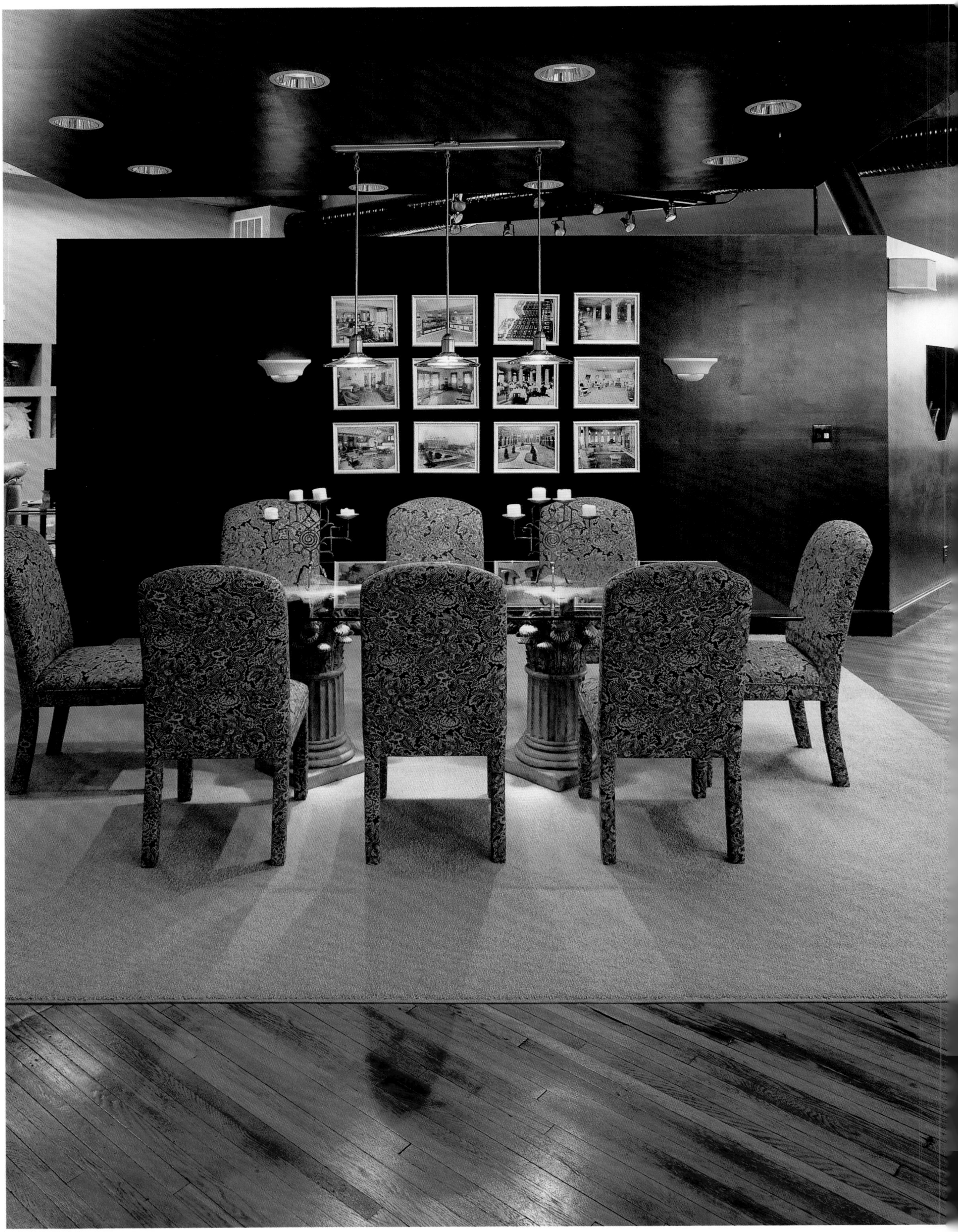

Ann Windle

Historic Name: CHARLES SHREWSBURY HOUSE

City: MADISON

County: JEFFERSON

Date of Construction: 1848

Architect: FRANCIS COSTIGAN

Architectural Style: GREEK REVIVAL

NATIONAL HISTORIC LANDMARK

In 1948, the Francis Costigan–designed Shrewsbury House overlooking the Ohio River in Madison was nearly sold and reconfigured into a low-rent boardinghouse and coffee shop. Destroyed, in other words. An American treasure lost.

But along came John and Ann Windle, newly arrived from Chicago in search of adventure and romance along *la belle rivière,* the beautiful river, as early French explorers called the Ohio. They bought and restored the twelve-room

house with thirteen fireplaces, a fifty-three-step spiral staircase, and big windows overlooking the river below.

In 1960, the Windles, who ran an antique business, formed Historic Madison to protect the lovely nineteenth-century riverfront homes from the scourge of development. Over 130 city blocks were placed on the National Register of Historic Places in 1973, largely due to the Windles' tireless preservation efforts. The Shrewsbury House is a Na-

tional Historic Landmark, one of only two such homes in Indiana.

John Windle, an accomplished violinist, died in 1987, shortly after co-authoring *The Early Architecture of Madison, Indiana,* a final tribute to his beloved river town.

The house was built in 1848 by Charles Shrewsbury, a salt-barge riverboat captain, flour manufacturer, and pork merchant. The floor-to-ceiling windows are thirteen feet tall. A man on horseback could step through the enormous front door. In 1872, Captain Shrewsbury tumbled to his death down the spiral staircase that he so loved.

"The captain's death was unfortunate," says the delightful Mrs. Windle, whose twinkling blue eyes sparkle like the river below on a moonlit night. Now in her ninth decade, she recalls in vivid detail the great moments spent in the house. The parties, lively literary discussions, musicales, the time it snowed and she and John laughed and tossed snowballs on the sweeping back lawns.

Several years ago, a Nevada gaming casino representative sat in her sunlit parlor seeking to enlist her support of a Jefferson County referendum to allow riverboat gambling. The riverfront below Shrewsbury House would be a fine location for a riverboat, golf course, hotel, and theme park, he told the astonished Mrs. Windle. "What you're proposing would be the worst thing to happen in Madison since the Civil War," she warned him. The referendum was defeated two to one, just as she predicted. "Can you imagine such a thing? A riverboat in front of my house," she says, tossing up her hands in disgust. "John would have shot him.

"Oh, John and I had such fun in this house," she exclaims. In the big house they found romance and adventure. They traveled extensively in search of seventeenth-century antiques and Chinese porcelain and silver, visited the world's great art museums, attended operas, and told jokes. When they returned, they sipped fine bourbon and watched the enchanted river through the enormous parlor windows.

She grew up in Chicago in a house with ten thousand books and parents who encouraged critical thought, curiosity, a life of literature, and laughter. Lincoln biographer and poet Carl Sandburg was a family friend. Ann graduated with honors from Wellesley College in 1933 and later flunked out of the London School of Motoring.

"Don't you think that's funny?" she laughs. "I've never driven a car."

Mrs. Windle has deeded the house and all its furnishings to Historic Madison, which will maintain it as a museum upon her death.

"I've never seen the sky so beautiful on the river," she marveled one spring day. "I was just born happy, I guess. Like Shakespeare wrote, 'A star danced and under that was I born.'"

Bob Wolfe

City: MADISON

County: JEFFERSON

Date of Construction: CIRCA 1835

Architectural Style: FEDERAL

LISTED IN THE NATIONAL REGISTER OF HISTORIC PLACES, *Madison Historic District*

When Bob Wolfe told friends he was restoring an old house on West First Street in Madison they pointedly asked how far west. Far, he said proudly. Right in front of the junkyard and across the street and next door to a series of unrestored, unrevitalized vinyl-sided working-class homes.

Restoring the first house in a neighborhood appealed to his anti-elitist, pioneer spirit. Not everyone has the money, time, or inclination to restore their home, but so what? The neighbors are proud, decent people and their homes neat and clean.

"I don't like grandeur for grandeur's sake. What is satisfying is three-fourths of my neighbors in those little shotgun houses have flowers on their porches in the summer," he says. "That's what I like about Madison, no matter where you go there are fancy homes and ordinary homes. I'm two blocks from The Lanier Mansion and a hundred yards from the junkyard and I like it."

He bought the rundown 1835 Federal-style home in 1990 after retiring from Miami University in Oxford, Ohio,

where he taught fine art and printmaking for thirty-one years. His grandmother was a cook at the university and his father drove a truck for the school. Bob was born in Oxford, graduated from the university, and spent his career there. He sadly watched the university and real estate speculators buy the big old homes and tear them down for parking lots or office space or chop them into student rental apartments. He owns five homes in old Oxford, including the house where he and his mother were born. He bought them to save them from the wrecking ball.

"Everyone left old Oxford and the city didn't care. People in Madison are concerned about protecting their neighborhoods and the city seems to listen," he says of his decision to join friends in Madison and buy the old brick house.

With the help of a former student and architect, the late Todd Mozingo (who had written his master's thesis on Madison architecture), Bob expanded the small house, adding a bathroom, a bedroom, a stone kitchen in the original basement, terraced gardens, and a unique stone shed

with a slate roof in the backyard facing the junkyard. He didn't remove the burn marks on the upstairs bedroom floor where house legend has it that Grandma Morrisey burned to death while smoking her pipe on the slop jar.

The antique furnishings are sparse. The artwork ranges from his own pastel painting of the late Pierre, the longtime family dog, to George Catlin lithographs and paintings and etchings from India, Thailand, and other world ports he's visited in search of beautiful things.

First Street parallels the Ohio River about a quarter of a mile away. During the flood of 1995 it filled his basement-kitchen with two feet of water from the swollen river. Like the vinyl-sided shotgun houses across the street and the nearby junkyard, he took the terrifying flood in stride. So what? It's part of the rhythm of life on the Ohio along West First Street, says the easygoing, unflappable Bob.

He takes daily walks or bicycle rides, marveling at the sights and sounds, the immensity of the great and mighty river flowing past "unfashionable," unrestored West First Street on its long, meandering journey to the Mississippi and on to the sea. The river is an eternal presence that never fails to inspire.

"The river is like the neighborhood," he says. "It's real."

Paul Yurkas

Historic Name: MORGAN-BOYD HOUSE

Town: MERRILLVILLE

County: LAKE

Date of Construction: CIRCA 1855

Architectural Style: ITALIANATE

To Paul and Catherine Yurkas it seemed like the historically correct thing to do—buy an old house to display their collection of nineteenth-century medicine bottles, marbles, and ceramic doll heads that they dug from old dumps in Lake County. Old bottles belonged in an old house, they agreed.

"We're bottle diggers," proclaims Paul, now retired after working forty years in the U.S. Steel mill in Gary. Bottle diggers locate old dumps, usually along riverbanks, dig down four or five feet and search for stuff. Paul and Catherine found thousands of bottles and other ceramic and glass things which are now piled, stored, stacked, and displayed throughout their old farmhouse on 73rd Street in Merrillville.

Paul quit bottle digging when Catherine, a short-order cook at the Temple Diner in Hammond, had a heart attack and died in 1993. "The big boom," Paul calls it. She re-turned home from a walk and collapsed. They'd been married thirty years.

The Yurkas house of bottles was built in the mid–nineteenth century along the Sauk Indian trail. In the early part of the twentieth century, it became the roadbed for the original Lincoln Highway, the first transcontinental highway across America. The Lincoln Highway from New York to San Francisco was completed in 1928 and ran right past the house that the Yurkases would one day fill with bottles.

The house was built by a dairy farmer named Morgan, who formerly lived in Furnessville in Porter County. Morgan bought about a thousand acres around what is now U.S. 30 through Merrillville. U.S. 30 in Lake County is possibly the most congested, commercially overdeveloped stretch of road in Indiana. U.S. 30 is now called the Lincoln Highway.

At the time that farmer Morgan built the seventeen-room house it was heralded as Lake County's premier residence, a modern marvel. It had an elegant three-hole, plaster-walled, carpeted outhouse, the envy of all the neighbors.

When Paul and Catherine bought the decrepit farmhouse in 1980, Merrillville was still relatively quiet. In the 1960s Paul remembers people leisurely riding horses through the deserted streets of Merrillville. "You'd get killed now, doing that," he says, rocking on his front porch, noting the traffic on 73rd Street.

"At rush hour I can't get out of my driveway," sighs Paul, although he doesn't much care because he's never in a hurry anyway. The house and the great fun that he and Catherine had in fixing it up and filling it with bottles highlighted his life.

"This house wasn't fit for humans," Paul remembers fondly. "My wife wouldn't live in it for a year, even though

it was her idea." Paul, who can repair anything, happily made the house inhabitable. He used his entire six-week vacation one year to rebuild windows. Every surface in the house needed extensive restoration. On weekends, they scrounged around condemned buildings and salvaged useful items, like tin ceilings and plumbing fixtures.

"This sink is from the old Gary National Bank, the toilet is from a dentist office in Hammond, and so on," explains Paul. Catherine wouldn't allow anything that detracted from the home's historic character.

"Get that outta there. You can't have that thing sticking out the window of an old house," barked Catherine when she came home one day and found Paul had installed a window air-conditioner. "So we stayed hot," shrugs Paul, thinking back to Catherine.

"Boy, we had fun here," he reminisces.

INDEX

BILL SHAW is a former feature writer for *The Indianapolis Star* and former national correspondent for *Time-Life* magazines. He has written extensively for *Life, In Style, People Weekly,* and *Reader's Digest* magazines, among others. He co-authored *Going Home to Nicodemus* in 1994 with former *Time* magazine editor Dan Chu and has contributed to several other books, including a 1987 Carnegie Foundation study of American higher education. In 1993 Shaw received the Peter Lisagor Award for Magazine Writing from the Chicago Chapter of the Society of Professional Journalists. He lives with his two dogs in the woods outside Jolietville, Indiana, and doesn't go out much.

MARSH DAVIS is the former Director of Community Services for Historic Landmarks Foundation of Indiana, the nation's largest not-for-profit preservation organization. While there, he contributed articles and photographs to the foundation's magazine, *The Indiana Preservationist,* and other publications, including *The Main Stem: The History and Architecture of North Meridian Street.* A native of Lake County, Indiana, Davis lived with his family in the Historic Meridian Park neighborhood of Indianapolis until moving to Texas in 2002. He is currently Executive Director of the Galveston Historical Foundation.

SPONSORING EDITOR: *Roberta Diehl*
COPY EDITOR: *Miki Bird*
BOOK AND JACKET DESIGNER: *Pamela Rude*
COMPOSITOR: *Tony Brewer*
TYPEFACES: *Trajan Display and Adobe Garamond*
PRINTER: *Four Colour Imports Inc. / Friesens*